Inspir
Women
Every Day

One-year devotional
by women for women

CWR

Copyright © CWR 2013
The readings in this compilation were originally published 2009 by CWR as bimonthly Bible-reading notes *Inspiring Women Every Day* as January/February, March/April, May/June, July/August, September/October, November/December 2009.
First published in this format 2013 by CWR, Waverley Abbey House, Waverley Lane, Farnham, Surrey GU9 8EP, UK. Tel: 01252 784700 Email: mail@cwr.org.uk Registered Charity No. 294387. Registered Limited Company No. 1990308.

For a list of National Distributors visit www.cwr.org.uk/distributors
Unless otherwise indicated, all Scripture references are from the Holy Bible: New International Version (NIV), Copyright © 1979, 1984, 2011 by Biblica (formerly International Bible Society). Used by permission of Hodder & Stoughton Publishers, an Hachette UK company. All rights reserved. 'NIV' is a registered trademark of Biblica (formerly International Bible Society). UK trademark number 1448790.
Other versions used: Amplified: Scripture quotations taken from the Amplified® Bible, Copyright © 1954, 1958, 1962, 1964, 1965, 1987 by The Lockman Foundation Used by permission. (www.Lockman.org) RSV: *Revised Standard Version*, © 1965, Division of Christian Education of the National Council of the Churches of Christ in the United States of America. NKJV: *New King James Version*, ©1982, Thomas Nelson Inc. NLT: Scripture quotations marked (NLT) are taken from the Holy Bible, New Living Translation, copyright © 1996, 2004, 2007 by Tyndale House Foundation. Used by permission of Tyndale House Publishers, Inc., Carol Stream, Illinois 60188. All rights reserved. *Message*: Scripture taken from THE MESSAGE. Copyright © 1993, 1994, 1995, 1996, 2000, 2001, 2002. Used by permission of NavPress Publishing Group. Phillips: J.B. Phillips *The New Testament in Modern English*, © 1960, 1972, J.B. Phillips, Fount Paperbacks. New Revised Standard Version Bible: (NRSV) copyright © 1989 National Council of the Churches of Christ in the United States of America. Used by permission. All rights reserved.

Concept development, editing, design and production by CWR
Cover image: Getty/altrendo images
Printed in Croatia by 1010
ISBN: 978-1-85345-997-9

Contents

 Welcome to this wonderful collection of devotional writings from women with as vast a variety of life-experience as those of you picking it up. Whoever you are, wherever you are in the world, and whenever you are commencing this compilation, I know you will be all the better for reading God's Word daily. We focus on themes such as worship, joy, disappointment and longing for more, and get to know some Bible characters too – including the amazing Esther.

As you allow the Word of God to dwell in you richly, I pray you will draw ever closer to the Lord who loves you unconditionally, passionately and extravagantly, and from that secure place of knowing how much the Father lavishes His love upon you, you will step out to love and serve those around you.

Lynette Brooks
Director of Publishing

See what great love the Father has lavished on us, that we should be called children of God! (1 John 3:1)

The hands of the Lord

Lyn Gitchel

Lyn Gitchel has taught Bible studies for many years and has much experience in establishing firmly committed Christians. Born and educated in England, Lyn worked as part of the team for the first Billy Graham Crusade in England in 1954. Ordained to the ministry in 1964, she worked with CWR in England before moving to the United States. Lyn and her husband pastored churches in America until his death in 1997.

The hands **of the Lord**

Isaiah 48:12–15

'My own hand laid the foundations of the earth, and my right hand spread out the heavens ...' (v.13)

What a boundless God we have! Imagine His greatness. To Him, the Bible says, the nations are simply 'a drop in a bucket' and all the dust contained on this earth He has weighed in His balances. Imagine how small the earth is to Him. If God's hand is larger than the expanse of space itself – and that is billions and trillions of miles beyond our comprehension – then see how small the world is to Him. It is less than a speck of dust and, when He takes it in His hand, it quivers as His breath blows upon it. Maybe that is what causes the world to turn – the breath of God!

But what is far more wonderful and beyond our understanding is that this great, great God could care so much about those minute beings of His creation upon this speck we call earth; that He should have stepped down and become involved with them. What a stoop was that! What condescension!

And now, having bought for us freedom from the power of evil through the blood of Jesus, He watches over us – each one of us – to be sure we have everything His love could shower upon us. We have hundreds of wonderful promises, hundreds of reassurances, hundreds of tokens of His love and care. He has never failed. That boundless God, whose hand is big enough to span eternity and space, has you and me snug in the palm of His great hand. As we begin a new year, walk with us on a search through the Scriptures as we look at those hands, the hands of God. Learn anew the wonder of being held by Him and see afresh the security it offers. Learn to rest on this fact: we are in His hands.

For prayer and reflection

Father, help me to grasp the truth that I am held firmly in Your hands. Teach me to rest in this and to live my life secure in this knowledge.

God's hands **overshadow us**

Sometimes we hit a spot in our lives when we are tempted to feel that God has forgotten about us. If we listen to our own thinking, it seems to us that we are of no use and that He cannot possibly be bothered with us. We long to be out working for Him yet duties and trials, from which we are unable to break free, keep us shackled. We tend not to look on home-style duties as 'His work' and we despair of ever being really useful to Him.

God has to draw near and change our thinking here, for caring for needs in our own home can often become one of the greatest fields of service we will ever have. It is at times like these that He will whisper in your ear, 'In the shadow of My hand I am keeping you because I am making you a polished arrow for Me. I am using you, even now. You may not feel it, but I am.'

With some of us it is a case of time. If God sent you out too soon you would not be ready. Rust would eat into your soul and tarnish destroy your witness. Time must be taken to make sure that the arrow is polished before putting it into use. Only then will it fly with certainty to its intended goal.

Even Jesus, perfect as He was, had to wait 30 years before it was time for Him to begin His ministry. He wanted to begin at the age of 12, but it was not the right time; at that age it was the custom for a Jewish boy to go into partnership with his father in his business. Jesus knew that His Father was God and was anxious to start working with Him. You would have thought that the sooner He began, the more He could have accomplished – but no, it was not the time. Like us, He had to wait until it was God's perfect time.

Isaiah 49:1–4

'... in the shadow of his hand he hid me ...' (v.2)

For prayer and reflection

Father, please teach me patience. You know how I love You and want to serve You. Help me to understand what working for You means.

7

God has **forgiving hands**

....

Isaiah 40:1–9

....

'… she has
received from
the LORD's hand
double for all
her sins.' (v.2)

For many years, this verse didn't make any sense to me. I wondered what was so wonderful about receiving double for our sins – as if we had to pay a double penalty or something similar. If God was promising that double would have to be paid for the sins of the people, why would Isaiah have been thrilled about this?

Then, one day, an old rabbi (whose name I have forgotten) explained the verse to me. This Jewish religious leader had become a follower of Jesus, so he fully understood what it meant to have sins forgiven.

The rabbi told me about an ancient Hebrew custom. If a man was deeply in debt and unable to pay, he would write the sum of the total owed on a piece of parchment and pin it up outside his tent door. There it would stay until a passing nobleman who was charitably inclined took pity on the poor man. Taking the piece of parchment down, the benefactor would then fold it – double it – and place it back on the nail, thus signifying that he was prepared to pay the debt in full on behalf of the man. This custom was known as 'receiving the double' – and it is to this that Isaiah refers.

But more than this: Isaiah is, in fact, referring here to the redemption of the nation and of all mankind. In Colossians 2:14 we find the same image again. There, Jesus takes down the list of our sins and nails it to His cross, paying the price and cancelling the debt against us forever. Never will we have to pay for our sins and failures. They are nailed to His cross and, through His death, we have 'received the double'.

....

**For prayer
and reflection**

....

**Father, write the
reality of this truth
on my heart. Help
me to understand
fully that the
death of Jesus on
the cross for me
has completely
wiped out every
trace of my sin.
All of it!**

God has **merciful hands**

You might think that King David would have said these words after Nathan the prophet had pointed out his sin. David had fallen for Bathsheba, the wife of Uriah the Hittite, sleeping with her in his absence. She became pregnant and went to King David with the news.

After failing to succeed in getting Uriah to sleep with his wife (and so cover up the pregnancy), David dealt with the situation by having him killed – in a discrete and roundabout way, of course. But he'd nevertheless committed murder – and it was sin. This sin was in addition to his previous sin of taking Bathsheba – and one wrong added to another will never make a right.

The prophet Nathan was sent by God to discipline David. When he pointed out that David had offended God by his actions, David admitted his sin – expecting God to punish him. God did punish David – but indirectly. He did not allow the child of the illicit relationship to live. King David accepted this – and mourned the loss of his child.

Sometimes, when we've turned aside from God and done something we feel really badly about, it's hard to forgive ourselves. It's sometimes easier to receive forgiveness from God than to forgive ourselves. I think that's why God dealt with David in this way – so that the child's presence would not always remind him of his wrongdoing. And notice how God's forgiveness is later shown. David and Bathsheba had another child, Solomon, who became the greatest among the kings of that nation. Solomon was also the king who built the Temple for the worship of God – yet he was the son of that same couple, David and Bathsheba. That's truly God's forgiveness.

2 Samuel 11:2–5; 12:7–14; 24:14

'... Let us fall into the hands of the LORD, for his mercy is great ...' (24:14)

For prayer and reflection

Father, sometimes I find it hard to forgive myself. I know You have forgiven me; help me also to forgive myself and others, so that my sin is completely wiped out.

God has **moulding hands**

Jeremiah 18:1–6

'But the pot he was shaping from the clay was marred in his hands ...' (v.4)

Clay is so very cheap that it really need not be used again – after all, it's basically just a certain kind of soil dug up from the ground. When a vessel goes wrong in the making on the potter's wheel, it might just as well be discarded and fresh clay taken to enable the potter to begin again. If a vessel is broken, it can be ground down to powder, then water added again to make fresh clay. But why do that when clay is cheap?

In this passage of Scripture God was demonstrating to Jeremiah the lesson of the potter: nothing is too much bother for Him! God does not have to remake a marred vessel any more than He had to tolerate humanity after the Fall. He could have wiped out Adam and Eve and started again with another perfect pair, but He did not. Why? The reason is simply this: it would have been wonderful if mankind had passed from innocence to perfection through testing and temptation, and if Adam and Eve had resisted every advance of the devil. But things didn't happen that way. So, because God is God, He did something greater. Instead of discarding the faulty vessels, His plan of redemption intends to make us, in the end, something greater than we could ever have been if we'd never been part of a fallen race. It's far more wonderful for man to pass from guilt, through redemption, to holiness!

This should be such an encouragement to those who are depressed because, to them, it seems that they fail constantly. Take heart! God is not dismayed. He takes marred vessels in His hands and remakes them, sometimes over and over again, until they become something greater than was possible any other way.

For prayer and reflection

Thank You, heavenly Father, for encouraging me that You do not discard vessels that become marred, but You work on them until they become what You want.

WEEKEND

God has reviving hands

For reflection: 1 Kings 18:41–46
'A cloud as small as a man's hand is rising from the sea.' (v.44)

God's people had strayed far from Him and heathen worship was taking place everywhere throughout the land. An evil king, Ahab, was ruling the nation – and his wife, Jezebel, was even more wicked. As a result, God had caused a three-year famine in the land and the people were suffering for lack of food and water. This was the setting for the event described in our passage.

Elijah called the nation together at Mount Carmel, denounced their apostate worship of Baal and presented a challenge to prove who was the true God. In competition with the heathen priests, Elijah called down fire from God. It consumed the sacrifice and demonstrated who was the real, living God.

After this triumph, Elijah told King Ahab to hurry home – as rain was on its way. He then went to pray for that rain to arrive.

And rain it did. Not right away, but as Elijah prayed the rain clouds began to appear. His servant saw the first rain cloud in the shape of a hand – the hand of God. They needed rain so badly – and here was God's answer.

Optional further reading
Read the whole story, beginning in 1 Kings 16:29 and continuing through to the end of chapter 18. It's an exciting one! A once-only-in-history happening!

God has **humbling hands**

1 Peter 5:6–7

'Humble yourselves, therefore, under God's mighty hand, that he may lift you up in due time.' (v.6)

We need to note here that the word is 'humble' not 'humiliate' which, unfortunately, is how some have read it. Nor does this verse say that God will humble us. It tells us that we have to humble ourselves under His hands.

God's will is always working for our best. Many people look at God's will as a negative thing – something to stop a person having fun. They think of God as a severe Master, looking down on us in order to make life difficult. But God is not like that. His heart is loving towards us in every way.

The directive to humble ourselves does not imply being knocked down, or even afflicting ourselves, in an effort to be humble enough to please God. Instead, it means having a positive, active attitude towards life whereby a person voluntarily adopts an unassuming outlook towards God to allow God's will, and only His will, to be worked out in his or her life. This means that there is no room for personal ego.

Having an unassuming attitude doesn't mean that we have to be like quiet little mice, either. Everyone needs to get on with daily life, just as before, only with an unassuming manner – free of personal ego and willing to give God space to dictate what happens next.

Most of us have met people who seem to have the ability to praise God in spite of everything. Instead of being pulled down by the circumstances around them, these people seem to live above them: their eyes are on the Lord and He is the total focus of their lives.

I think this is what it means to be humble in the real sense – to live, not for yourself, but for Him; unassuming and pliable in His hands.

For prayer and reflection

Teach me, heavenly Father, what it really means to humble myself under Your hands. I want to live my life without personal ego trips; I want to be totally focused on You.

God has **delivering hands**

Moses spoke these words at the time when God gave him instructions about keeping the Passover. This event was to be celebrated annually as a memorial of the Israelites' release from slavery. The bondage of the Egyptians had been hard and the oppression severe. The Israelites had cried to God in their misery and He had sent them a deliverer to lead them out of Egypt. The key for their deliverance was to be the blood of a slain lamb painted, in an act of faith, on the doorposts of their houses the night before their release.

God could have brought the Israelites out of Egypt without that final miracle, but it's as if He wanted it recorded in written history, for all to see, that deliverance comes by the blood of a lamb.

And it was a threefold deliverance. Firstly, it was deliverance from death. The plague hit the firstborn of every Egyptian family and they died, but the blood of the lamb protected the Israelites. Secondly, it was deliverance from slavery and oppression. After the devastation of that night, Pharaoh set the Israelites free and the Egyptian people begged them to leave. So we can picture that the blood of the lamb also delivers from the slavery of sin, addictions, depression – and anything else that holds us in an evil grip. Thirdly, it was deliverance into a new life – a life that, while the journey through the wilderness to the promised land might have been difficult and arduous in places, was also a time of miracles, as God provided for their every need.

God wrote these truths in His Book – for us to know that by the blood of the Lamb of God, Jesus, we have deliverance from slavery, oppression, addictions and evil and we have the way into a new life.

Exodus 13:3–10

'… the land of slavery, because the LORD brought you out of it with a mighty hand.' (v.3)

For prayer and reflection

The blood of the lamb, painted on the doorposts of their houses, protected the Israelites only if they stayed inside. May God help us always to stay inside His protection.

God has **guiding hands**

Ezra 7:1–28

'Because the hand of the LORD my God was on me, I took courage …' (v.28)

You really need to read the whole of the book of Ezra to get the full picture here. It describes events taking place during the reigns of at least three Persian kings.

Some of the Jewish exiles, taken to Persia many years before, returned to their homeland in order to rebuild. Work was slow and they encountered many problems, mostly from people living in neighbouring countries who remembered the former power of the Jewish nation and were afraid of this happening again. These neighbouring people sent a letter of complaint to the Persian king and, for a time, the work was stopped.

It was the prophets Haggai and Zechariah who got the rebuilding work restarted some years later. Two men, Zerubbabel and Jeshua, began the rebuilding, the prophets working alongside them. Once again a letter of complaint was sent to the Persian king (a different ruler this time) but the complainers didn't get the response they expected – it went right against them. The king ordered them to leave the builders alone – and also to pay part of the cost!

In time, the Temple was completed – and this is where Ezra comes onto the scene. Descended from Aaron, he was a teacher of the Law. When he requested permission to return to Jerusalem and function there, the king not only granted him permission but appointed him Chief Justice – not only over the Jews but over the complainers as well! Surely the hand of the Lord his God was in this!

The whole story is a remarkable example of how God turns things around to bless those who obey Him. Note how the complainers were forced to come up with the finances for the project they fussed about, and how Ezra became Chief Justice over them as well!

For prayer and reflection

Father, I want to be so in the centre of Your leading that I can know and be sure of Your hand upon me.

God has **anointing hands**

Three kings were seeking the counsel of the prophet Elisha. Joram, son of the evil King Ahab, was now king of Israel, while Jehoshaphat, a godly king, ruled in neighbouring Judah.

Forced to pay tribute to Israel, the country of Moab had rebelled, refusing to pay. Seeking the help of King Jehoshaphat, King Joram set out to invade Moab. Passing through Edom, the two kings gained the help of the king of Edom. The three armies travelled for seven days towards Moab.

Then the unthinkable happened: they ran out of water to drink and to water their horses. The kings were close to despair when an army officer reminded them that they were in Elisha's territory; they could seek counsel of this prophet of God. Elisha agreed to talk with them. After hearing their dilemma, he called for a harpist. While the harpist played, the anointing of the Holy Spirit fell on Elisha and he gave the kings their answer: God would supply water by a miracle and give them victory as well.

The following dawn water was flooding the valley. The sun shone red on the water and the Moabite army, mistaking it for blood and assuming that the kings had fought and slaughtered each other, advanced – and lost the battle.

There is a mighty power in music when it is focused on praising God. We see this even today. It still opens the door to anointing – a term we use to describe the coming of the Holy Spirit into a situation and His resting upon a person to enable God to use him or her. Praise music has a particular way of helping this to happen by apparently connecting us to God in some special way so that He can allow the Holy Spirit to move through us.

2 Kings 3:14–27

'While the harpist was playing, the hand of the LORD came upon Elisha …' (v.15)

For prayer and reflection

Father, help me to recognise the power in music and to understand that it will help me reach out to You. Help me to be discerning about the kind of music I listen to.

God has **encouraging hands**

**1 Samuel
23:15–18**

'And Jonathan …
went to David …
and strengthened
his hand in God.'
(v.16, AV)

David was having such a bad time! King Saul was after his life and David was in hiding. He'd done nothing wrong – it was just that Saul was jealous of him. A group of loyal fighting men had attached themselves to David and, along with them, he lived in caves in the hills, carrying out a sort of guerilla warfare.

The Philistines had attacked the town of Keilah and David and his men planned to go and help the city. David took counsel with the Lord and the answer came back clearly that they should go. They did, and won, but when King Saul heard about it (as was inevitable) he decided that this was his opportunity to trap David. It would be easier to do so inside a city than in the hills. When God warned David that the people of Keilah would hand him over to King Saul, he and his men left Keilah and went back into the hills.

I am sure that it must have been really devastating to David to know that, after saving them from their enemy, the residents in Keilah would have handed him over to his own death. It was at this point that his old friend, Jonathan, the king's son, came out to him to reassure and encourage him. The Authorised Version puts this so beautifully when it says that Jonathan 'strengthened his hand in God'.

This ministry of encouragement is a real outreach from God Himself. An old poem reminds us that the only hands God has today are our hands – and how true that is! Through us, He can reach out and touch the people who need to know that He cares about how they feel. Through us, God can let them experience His encouraging hand reaching out to them.

**For prayer
and reflection**

**Heavenly Father,
help me to be one
of those people
who reach out to
others in need of
encouragement.
Help me to be
Your hand
touching them.**

WEEKEND

God has upholding hands

For reflection: Psalm 37:23–29
'… though he stumble, he will not fall,
for the Lord upholds him with his hand.' (v.24)

The picture that immediately comes to mind is one of a parent with his child. The young child, a toddler perhaps, is walking beside his father and the father is holding his hand. The child trips but does not fall, because the father tightens his grip and holds him steady. If the child were to take his hand out of the father's hand and run ahead, as children love to do, he would not have that same protection.

Then, there are also the stops. When it's time to cross the road, the hand of the parent restrains the child so that he does not run out into the traffic and become involved in an accident. There are other times to stop too: pauses to rest, to look at something new, or even to allow another person to get ahead. All these times to stop are caused by the restraining hand of the father and have a purpose.

God uses these illustrations to show His hand at work in our lives – He holds us and sometimes restrains us.

Optional further reading
Psalm 37:1–40. Discover all the other truths laid out within this psalm.

God has **faithful hands**

1 Kings 8:15–21

'Praise be to the LORD, the God of Israel, who with his own hand has fulfilled what he promised …' (v.15)

The Israelites were now firmly established in the land God had promised to them. They had come out of Egypt, passed through the years in the wilderness and entered the promised land. Over the course of time, a monarchy had been set up and King David had ruled the country, a wise and God-fearing king. As the people were now permanently established in the land, he had wanted to build a permanent temple in which to hold services, to replace the temporary tent they'd been using. However, God forbade him, saying it was not yet time for that. After David's death, his son Solomon came to the throne, whom David had commissioned to build the Temple.

In our reading today, the Temple is now complete and the Israelites are ready to move in the furniture, including the most sacred article of all: the ark of the covenant. When everything is ready, the glory of the Lord descends and fills the sanctuary, and the amazed people actually see with their own eyes the evidence of God's presence. King Solomon prays and then speaks the words we read today. He blesses the God who has fulfilled what He has promised to do. He hasn't failed one iota!

It isn't that God doesn't choose to fail – though even that would be wonderful. It is that because He is God He cannot fail. Simply cannot! If He could fail, He wouldn't be God.

If you still haven't seen the hoped-for answer to a prayer you've been asking, remember that there are three ways in which God can reply: 'Yes', 'No' or 'Wait'. We need always to remind ourselves that God knows what is best in any situation we bring to Him and to rest in that assurance. He knows the best time, too.

For prayer and reflection

I do realise, Father, that You absolutely cannot fail. Help me to rely on Your judgment and to rest in the assurance that You really do know best.

God has **limitless hands**

The 'ups and downs' of life are more than a little disconcerting. As Christians, we may feel that we should be able to be joyful all the time – and then we hit a low spot and it causes us distress. The highs of the mountaintop experiences are far easier to deal with – and far more enjoyable too! We can be like Peter who, when he experienced the wonderful sight of Jesus at His transfiguration, wanted to build a tent around the experience and keep it like that all the time. But there always has to be a 'coming down'.

There is always a valley between the mountains – that is the way things are – and the fact that you and I suffer our 'down times' of depression is all a part of life. If life were all valleys, it is true that there would be no climbing to be done, no difficult, steep pathways – but there would be no downhill runs either. If life were all mountaintop experiences, we would become cold and icy up there and the freshness would turn into biting bitterness. There have to be mountains and valleys, ups and downs, different times and seasons of life (Eccl. 3:1–8). God made it that way.

All we need to do is realise that the depths, the down times that cause us such distress and heartache, are also part of the overall plan. The earth runs with ups and downs, highs and lows: high tide and low tide, summer and winter, night and day. Those down times, although they may not be enjoyable, are in His hands just as much as the mountaintop experiences. We need to realise that we need them because we could not stand the exhilaration of the mountaintop for long. Hold on! It's all part of His plan.

Psalm 95

'In his hand are the depths of the earth, and the mountain peaks belong to him.'
(v.4)

For prayer and reflection

Heavenly Father, I do understand that You created the whole world to run on ups and downs – but I find the down times in my own life difficult. Help me, please.

God has **mighty hands**

Joshua 4:19–24

'… the hand of the LORD is powerful …' (v.24)

You need to take the time to read the whole of this story (Josh. 3:1–4:24). The Israelite people had reached the very edge of the promised land but they still had the River Jordan to cross and, at that time of year, it was in flood and too deep to wade through. So God told Joshua, who was now their leader, to instruct the priests carrying the ark of the covenant to go ahead into the water. The moment their feet entered the water, the river dammed itself higher upstream and stopped flowing down to where they were. The people crossed the river on dry ground, the Scriptures say, while the priests holding the ark stood still in the centre of the riverbed.

In addition to this, Joshua had instructed that one man from each of the 12 tribes should take one stone from the centre of the riverbed where the priests stood and bring it with him to the other side. There, the 12 stones were set up as a memorial to the miracle.

A memorial is built to preserve a memory. This memorial was to remember a truly remarkable miracle of God, as great as the one experienced by the parents of the Israelites 40 years earlier, when crossing the Red Sea.

God is absolutely awesome and the accounts of these miracles are incredible. It is this same God whom we serve today. Sometimes we have to remind ourselves of that fact. With all the helpful goods and services available to us in modern life – health care, electricity, transportation etc – we don't rely on God's miraculous power as much as the Israelites had to. Maybe we need to rethink – and rely on God a little more! He hasn't changed!

For prayer and reflection

Almighty God, give me a deeper concept of Your awesomeness and Your mighty power, and let me see how very great You are. Enlarge my vision of You.

God's hands **reveal the plan**

King David was a good and God-fearing king. In fact, he was an example of someone who was sincerely devoted to his God. His psalms are full of praise and understanding of the majesty of God; and his life showed that he would turn to God in prayer whenever he had a problem, whatever it was.

David had longed to be the one who would build the Temple of worship for God, but the Lord had restrained him, telling him that his son, Solomon, would do it. This passage of Scripture recounts the time when King David called his officials together and, in front of them all, commissioned his son to build the Temple. David said that God had given him a detailed plan for the building of the Temple and he passed it on, in writing, to his son, Solomon. 'I have [it] in writing from the hand of the Lord upon me ...' he said.

Reading this passage shows us something else amazing that is the result of the 'hand of the Lord' being upon one of His servants – it is the means of God revealing the plan He has in mind. David wanted to do things one way; God checked that and showed him the way He wanted things to be done. It's also a very beautiful picture. It describes the hand of the Lord resting on the hand of His servant, David, as he wrote; guiding David in the words he set down on paper. In this instance, the hand of God refers to the ministry of the Holy Spirit when He is resting on a person under particular anointing.

When the Scripture is so descriptively beautiful it stirs our imagination and moves our hearts. Surely it should be our desire always to have the hand of the Lord upon us – and His Holy Spirit guiding us from within.

---

1 Chronicles 28:9–20

"'All this," David said, "I have in writing from the hand of the LORD upon me ...'" (v.19)

For prayer and reflection

Father, I want to live my life with Your hand always resting on me. I want to be guided by Your hand and, most of all, I want You to be seen at work in me.

God's hands **can be condemning**

....

Daniel 5:1–30

....

'Suddenly the fingers of a human hand appeared and wrote on the plaster of the wall …' (v.5)

Belshazzar, the king, was the son of the famous Nebuchadnezzar who had besieged and captured Jerusalem, then carried away captives to Babylon. Daniel was among these captives, but because the hand of God was upon his life he had risen to an important place in the kingdom under Nebuchadnezzar. He was known to be able to interpret dreams and visions. Through various happenings, most of which involved Daniel, Nebuchadnezzar had come to respect Daniel's God.

The king's son, Belshazzar, did not share this respect for God. He held a feast and, amid drunken debauchery, commanded that the vessels of the Temple, which they had plundered in Jerusalem and brought with them to Babylon, be brought for them to use. This was outright blasphemy.

When the writing '*Mene, mene, tekel, parsin*' appeared on the wall, King Belshazzar summoned his own wise men and magicians but none of them was able to tell him the meaning of the words. It was the queen who pointed out that Daniel would be able to interpret them. Daniel told King Belshazzar that he, as king, had been judged by God. That night the armies of Media-Persia invaded, the king was killed and the kingdom lost to the enemy.

The '*tekel*' was used as a measure in balances. The last word, '*parsin*' is exactly half the measure of each of the first two ('*mene, tekel*'), indicating that, in God's sight, the king failed to measure up.

In our own lives, God does not expect us to measure up to His expectations as much by the things we do, as by the respect and honour we pay to Him. He expects us to honour Him by putting Him first in our lives.

....

For prayer and reflection

....

Father, Your Word instructs us to pray for kings and those in authority in our nation. I do pray that we may always have a God-respecting ruler or president.

WEEKEND

God has restraining hands

For reflection: 2 Chronicles 30:1–12
'Also in Judah the hand of God was on the people
to give them unity of mind …' (v.12)

Hezekiah, a good king, wanted the people to turn back to God. The whole nation had been worshipping idols and, when it came to religious observance, the people had been doing whatever they felt like. Many of the practices in heathen worship were totally disgusting, some even involving the sacrifice of children. God hates idolatry.

Hezekiah decided that it was time to invite the nation back to the worship of the one true God, so he sent letters around the country inviting the people to a Passover celebration. Some ridiculed the messengers, but others were open to the suggestion. God moved on the tribe of Judah, causing them to obey, and they were joined by people from among the other tribes. Finally a crowd came. The people discovered that when they obeyed God they had a good time – so good that they decided to prolong the celebration!

Although God does allow us to make our own choices, there are times when He gives us a little push! Sometimes we need that. Deep in our hearts we want to serve Him, but things may have got out of control. At times God helps us to make the right decision by holding onto us firmly, restraining us.

Optional further reading
Now go back and read the whole of 2 Chronicles 30 and the first verse of the next chapter. Make a note of the results when people obey the Lord.

God has **loving hands**

Job 2:1–13

'What? shall we receive good at the hand of God, and shall we not receive evil?' (v.10, AV)

The argument between Job and his wife recorded here is one that is played out many times in life. We know for sure that good comes from God. Most people will say that evil comes from the devil and, of course, this is true. But then the question arises as to why good people suffer or why Christians get sick. Some preachers will tell you it is simply that we live in a wicked world and troubles are inevitable, but that is not a complete answer if God gives only good — because we are God's people and we belong to Him.

I am glad that God set down one answer here in the book of Job. Note well who started off this situation. It wasn't Satan; it was God. Look at Job 1:8 and notice how God raised the question of how much Job loved and feared Him. It was God who challenged Satan to refute the fact. Satan took up the challenge and obtained God's permission to put Job to the test. Knowing that Job would come out of it all right, God gave His permission and Satan went to work inflicting Job with troubles and sickness. Here we can see for sure that sickness and evil do come from Satan, but we also see that this does not happen without God's permission.

I am sure that you, like me, have been through difficult and painful times when it has been very hard to thank God for the circumstances we find ourselves in. In remembering Job's story, we can still take comfort from the truth that God is greater than all our circumstances and can work in everything for our good (Rom. 8:28). It may even be that God has been bragging about us — and is allowing us a time of testing: not to punish us but, ultimately, for our good because He loves us.

For prayer and reflection

Father, it's hard to understand that good comes from You — and yet we also get sick and have troubles. Help me to grasp this truth in the right way.

God has **ministering hands**

It would have been very precious and moving if Jesus had merely bent down that night to wash the disciples' feet. After all, He was their Master and it was more their task, as servants, to do that for Him. But, in this passage, the Scriptures add something even more significant than that. They give a picture of Jesus, who was perfect and totally sinless, knowing, at that precise moment, exactly who He was. He knew that He was God.

Here we have, embodied in human flesh, the Creator Himself – for the Bible tells us that all things were created by Him – wrapping a towel around Himself and washing the feet of 12 rugged and uncertain disciples. This was the last time Jesus would eat a meal with His disciples and I think that He wanted to assure them that, whatever happened in the hours to follow, He loved them. After all, Jesus' love prompted Him to do this: a love so boundless and unfathomable that it sent Him to walk the road to Calvary and to die on the cross for you and me. He stooped, that great Creator, and washed His disciples' feet – and then gave them a command that they, too, should minister to others in the same way that He had ministered to them. Can anyone retain his or her own pride after that?

How much more do we have to be humbly willing to walk in Jesus' footsteps and minister to others on His behalf? It's up to us to take something of that same boundless love to others and to show them an expression of those ministering hands. It may not always seem easy and, for some of us, it may seem sometimes that there is nothing we can do. But there is. There always is. God has a work for each one of us – and that includes you.

John 13:1–17

'Jesus knowing that the Father had given all things into his hands ...'
(v.3, AV)

For prayer and reflection

Help me, Father, to appreciate Jesus' incredible love deep inside of me and then to be able to minister that same love to other people.

God has **healing hands**

Matthew 8:14–17

'He touched her hand and the fever left her …' (v.15)

For prayer and reflection

Dear Lord, I bring to You every situation in my own life and family that needs Your healing touch today. Help me to believe that You will turn things around and meet my need.

No one would doubt that if Jesus was God, then His hands were God's hands, extended to the world through the Person of His Son. In today's reading, Peter witnesses the touch of God's hands in his own home, as Jesus ministers to his sick mother-in-law. Maybe Peter was torn between wanting to be with Jesus and feeling that he ought to be at the side of his sick relative – we don't know. All we do know is that Jesus had just told a centurion asking for healing for his sick servant that He would come to his home to heal the servant. At this, the centurion had argued that he was unworthy to receive Jesus at his home and that, if Jesus would just speak the word, He would not need to come in person. Marvelling at the man's faith, Jesus agreed, telling him that because he'd believed, his request was granted.

After this, we read that Jesus entered Peter's home and found Peter's mother-in-law sick and in bed. Jesus touched her hand and immediately she was healed.

Perhaps a situation in your home or family needs healing today: not necessarily a physical sickness – maybe an emotional need or a broken relationship needing the touch of the mighty hand of God. God's hands are healing hands: right throughout the Old Testament and on into the ministry of Jesus. Recognise afresh, today, that God is Master over every situation and that nothing is beyond His power to heal. Bring the situation in your home or family to Him and ask the Sovereign Lord to touch it with His mighty hands. Believe that God's healing power can transform the people and the situation – physically, emotionally and spiritually.

God has **life-giving hands**

Matthew 9:18–26

'… he went in and took the girl by the hand, and she got up.' (v.24)

When called to the death of Lazarus, Jesus did not say, 'I am the resurrection and the life', because one day He was going to conquer death and rise from the grave. He claimed to be the resurrection – in person – and that's why death could not hold Him. It could not keep Him down. That's also why He was able to call Lazarus back from the dead and impart to him new life – even after Lazarus had been dead for four days.

Jesus is Life itself. He does not merely give life – He is Life!

There was nothing exceptional about the little girl in today's passage when, as a result of some sickness, she died. What was exceptional was that when Jesus took her by the hand, He pulled her back from the grave to life once again. Through His touch, life, the life of the eternal God, flowed back into her and she opened her eyes and lived again.

Did you notice that Jesus pulled back from the grave people from three different age groups? There was the older man, Lazarus; the widow's son who, it seems, was probably a young man; and this child. Maybe that is just coincidence, but maybe it's not. Perhaps Jesus was demonstrating that the hands of Almighty God can reach out to people of all ages: whether to your elderly relative who needs His touch, a brother or sister of your own age, or a little child. No one is beyond His reach. It is also true that, if these three people were already dead, they couldn't reach out to Jesus for themselves. It took relatives to reach out for them. You may have relatives who need His touch; reach out on their behalf today and believe that God will touch them. He will!

For prayer and reflection

Heavenly Father, I am bringing to you members of my family: elderly relatives, young people and children – whoever they are – that You would minister to them today.

God's hands **lead us**

....

Mark 8:22–26

....

'He took the blind man by the hand and led him outside the village.' (v.23)

You'd have thought that Jesus would have saved time if He'd simply touched the sick and, instantly, they'd been healed. After all, in the book of Acts, the sick were laid beside the road so that even the shadow of Peter might fall on them as he passed by.

I am sure that Jesus could have just gone around touching people and they would all have been instantly healed, but He did not choose to treat people in this impersonal way. No two people who came to Him for help were ever ministered to in the same way by the Master. He did not have a routine way of doing things. Each person was an individual to Jesus – and each person's needs required a special touch from Him. Such was His loving compassion and tenderness.

We don't know why Jesus did not choose to heal this man in the place where he came to Him. We can't tell whether the crowd was hostile or unbelieving or whether, perhaps, Jesus wanted to walk this man away from the crowd and out of the village just to talk with him. But one thing we do know, Jesus took the blind man by the hand and led him outside the village. And, after healing him, Jesus told the man not to go back into Bethsaida again.

Some of us are like this man. You may have asked God for healing or for the answer to some other prayer and God does not seem to be answering. Perhaps there is still a road you have to walk with Him, led by His hand, before that answer will become possible. Maybe God has to take you by the hand, just as Jesus did this blind man, and lead you to a different place before He can meet your need. Take His hand and trust Him.

....

For prayer and reflection

....

Father, show me the reason for the delay in the answer to my prayer. Is there somewhere you have to take me to, or something you have to deal with in my life?

WEEKEND

God has proud hands

For reflection: Isaiah 62:1–7

'You will be a crown of splendour in the Lord's hand …' (v. 3)

It is said that God will reward us with a crown after we reach heaven. Maybe there is a special crown of reward for us – a crown that we will be able to lay at His feet in worship. But what is hardly ever considered is what is said in this passage of Scripture. Here it tells us that we will be a 'crown of splendour in the Lord's hand' and a 'royal diadem in the hand of [our] God'. And that's a promise – one that can be relied upon.

While it is truly wonderful that we are precious to God Himself, there is another wonderful thing to consider here. He holds the crown in His hand; it is not on His head. Why? He holds it in His hand so that He can admire and cherish it for all eternity. Imagine that! You and I are so precious to Him that, not only does He mould and polish us to shine with His glory, but He also holds us in His hand so that He can cherish and admire us!

Optional further reading

Turn to Revelation chapters 21 and 22 and read about the New Jerusalem, the Bride of Christ. Remember that the New Jerusalem consists of redeemed people (like you and me) shining with His glory.

God's hands **lift us up**

Mark 9:14–29

'But Jesus took him by the hand and lifted him to his feet, and he stood up.' (v.27)

After being on the mountain where they had experienced the transfiguration of the Lord, Peter, James and John, the disciples, might have seemed equipped to help this demon-possessed boy. They had just come down from the most wonderful experience of their lives. Alone with Jesus, they'd been transported into a new realm of spiritual experience where they had seen the majesty and divinity of the One whom they served. They had even heard the audible voice of the Almighty God and it would seem that these things would have qualified them to be the greatest miracle workers there had ever been. But they did not volunteer to be the ones to help this boy. The other disciples had not been able to do so either. Only Jesus was able to perform this particular miracle.

God favours men and women with mountaintop experiences and portions these out as He pleases, but it is not these experiences that equip us to be able to cast out demons, deliver the sick and lift up the oppressed. Visions and mountaintop experiences do not make a person more effective for God, nor can we wish our way into a ministry of miracles. We cannot believe our way into it either. There is only one way to become an effective vessel for the power of God to minister through us and it is the way Jesus took. He spent time in prayer and fasting, and trod the road of the cross. The price was great and the way was hard. It still is.

Because of the way Jesus chose to live His life, His hands were hands that could lift a person up and free him or her from oppression and the work of Satan. May God make us willing to pay the price, so that we may also be effective ministers for Him.

For prayer and reflection

Lord, I do want to be a vessel through which Your miracle power can flow. Please help me to be willing to follow Your example of prayer and fasting.

Jesus' hands **identify Him**

I t was not so much that the disciples could not recognise the Lord when He appeared to them after His resurrection. They knew who He was for sure. They knew Jesus well and had lived with Him continually for so long that it would have been impossible for Him to have appeared to them, even in His new resurrection body, and for them not to have recognised who He was.

It was necessary for Jesus to draw attention to His hands, His feet and also His side (John 20:27), for two reasons. Firstly, to show them that the crucifixion really had happened and that it was not just a nightmare. Jesus wanted the disciples to know that the cross was indeed a reality and that He had really died. He wanted them to be certain that He had not escaped death and simply come back from hiding to be with them again. No, the cross was a reality: the disciples had to understand that. Secondly, Jesus wanted the disciples to know that whereas He had truly died, He was now truly alive again. It was no ghost they were seeing. He was real – and His body was real. Jesus told them to touch Him and to feel the wounds for themselves. He was flesh and blood, not a ghost, and His wounded, nail-scarred hands proved it.

If Jesus had appeared to them as a spirit, He would not have been the conqueror over death. He would have still been dead. But the resurrection was a reality. He, the same Jesus, was alive again. His hands bring us the same message today. We can see those nail prints and know that He has died in our place, then risen from the grave, victorious over Satan and death. Glorious Lord! He has the victory!

Luke 24:36–49

'Look at my hands and my feet. It is I myself! Touch me and see …'(v. 39)

For prayer and reflection

Lord Jesus, I rejoice today in Your victory over death and Satan. I place my hands in Your nail-scarred hands and feel Your presence as I walk with You. Thank You that You are with me every day. Praise You, Lord!

Longing
for more

Beverley Shepherd

Beverley is a trainer, writer and executive coach. She specialises in the areas of leadership, team development and stress management. One of her passions is the encouraging and equipping of Christians in the workplace and in 2011 she established PrayerWorks on behalf of LICC. A regular speaker, Beverley has written several books including *Insight into Stress* and *Created as a Woman*.

The **disciple**

Luke 5:1–11,
27–32

'So they pulled
their boats up
on shore, left
everything and
followed him.'
(v.11)

**For prayer
and reflection**

**Lord, I am
struggling –
caught between
the desire to
follow You and
the fear of moving
out of my comfort
zone. Yet I also
know that life
without You isn't
worth living.
Please help me.**

Those that responded to Jesus' call to follow Him were known as His disciples. The concept of the disciple was a familiar one at the time of Jesus. Young men who had excelled in their study of the Scriptures would apply to their chosen teacher or rabbi to become his disciple. 'The goal of a disciple wasn't just to know what the rabbi knew, but to be just like the rabbi.'* Hence the rabbi would question the prospective disciple to evaluate whether the young man had the potential to teach what he taught and do what he did. If he thought that the young man was fully suitable, then he would say 'Come, follow me'.

There was one central difference between Jesus' disciples and those of other rabbis: Jesus' disciples did not apply to Him – He chose them (John 15:16). In doing this, Jesus declared His belief that they could learn to be like Him and do what He did.

So the decision to follow Jesus is a decision to become His disciple – to become like Him; to learn to do what He did – not in our own strength, but through His Spirit dwelling within us. And Jesus believes we can!

As I search the Scriptures I see no second category of believer in Christ. I can't find anyone who gave mental assent to the truth: 'Jesus, the Son of God who paid the price for our sins, rose from the dead and secured us a place in heaven' – and yet was not a disciple (ie an imitator of His life). The title 'Christian', first used in Antioch, was only applied to disciples and meant 'little Christ'.

Jesus promises abundant life to those who follow Him – and that life is His own.

*Rob Bell, *Velvet Elvis* (Grand Rapids: Zondervan, 2005) p.129.

How dissatisfied are you?

Waiting in the doctor's surgery one day I began reading a magazine article inviting you to be your own 'life coach'. It asked you to grade your satisfaction with different areas of your life: work, relationships, health etc. The scale ran from '0' (denoting that you were totally dissatisfied) to '10' (indicating that you were completely satisfied). I completed the exercise and then read the comments: 'Beware any areas in the 4–6 range,' it said, 'these are the areas you may not be sufficiently dissatisfied with to do anything about.' Wise words. Change is demanding – it takes time and effort. There is a cost involved. Vague dissatisfaction may not be sufficient motivation to pay the cost.

But there is also a cost in staying the same; a cost in answering the call of Jesus to follow Him with: 'Not yet' or 'Only so far' or 'If you lead in the direction I choose'. 'Non-discipleship costs abiding peace, a life penetrated throughout by love, faith that sees everything in the light of God's overriding governance for good, hopefulness that stands firm in the most discouraging of circumstances, power to do what is right and withstand the forces of evil. In short, it costs exactly that abundance of life Jesus said he came to bring (John 10:10).'*

Just as an encounter with Jesus turned the woman at the well's flickering flame of 'longing for more' into a blazing fire, allow God to turn vague desire into deep hunger, and dissatisfaction with your life into a firm decision to place yourself before Him and allow Him to change you. The first stirrings of 'longing for more' are evidence that God is already at work in your life.

*Dallas Willard, *The Spirit of the Disciplines* (London: Hodder & Stoughton, 1996) p.274.

John 4:1–15

'… whoever drinks the water I give him will never thirst.' (v.14)

For prayer and reflection

Note down different aspects of your Christian life and score them on a 'thirsty' scale: 0 = parched and 10 = already drunk deeply. Reflect on your scores.

Spiritual **disciplines**

....

Colossians 3:1–17

....

'… since you have taken off your old self with its practices and have put on the new self …' (vv.9–10)

Throughout the centuries, the Church has understood that a believer requires discipline (in the sense of instruction and training) to be a disciple. Spiritual disciplines are intentional practices that give space in our lives for the presence of Jesus to transform us. They include solitude, silence, prayer, fasting, study, worship and celebration – and are designed to replace the habits of our former non-believing thinking and behaviour with ones that fuel our desire to know and love God.

Why are our habits so important? A habit is a tendency to perform certain actions or to behave in a certain way without thinking – on automatic. Unless our beliefs transform our habits, our desire to become more like Christ will be hampered. In the *Screwtape Letters* an older, experienced devil writes with advice to his nephew: 'My dear Wormwood, I note with grave displeasure that your patient has become a Christian … There is no need to despair … All the *habits* of the patient, both mental and bodily, are still in our favour' (my emphasis).*

So how do we change our habits? Willpower is seldom enough when habits are built on wrong beliefs about God, ourselves or others. The spiritual disciplines allow us to place ourselves before God so that He can transform us. Just as the goal of going to the gym is not to do various exercises for their own sake, but to get fit, so the disciplines contain no merit of themselves. 'It was this important truth that the Pharisees failed to see. The Disciplines place us before God; they do not give us Brownie points with God.'**

For prayer and reflection

Think of a time when you undertook to change a habit (eg smoking, unhealthy eating, criticising). What was involved in making the change?

* C.S. Lewis, *The Screwtape Letters* (London: HarperCollins, 1942) p.5.
**Richard Foster, *Celebration of Discipline* (London: Hodder & Stoughton, 1989) p.12.

WEEKEND

Longing for more

For reflection: John 10:10
'I have come that they may have life, and have it to the full.'

These notes are born out of a heart cry – a cry that first clamoured for my attention nine months ago and has increased its insistence ever since. One day, whilst spending time with God, I found myself shouting: 'There must be more, Lord! There must be more!' More to Christianity than my life evidences … more to life-changing, world-shaping community than my church experience indicates … MORE!

When Jesus called the first disciples with the words, 'Follow me', they had to make a decision – based not on knowledge of the route, nor guarantee of the destination, nor promise of comfort on the way, but on a deep desire to be with Jesus and to know Him better. More than anything they wanted to know this man who could lead them to life that was 'more'.

Are you longing for more? As we travel together let's seek to understand what that 'more' is and begin to walk in the fullness of it. Why not use a journal to note down your reflections each day?

For reflection: John 1:35–51. Why did the first disciples follow Jesus?

Optional further reading
Psalm 42:1–2. Ask God to increase your thirst for Him.

The **risk factor**

Luke 10:38–42

'… you are worried and upset about many things, but only one thing is needed.' (vv.41–42)

Committing to anything new carries a risk factor. Will the effort involved lead to the results I am hoping for? This is particularly true of the spiritual disciplines because they place me before God but, of themselves, do not change me. It is God who does the work of transformation in me. To embrace the disciplines requires faith because, from the world's point of view, they seem non-productive. Since we cannot measure the 'product' of time spent developing our relationships with God and with others, it takes a risk to invest time in these ways.

We live in a world addicted to activity: we work in cities where we are forever rushing to meet deadlines; we shop in supermarkets where the words 'instant', 'quick' or 'rapid' sell products; and we worship in churches that praise 'the active Christian'. We also live in homes where everyone is on the go – or have collapsed, exhausted, in front of the TV. Although Paul says that we are not to allow the world to squeeze us into its mould (Rom. 12:2), it is often hard to go against the flow.

Similarly, in church, we say that we value godly character but what is 'rewarded' and praised is activity. We value our Marthas and criticise our Marys: 'Lord, don't you care that my sister has left me to do the work by myself? Tell her to help me!' So, often, the result is a full church programme but little impact on our towns or cities.

Why do we choose to be so busy? Because 'being busy producing and consuming can be a substitute for facing the deeper realities of life'.* Hence it is important to recognise that we will have to continually confront our addiction to busyness and our need for instant results.

For prayer and reflection

Lord, thank You that Mary chose the better way – please help me to do the same. Amen.

* Abbot Christopher Jamison, *Finding Sanctuary* (London: Phoenix, 2006) p.21.

Our **Personal Trainer**

The Holy Spirit does the work of reproducing the character of Jesus in us. Does that mean we are passive and have no role in this transformation? No! We can either co-operate with the Holy Spirit or block Him.

At the gym, a personal trainer does not exercise for me – he gives me instructions on how to use the machines, observes my progress, suggests changing the settings to make the exercise more beneficial and corrects any wrong technique on my part. Similarly, the Spirit of Jesus helps me as I seek to become more like Christ. As He whispers, 'This is the way; walk in it' (Isa. 30:21), I am faced with a choice: to walk God's way or to go my own. Consistently ignoring the Spirit's promptings leads to increasing deafness – we'll no longer hear His voice, and so block His activity in our lives.

If the goal of a more disciplined spiritual life is to become increasingly 'like Christ', then how will I know that progress is being made? It will, over time, be evident in my daily living, in my interactions with others. Instead of hating my enemies, I will love them; I will learn to turn the other cheek rather than hit back either verbally or physically; I will go the second mile rather than harbour resentment (Luke 6:27–36); and I will see God's resurrection power at work in me and through me.

Even writing this, I'm aware of how far I still have to go on this journey – but I'm encouraged by two facts: (1) Jesus believes that I can do what He did, for otherwise He would not have chosen me and called me to follow Him; (2) He sent the Holy Spirit to instruct me, comfort me, train me and remind me of all He has said. Those facts are true for you too!

John 14:15–31

'... the Holy Spirit ... will teach you all things and ... remind you of everything I have said to you.' (v.26)

For prayer and reflection

Lord, I thank You for Your Holy Spirit – give me ears to hear what He is saying and a desire to follow His guidance. Amen.

Solitude

Luke 4:1–21

'Jesus, full of the Holy Spirit … was led by the Spirit in the desert …' (v.1)

Solitude is the practice of spending time alone with God in an environment where you are free from distractions and will not be interrupted. There is nothing to 'do'. Greta Garbo is famous for the declaration, 'I want to be alone', but few of us really seek solitude. We may desire a break from the constant demands we face and see it as our right to have more 'me time' (ie time where I'm free to set the agenda according to my own needs and wants). But most of us are apprehensive about true solitude – we don't enjoy being alone.

In 'aloneness' we come face to face with ourselves and with God. There's nowhere to hide and no one else to meet our needs or to distract us. Our props of meetings, radio, TV, books, telephone, work and friends are removed, leaving us vulnerable. In solitude, we take the risk of feeling the full extent of our emptiness and we are brought face to face with our compulsions. Who are we, when productivity, visibility and recognition are removed?

Jesus repeatedly sought time alone with His Father – 40 days in the desert, nights alone on the mountainside and early morning times of prayer in solitary places. He longed for uninterrupted communion with Father God – He needed it! How else could He resist the temptations of the devil and know what the Father wanted Him to do?

We need solitude too. Here we develop an intimacy with the Lord and delight in His company. We are freed from the patterns and pace of this world. He answers the question of our identity with His love, stills our busyness with His peace, and touches our woundedness with His healing. 'Who is this coming up from the desert leaning on her lover?' (Songs 8:5).

For prayer and reflection

Father, please show me how to build times of solitude into the pattern of my life and forgive me where I have avoided intimacy with You.

Silence

O ur world is full of noise. We seek noise, be it from the TV, radio, iPod or our mobile phones. Encouraged to be 'in communication' at all times, we don't 'waste' precious minutes. Yet, in this buzz we often have very little worth saying. Endless words, but little wisdom.

The discipline of silence is twofold. The first aspect is to seek outward silence as a means of freeing myself from the distraction of noise and gradually coming to inner stillness. This allows me to be totally present to God: 'Be still, and know that I am God' (Psa. 46:10). Over time we learn to carry that stillness with us – even into our noisy world. This enables us to embrace the second aspect of silence: control of the tongue. James says that a person who is never at fault in what he or she says is perfect. I've rarely regretted being silent, but often regretted things I've said.

We use words to manage and control situations and people. So to remain silent is to embrace helplessness and to trust God to fight for us. In one situation, a few years ago, I felt God ask me to leave my reputation in His hands and not seek to vindicate myself. It was a hard yet valuable lesson that brought new understanding of Jesus' silence before His accusers. It also highlighted my unhelpful concern with what others think of me, and my need to have my actions and motives 'understood'.

Have you ever been at a party where the music was so loud you couldn't hear what others were saying? Gradually you don't even try to compete – conversation dies. At times the noise of our lives is so loud we cannot hear God. When we turn down the volume we begin to hear more clearly – God and others – through silence.

James 3:1–12; Proverbs 10:19–21,31; Exodus 14:13–14

'The LORD will fight for you; you need only to be still.' (Exod. 14:14)

For prayer and reflection

Lord, please help me to become still and listen to You.

The fruit of solitude and silence

1 Kings 19:1–18

'And after the fire came a gentle whisper.' (v.12)

Elijah fled into the desert – worn out, alone and scared for his life. After 40 days the voices of self-justification ('I have been very zealous for the Lord God Almighty') and of self-pity ('I have had enough, Lord') had stilled; God has spoken and ministered to him physically, giving him new perspective and direction. He has been restored. We can't all take 40 days 'out', but regular times of solitude bring rich fruit.

In solitude we learn how much we are loved by God. Loved, not for what we do or achieve, but for who we were created to be. In His love, God sees us. Here we begin to realise that God doesn't need us to do anything for Him. Lovingly He may show us what He is doing and invite us to participate – as He did for Elijah. Our identity rests in the security of His embrace. 'When we are willing to wait in solitude and silent prayer before God, the Holy Spirit begins to re-centre our lives, picking through all the distracted fragments and confusion, to the heart of who we are, to the place where God's love waits to welcome us.'*

Loving God and loving our neighbour is the great calling of our lives. We love because He first loved us. As we allow God to fill the void within us we are free to move towards others with love, secure in our own identity, and desiring to bless them instead of demanding they fill our emptiness. We have been enabled to face our own weaknesses and so are less eager to point out the speck in our neighbour's eye. Compassion is born.

My own experience is that times of solitude create a place of stillness within me. In this place I hear more clearly what God is saying and gain His perspective on my life.

For prayer and reflection

What would stop you spending an hour, in silence, alone with God, at some point in the coming week? Will you let it stop you?

* David Runcorn, *Space for God* (London: Daybreak, 1990) p.23.

WEEKEND

Spiritual detox

For reflection: Romans 12:1–21

The apostle Paul urges: 'Do not conform any longer to the pattern of this world …' (v2)

For those of us who work/study in organisations that claim no Christian ethos, live alongside non-believing neighbours, read magazines/books and watch TV (ie the normal context for living our lives), we will be aware of the pressure to conform to the pattern of this world. We do not have, nor probably want, the option of monastic life. We like to think of ourselves as individuals but the truth is, without deliberate action on our part, we will be squeezed into the world's mould. Just as normal patterns of eating leave toxins in our bodies, so normal patterns of living leave toxins in our spirits. So how do we detox or cleanse our spiritual system?

Of the many spiritual disciplines, I am going to focus initially on the 'detox' disciplines of solitude, silence and fasting. They confront our addiction to the pattern of this world.

Optional further reading

Richard Foster, *Celebration of Discipline* (London: Hodder & Stoughton, 1989) – a very practical guide to the disciplines.

Dallas Willard, *The Spirit of the Disciplines* (London: Hodder & Stoughton, 1996) – a clear philosophy, theology and psychology of spiritual growth.

Fasting

'When you fast, do not look sombre as the hypocrites do …' (v.16)

I enjoy food! If their choice of birthday cards is evidence, my friends believe me to be addicted to chocolate. It's easy to think that what we eat and drink has little relevance to our spiritual life, yet the Bible has a lot to say on this subject. If any area of your life is controlled by anything other than God, it's out of control. Fasting, more than any other discipline, reveals the things that control us (not just food). Anger, bitterness, fear and pride can quickly surface.

Fasting is the practice of abstaining from all food for a period of time. It is usual to drink water. The Bible speaks of fasts for anything from one to forty days. Some are partial fasts (abstaining from certain foods – Dan. 1:12; 10:2–3). Fasting from food enables us to feast on the Word of God and to spend time in prayer. Yet those for whom fasting is not a regular discipline may initially find that all they think about is food! It's therefore helpful to make a 24- or 36-hour fast a regular part of our week.*

The Old Testament prophets often called the Israelites to times of mourning and national repentance. Esther called the Jewish people to fast as she prepared to confront the evil Haman's schemes. 'When you fast …' were Jesus' words. Jesus fasted, as did His disciples, and it was the normal practice of the Early Church.

Jesus was concerned with our motivation when fasting. We don't fast to impress others, lose weight or feel morally superior. We fast to draw closer to God, to stand against evil and to break the hold of the worldliness in our lives. The prophet Isaiah spoke out strongly against fasting as a mere ritual (Isa. 58).

For prayer and reflection

Father, please use fasting to reveal the things that control me and to break their power. Amen.

*If you've never fasted before, begin slowly, perhaps missing just one meal – reading the Bible and praying instead. If you are pregnant, breast-feeding, ill, severely underweight or have diabetes, do not fast.

The 'rewards' of fasting

Jesus says that fasting is rewarded by our Father, but it's not a way of manipulating God. I remember fasting to hear from God over an issue. I did hear – His answer was 'No!' Then it dawned that I'd thought my fasting would 'earn' me a 'Yes!'

We seek to be people who are not conformed to the pattern of this world; our appetites play a vital part in this. In an age where appetites are out of control – witness the rise in obesity, pornography and general consumption – our appetites for food, drink, material possessions, physical love and entertainment can easily take a wrongful place in our lives: we become enslaved to them. 'Refrain from gluttony and thou shalt the more easily restrain all the inclinations of the flesh.'* Through self-denial we begin to recognise what controls us – and fasting helps us to bring our lives under God's control.

Most importantly, fasting humbles us and confirms our absolute dependence on God alone. When King David's prayers had returned to him unanswered, he humbled himself with fasting (Psa. 35:13–14). He knew that God promises to hear those who humble themselves and seek His face (2 Chron. 7:14).

Fasting leads to an increased hunger for God and often 'breakthroughs' in prayer. Daniel humbled himself through a partial fast for 21 days and God's messenger, who had been resisted by a demon, was freed to come to him. The experience of many people committed to prayer is: 'Fasting multiplies the effect of prayer at least several times ... Fasting will touch things that prayer alone will not affect.'**

* Dallas Willard, *The Spirit of the Disciplines* (London: Hodder & Stoughton, 1996) p.172.
**Cindy Jacobs, *Possessing the Gates of the Enemy* (London: Marshall Pickering, 1993) p.95.

Daniel 10:1–19

'But the prince of the Persian kingdom resisted me twenty-one days.' (v.13)

For prayer and reflection

It helps to plan and prepare for a fast. When would you have the opportunity to fast in the coming week? Prepare the day before by cutting down on coffee and rich foods.

Lectio divina

Psalm 1:1–6;
Joshua 1:6–9

'… and on his law
he meditates day
and night.'
(Psa. 1:2)

O ne way to be in silence creatively is through *lectio divina* or 'divine reading'. This involves reading and meditating on a passage of Scripture; holding a Bible verse or passage in the mind, pondering it from every angle, until it begins to affect the deepest parts of one's being. It's different to Bible study, in that you internalise and personalise the passage so that it becomes a living word addressed to you.

Meditation can best be understood by comparing what happens in the digestive system of animals that 'chew the cud' or ruminate, such as cows or sheep. The animal bolts its food down and then later regurgitates it out of its stomach and back into its mouth. It does this several times, a process that enables the food to be thoroughly digested, whereupon it is absorbed into the animal's bloodstream, so becoming part of its life. Rumination and meditation are parallel words. When a Christian takes a phrase or verse of Scripture and begins to meditate upon it, the power resident in God's Word is absorbed into his or her inner being, producing spiritual energy and faith.

So how do we meditate? Read the verse(s) many times until you visualise the setting. Imagine yourself there: what do you see, hear, smell and feel? Listen to what the words are saying. Who is speaking in the passage? Observe the reactions of those to whom the word is addressed. Ask the Holy Spirit whether the word applies to you. Quietly and gently He will speak. Open up your heart to Him – His Word may reassure, convict, encourage or reveal a wrong attitude towards God or another. Write down what God says and pray it back to Him. Through this, the Word of God becomes part of you and is worked out in your life.

**For prayer
and reflection**

**Meditate on
Psalm 119:
103–105.**

Prayer

Prayer is the heart of relationship with God. Through prayer we draw close to Him; we listen to Him; we share our desires and our concern for others. It's like having a heart-to-heart with your best friend or your loving dad. Jesus addressed God as 'Abba' or 'Daddy'. Too often, our model for prayer has been the presentation of a 'shopping list' to God, with the proviso, 'according to Your will'. We almost fear Him speaking in case He has a 'to do' list for us that we're required to fulfil. No wonder many of us say 'I'm not very good at prayer' or 'I know I should pray more'. 'Real prayer comes not from gritting our teeth but from falling in love.'* Relationships take time – and so it is with learning to pray.

In a world where we want action and instant results, it takes faith to pray – to believe that the most powerful 'activity' we can engage in is to speak with our heavenly Father about a situation and to listen for His wisdom. Prayer is the God-given key enabling us to partner with Him in changing lives, situations, our world – and God is committed to partnering with His people.

One form of prayer I find helpful is 'soaking prayer'. The emphasis is on rest, as opposed to striving, in prayer. You lie or sit in a comfortable position and use softly playing, intimate worship music to help you quiet your soul and draw near to God. It may take a little while for the 'quietening' to happen and an awareness of God's presence to develop, so it's often helpful to 'soak' for 30–60 minutes. 'With simplicity of heart we allow ourselves to be gathered up into the arms of the Father and let him sing his love song over us.'**

* Richard Foster, *Prayer* (London: Hodder & Stoughton, 1992) p.3.
**Ibid., p.4.

Luke 11:1–13

'When you pray, say: "Father, hallowed be your name …"' (v.2)

For prayer and reflection

Lord, please teach me to pray and give me the desire to spend time with You – sharing the things on my heart and listening to Yours.

The prayer **of examen**

**Colossians
1:3–14**

'… asking God to
fill you with the
knowledge of his
will through
all spiritual
wisdom …'
(v.9)

In the prayer of examen we review the day with God, asking for His perspective on it and seeking to discern His hand at work. We ask God to search us: to show us what was in line with His priorities and where we have taken a wrong route or shown an ungodly attitude. 'I the Lord search the heart and examine the mind …' (Jer. 17:10). The aim is to become increasingly aware of God's presence throughout the day.

Questions to ask ourselves about the day include: What am I most thankful for? What did I find most difficult? When did I feel most alive? What drained me? When was I most aware of God's presence? When did I feel most connected to others? When did I give/show love today?

Questions to ask God (allow the Holy Spirit to bring insight): What was important to You in my day? When did I display the family likeness? Where would You have had me act/think differently? What am I to learn from today?

The Holy Spirit's examination of our thoughts and actions may well cause thankfulness and celebration, or spotlight areas of sin or rebellion. As we surrender our wrong attitudes and behaviours to the forgiving love of Christ and choose to change, He will give us the strength to live differently.

Over time we become more aware of the Spirit's promptings throughout the day – we begin to notice the person to whom God wants us to give attention; the word He would have us speak or refrain from saying; and, most importantly, what He is doing in each of the circumstances of our lives. We become more attuned to Jesus' presence in every situation and stay connected with Him.

**For prayer
and reflection**

**Replay the last
24 hours in your
mind, asking God
to give you insight
into all that
happened.**

WEEKEND

A healthy appetite

For reflection:
'Taste and see that the Lord is good;
blessed is the man who takes refuge in him.' (Psa. 34:8)

A man I met recently had been on an eight-week programme to clean out the toxins from his body. By the end of that time his taste in food had totally changed and flavours were more intense. He now desired nutritious natural foods and rejected foods full of artificial flavourings.

Similarly, the disciplines of solitude, silence and fasting, together with others such as simplicity and chastity, are ways of changing our spiritual taste buds. Instead of longing for some of the junk food that has filled our lives: relentless busyness, mindless entertainment, comfort eating or retail therapy, we can now taste and see that the Lord is good. We long for Him to come and fill our lives and restore our souls.

During this week we have studied the disciplines of *lectio divina*, prayer and worship. These help us to seek God's face and hear His voice. Take time this weekend, whenever possible, to remember all the evidence of God's goodness in your life. Taste and see that He is good!

Optional further reading
Jeremiah 17:5–8

Worship

John 12:1–8

'… she poured [the perfume] on Jesus' feet and wiped his feet with her hair.' (v.3)

For prayer and reflection

Lord, I long for a worshipping heart. Please teach me to be more like Mary and to worship You extravagantly for who You are. As I come to You in adoration, may I be transformed by Your presence and carry Your aroma into a hurting world.

Human beings were designed to worship, and we worship whatever gives our life meaning. For some, that is their work; for others, their family, sport, wealth, appearance or popularity etc. What we truly worship reveals what we value most and, ultimately, the type of person we are seeking to become. The true disciple worships God and God alone: 'Worship the Lord your God, and serve him only' (Matt. 4:10).

Worship changes us. 'In that place of beholding the Lord in worship, we are transformed. Since we always become like whatever we worship, there is nothing greater that God could want for His people than for them to worship Him, for there is nothing greater than Himself.'*

Consider Mary: she broke the alabaster jar of nard, an expensive perfume, and anointed Jesus with it. She poured it on His feet and wiped His feet with her hair. After honouring Him in this way she would have smelt just as much of the perfume as Jesus did. Mary would have left the place of worship drenched in the aroma of Christ, changed.

True worship is costly. For Mary it cost not only the expensive perfume but the criticism of others. Often we find it easier to work for God than to worship Him. In our busyness we hide from intimacy with Jesus. Yet 'unless we are involved with Jesus Christ in a loving and adoring relationship we have nothing of eternal value to offer a dying world … our work for God must flow out of our worship.'** It is as we seek God's presence in the private place of worship that we will know it in the public place of work.

*Bill Johnson, *Face to Face with God* (Lake Mary, Florida: Charisma House, 2007) p.53.
** Selwyn Hughes, *7 Laws of Spiritual Success* (Farnham: CWR, 2008).

The God **we adore**

O ur view of who God is will determine how truly we worship. If I doubt His character (is He good?), His competence (is He able?), or His commitment (does He love me?), then I will be limited in my worship. The psalmist describes God as the Most High, the Almighty, the LORD and 'my God'.

Most High: Some years ago I went travelling in southern China with my little brother. My 'little' brother is six foot six – a good twelve inches taller than most of the men in that province. I was with the guy who was definitely the 'most high' – and it felt so safe. Our God is the biggest! There is no other power that comes close to being as tall as our God – so with Him we are safe!

Almighty: On that same trip we journeyed on to Nepal and did a three-day trek in the hills around Pokhara. It seemed pointless to take two rucksacks, so I transferred my belongings into my brother's for him to carry. He has broad shoulders so the extra weight presented no difficulty for him. Jesus is closer than a brother and He is Almighty – well able to carry not only our burdens but also our very selves. Will we let Him?

The LORD my God: Wherever you see LORD in capital letters in your Bible it refers to 'Yahweh' – the name by which God committed Himself in covenant love to His people. He loves us and nothing is going to change that. Moreover, His love is personal – He is not just 'our' God but 'my' God. He loves me, Beverley Shepherd, and He loves you.

It was this complete assurance in the God he adored that enabled the psalmist to trust God and worship Him. It also gave him the confidence to declare God's goodness to others: 'Surely he will save you ...' (Psa. 91:3).

Psalm 91:1–16

'He is my refuge and my fortress, my God, in whom I trust.' (v.2)

For prayer and reflection

Lord, thank You that You are the Most High, the Almighty, the Lord and my God. I trust You, I worship You, I love You.

Fruit – **the mark of a disciple**

'This is to my Father's glory, that you bear much fruit, showing yourselves to be my disciples.' (v.8)

Jesus is quite clear with His disciples – they were chosen to bear fruit; fruit that will last. Fruit, therefore, is not an optional extra in the Christian life – but the mark of discipleship. Just as an apple tree is so called because it produces apples, so a disciple is so named because she produces Christlike fruit.

What is that fruit? We are called to be imitators of Christ, so the fruit we bear will be the same as is evidenced in His life. A scan of the NIV Bible section headings in Mark 1:14–2:12 is revealing. They read: 'The Calling of the First Disciples'; 'Jesus Drives Out an Evil Spirit'; 'Jesus Heals Many'; 'Jesus Prays in a Solitary Place'; 'A Man With Leprosy' (who is made clean); and 'Jesus Heals a Paralytic' (forgiveness of sins). No wonder, in Mark chapter 3, we read the heading 'Crowds Follow Jesus'. If your life is similar to mine then you'll have seen some of this fruit but, for me, 'much fruit' would be a massive exaggeration! I want more!

It's tempting to make excuses for my lack of fruit, or even to relegate miracles of healing and deliverance to a previous era, but *current* evidence of God's moving in power does not allow me to do this. God's call on my life to bear much fruit, both in character and deed, prohibits my ducking this issue. 'Powerlessness demands an explanation or a solution. Blaming God seems to be easier than it is to take responsibility and pursue an encounter with Him that changes our capabilities in ministry.'*

I'm led to the conclusion that any 'lack' in this area must be a result of 'intermittent abiding' – a failure to 'remain'. It's therefore important to understand the 'what' and 'how' of abiding – questions we'll explore next.

Father, I long to bear much fruit and bring You glory. I want to 'remain' in You.

*Bill Johnson, *Face to Face with God* (Lake Mary, Florida: Charisma House, 2007) p.105.

Abiding

Psalm 27:1–14

'My heart says of you, "Seek his face!"' (v.8)

We are called to be fruitful, but we cannot strive to bear fruit. We can only aim to abide, because fruit comes from abiding or 'remaining' (John 15:4). 'Abiding' speaks of partnership – I in Him and He in me. It is in this partnership that I am empowered to be all that God intended me to be, and do all God assigned me to do.

There are two central strands to abiding: intimacy and obedience. They are exemplified in the life of Jesus. His lifestyle of fasting, spending time alone with God and praying through the night led to a total oneness with the Father: 'I and the Father are one' (John 10:30). The aim of each of the spiritual disciplines we have been studying is greater intimacy with Jesus through spending time with Him, worshipping Him and detoxing our lives of anything that would hinder our relationship. The disciplines help us to focus on the most important quest of our lives – seeking His face.

Henri Nouwen writes of seeking Mother Teresa's advice at a time when he was struggling with many problems and difficulties. 'Mother Teresa looked at me quietly and said: "Well, when you spend one hour a day adoring your Lord and never do anything which you know is wrong ... you will be fine!" ... I knew that she had spoken the truth and that I had the rest of my life to live it.'*

'As the Father has loved me, so have I loved you. Now remain in my love' (John 15:9). It is in the place of 'remaining in His love' that we hear His voice. It is in the place of intimacy that 'the Father will give you whatever you ask in my name' (John 15:16). It is in this place of connectedness with Jesus that we become fruitful.

* Henri Nouwen, *Here & Now* (London: Darton, Longman & Todd, 1994) p.75.

For prayer and reflection

Jesus, the cry of my heart is to love You more and to seek Your face. Deepen my desire for You and draw me closer to You.

Hearing His voice

John 10:1–18

'… his sheep follow him because they know his voice.' (v.4)

Jesus' life was one of radical obedience to His Father. He only did what He saw the Father doing and only spoke what He heard from the Father. Whilst the commands of God are recorded for us in the Scriptures, it is through continual listening to His voice that I understand how to apply them to my life. Intimacy is necessary for obedience. Recently I felt that God was asking me to visit a church in Redding, California for several weeks. I wanted to be sure that I had heard Him correctly so I submitted this thought to prayerful friends. They also believed it was from God. Nervously sitting in the departure lounge I was still only 80 per cent sure that this was what God wanted, but I knew that, even if I had got it wrong, He would still honour the trip as my desire was to be obedient. The visit was life-changing.

Obedience without intimacy leads to a sense of slavery, as the older brother in Luke 15 exemplifies: 'Look! All these years I've been slaving for you and never disobeyed your orders' (v.29). How the father's heart must have ached on hearing this. The elder brother had failed to realise that everything the father had was his; he was as relationally distant from the father as the younger son had been while away. 'Ignoring God while pretending to serve Him is a serious violation of relationship and cuts us off from being able to do the very thing we were put on the planet for – to live our lives to honor the One to whom we will give account.'*

When intimacy and obedience go hand in hand, life becomes an adventure. In my experience, God rarely gives me the 'whole' picture, expecting me to trust Him for what's around the next corner. My role is to follow His lead.

For prayer and reflection

Jesus, please help me to hear Your voice more clearly and so to follow Your lead more closely.

* Bill Johnson, *Face to Face with God* (Lake Mary, Florida: Charisma House, 2007) p.31.

WEEKEND
Longing for more

For reflection:
'Be imitators of God, therefore ... and live a life of love ...'
(Eph. 5:1–2)

M y prayer is that these studies are deepening your desire to know more of God – to experience the reality of His presence. God has given us the awesome responsibility of representing Him to this world. We can only do this if we imitate His nature and carry His presence.

Moses knew the importance of God's presence: 'If your Presence does not go with us ... How will anyone know that you are pleased with me and with your people ...? What else will distinguish me and your people from all the other people on the face of the earth?' (Exod. 33:15–16). We will only know God's presence in the public places of life if we seek Him in the private place. If we fail to seek His presence we will be indistinguishable from our non-Christian neighbours.

The spiritual disciplines are a means to an end. They are tried and tested ways of seeking intimacy with God – and it is intimacy and obedience that lead to fruitfulness! Are you longing for more? Then don't stop till you find it!

Optional further reading
All of Bill Johnson's books are life-changing. I particularly recommend *Face to Face with God* (Lake Mary, Florida: Charisma House, 2007).

Commanded **to love**

John 15:1–17

'This is my command: Love each other.' (v.17)

Returning again to Jesus' teaching in John 15, love was to be the hallmark of genuine discipleship: love that expressed itself in sacrifice – the laying down of our lives – not just some warm gooey feeling. Obedience to the command to love will affect all aspects of our lives – our attitude to work, finances, time etc. We're commanded to be the pipelines of God's blessing into this broken and hurting world. Our homes, streets, towns and cities will be different because we live there; our workplaces and schools changed because we work or study there; and the poor and hungry fed and clothed because our resources are available to them.

I don't know about you but, in my own strength, I cannot love like this. This world has schooled me to think more of my rights than my responsibilities, to value security over generosity and comfort above sacrifice. Yet I now belong to God's kingdom and His principles are so very different. We find life by dying; we gain through giving; and we're promoted through humbling.

The good news is that I'm not expected to love in my own strength, but to love as I am loved. My love for others will be the fruit of my love relationship with Jesus. In intimacy with Him are all the resources needed for loving others, especially joy ('my joy may be in you', v.11) and wisdom ('everything that I learned from my Father I have made known to you', v.15). Faced with the endless needs of the world we may wonder where to begin. The starting point is always our 'Yes' – coming into agreement with the Father that we want to imitate His heart of love. We then watch daily for opportunities to love and serve others, listening to His voice for wisdom to tell us how to do so.

For prayer and reflection

Lord, I say 'Yes' to Your command to love – please be my strength and my joy in living it out.

How desperate are you?

This woman was desperate! She had been bleeding for 12 years and was ceremonially unclean as a result. This would have left her isolated – anyone who touched her would have been made unclean as well. It was reckless to go into the crowd pressing around Jesus. If people had known of her condition she would have been rebuked and criticised. Surely, if she were meant to have an encounter with the Son of God she should have waited patiently at home for Him to visit? Perhaps, her friends would have told her, this weak and isolated life was her lot – one she should bear with acceptance. (Personally, I prefer friends who will demolish roofs to lower me into the presence of God!)

But this woman longs for more. When she hears about Jesus hope is reborn in her. She knows that 'If I just touch his clothes, I will be healed' (v.28). She believes that Jesus is the Messiah and as such there will be healing in the corners (wings) of His garment (cf. Mal. 4:2).

She takes a huge risk, but then faith is spelt 'RISK'. Jesus tells her that her faith has drawn the power for healing from Him. She refuses to wait at home hoping that God will show up – she goes after Him! My own personal quest for more of God has led me to go where I know He will be tangibly present – conferences with John & Carol Arnott, Rolland & Heidi Baker; a visit to Bethel Church, Redding, CA – and to bring back to others what I have found.

The healing this woman gains equips her for a life of community and co-labouring with God in a way she was unable to do before. Encounter with God transforms us and enables us to become agents of transformation. Are you desperate enough to pursue God?

Mark 5:21–34

'When she heard about Jesus, she came up behind him …' (v.27)

For prayer and reflection

Lord, I want to encounter You – make me desperate enough to push through the crowds to touch You.

Resting
in God

Sheila Jacobs

Sheila Jacobs is a writer of fiction and non fiction. She is the
author of a number of Christian novels, one of which won
the CBC Gold award for Published Children's Books 1998.
A freelance editor, she has been involved in the Christian
publishing world for many years. She is single, enjoys the
countryside, street evangelism, and loves speaking about
Jesus and praying for people.

Are you **weary?**

'Come to me …
and I will give
you rest.' (v.28)

I was in my mid-twenties when I became a Christian. A feeling began to grow inside me that God had 'a work' for me to do, but I didn't know what. I studied with the London Bible College (now the London School of Theology) by extension studies and then went into youth evangelism. But I was ill with what was later diagnosed as Ménière's disease. I couldn't work, I couldn't do anything, and I was distraught.

'I just wanted to work for You!' I wailed to God. And He said: 'I don't want you to work for Me. I want to do My work in and through you.' This challenged and changed my whole way of thinking and it was at this point I really began to 'let go and let God'. One of the things I'd always wanted to do was to write and publish a novel. But no one was interested in my fiction! So right then, I let it go; I gave it to God. And I had total peace about it.

Amazingly, within six months my first novel, *Aliens and Strangers*, was accepted for publication, followed by seven more. It was then I really began to 'get it' – it's only when you let go that God can do His work. What was the hindrance? Me.

For prayer and reflection

Dear Lord, I am weary of striving in … [name the area]. I give this situation to You now. I'm sorry I haven't let You have Your way before. Thank You, Lord.

We can so often get in the way of something God wants to do in our lives. Sometimes He waits for us to be exhausted and ready to give up and then He says, 'Can I take over now?' What a shame we have to get to that point before we let God do what He wants to do. Are you at that point now? Are you weary of striving and trying? Let God step in and take over. Enter into the rest Jesus promises. You won't be sorry.

Relax!

What did God do on the seventh day? And what did Adam do? God had finished all His work and rested but, for Adam, this day of rest was his first full day alive. What a lesson for us – resting before we even begin! But that is the way it works in God's kingdom.

God invites us to enter His Sabbath-rest, where we can see and understand that all has been done; all has been finished. The work is completed. Everything we need for salvation, being made right with God and then living to please Him, has been accomplished. God has done it all.

We see an interesting picture of our attitude to God's finished work in the story of 'The Lost Son'. He can do nothing to save himself, so he returns knowing he is dependent on his father's mercy (Luke 15:11–32). The father rushes to him and can't wait to put the robe and the ring on him. The young son receives these things in humble gratitude; he hasn't earned them and he doesn't deserve them. But look at the elder son's attitude – he's been slaving for his father for years and he seems pretty bitter about it. That's grace versus works, isn't it? Free, unmerited favour versus joyless slaving!

God longs to clothe us, to equip us, to bless us with His favour. He doesn't want us to spend our Christian lives slaving miserably for something He has already freely given us; something that should just be received with joy, as we let Him equip and empower us.

Ask yourself whether you are like the prodigal or the elder brother. And if you realise that your Christian life is more like that of the elder brother, what can you do to begin to change – today?

Hebrews 4:1–11

'… anyone who enters God's rest also rests from his own work, just as God did from his.'
(v.10)

For prayer and reflection

Reflect on the fact that you don't have to do a thing to make yourself right with God. He has done it all. Just receive what He has done and thank Him for His wonderful love.

61

The **greasy pole**

'… not by works,
so that no-one
can boast.' (v.9)

Cathy says: 'In my family, it was all about achievement. I passed the 11 plus, and everyone was so pleased with me. Then my cousin Amelia passed and went to a better school so she was the favourite. But she slid down the greasy pole of approval when she failed her GCSEs. So I was at the top, especially when I went to a good university. Then Amelia married a really wealthy man. So she was top. It was so performance-related. You were loved and accepted because of what you did, not because of who you were.'

Obviously, this kind of upbringing will affect a person's idea of what God expects of them. So, aren't you glad that God is not like this? He accepts us because of what His Son did, not because of what *we* did. Jesus died on the cross to pay the penalty for our wrongdoing. And He rose from the dead, His sacrifice accepted, and gives us power to live in Him and for Him.

Ephesians 2:8–9 tells us it's not by works, but by grace – God's free favour. Our sins made us His enemies (see Rom. 5:8–10) but He prepared a rescue operation even before we knew we needed rescuing! The restoring of our relationship with Him was His idea, not ours. Of course, this doesn't mean we can then sit back and do nothing once we know and believe in Jesus. James 2:17 says that faith without works is dead; actions show what the heart believes. The reason we do things for and in Christ, trusting in His power, is because we are grateful and we love Him – not because our works make us acceptable.

Do you ever feel accepted only because of what you do? Know that if you 'did' nothing more for Jesus, He would love you just the same.

For prayer and reflection

Meditate on the cross and on what Jesus has done for you, then thank and praise Him.

WEEKEND

Resting in God

For reflection:

'… for anyone who enters God's rest also rests from his own work, just as God did from his.' (Heb. 4:10)

Throughout this next month we will be looking at the idea of resting in God. That is, letting go, letting God, and simply not striving any more. Is this a radical concept? No. It's freedom.

But how many of us live in that freedom? How it must grieve the heart of God when, after receiving His wonderful free gift of salvation, we then try to do His works in our own power. Why do we act like this? Well, I think it's because we so often fail to grasp the idea of grace – God's free, unmerited, unearned favour.

So what does it mean – to rest in God? Does it mean that we accept Jesus as Saviour and then sit back and do nothing to help further the kingdom of God in our own lives and in the lives of others? No, of course not. Truthfully, *resting* in God is the first step to *moving* in God. Do you want to move? Then rest!

Optional further reading

Sit, Walk, Stand, by Watchman Nee (Eastbourne: Kingsway, 1994. First published 1957).

It's all **about Him**

**1 Corinthians
1:18–31**

'… Christ Jesus
… has become
for us … our
righteousness,
holiness and
redemption.' (v.30)

**For prayer and
reflection**

**Thank You, Lord,
that Jesus is *my*
righteousness,
holiness and
redemption
and that His
righteousness is
available for us
all. I lift [.........]
to You. Praise
You that nothing
is impossible for
You. Amen.**

One thing that changed my thinking forever was really understanding the fact that Jesus is *my righteousness*. All His righteousness is transferred to me! That's how God sees me – clothed in Christ. Because of Jesus, I am seated in the heavenly realms with Him (Eph. 2:6). That's where I am and that's who I am. Philippians 3:9 says that my righteousness comes from God and is by faith.

If my righteousness is Christ's, not my own, that brings me to an even bigger thought. It means that anyone can be saved, no matter how evil, how terrible, how far away from God they are – if they turn to Him, they will receive His righteousness. I remember listening to a speaker who'd led a very bad life before coming to know Christ. Someone muttered, 'Look what he's done! He shouldn't even be out of prison, much less sitting here with us.' But what you've done cuts no ice with God. Jesus didn't die just for the 'little' sins – comfortable sins we don't mind confessing. It's the 'big stuff' too; the stuff we don't like thinking about. So no one is beyond God's reach; He has done everything necessary for them to be saved.

Is there anyone in your life you can't quite believe could ever become a Christian? Remember: Jesus' righteousness is a gift; righteousness isn't something we can work for or work up. Again it's a case of resting in God, accepting what He has done. Don't be disheartened – pray for the ones you love who don't know Jesus. Lift them up to Him and ask Him to reveal Himself to them and to turn their hearts to Him. Nothing is impossible for God.

Precious and honoured

'**D**o you realise,' my friend said, 'even if you just sat there and did nothing for Jesus ever again, it wouldn't affect His love for you? He just wants to be your friend.' I needed to hear those words when I was so ill that I could hardly move, let alone work for God. But those words were key in the process of my finding freedom, as they set me free from the thought of having to work, work, work to gain God's approval.

One of the loveliest passages of the Bible is Isaiah 43. This is like God's personal love letter to each one of us. We are redeemed, so we needn't fear. We are known by name; we are His. Jesus said we would have trouble in this life (John 16:33) but in those tough times He promises to be with us (see also Heb. 13:5b). He will make sure that troubles don't swamp us.

To be known, with all our faults and failings, and loved anyway, is a wonderful thing. I remember as a child doing something my mum didn't approve of. I didn't do it again because I didn't want to grieve her. I loved her and, although I'd let her down, I knew she loved me. That kind of acceptance is God's acceptance. Think of the person you love most in the world and remember: this is how God loves you – and much, much more.

It's of course good to have an attitude of gratitude and to want to please Him. But we don't need to do anything to try to gain what is unconditionally given to us – His love and acceptance in Christ. Today, rest back in His perfect love for you, knowing that you are precious and honoured in His sight. Believe it? You should. He said it.

Are you feeling challenged by what you have read so far? Would you like to know Jesus better and be able to really rest in His unconditional love for you?

Isaiah 43:1–5a

'... you are precious and honoured in my sight ... I love you ...' (v.4)

For prayer and reflection

Read through Isaiah 43:1–5a again, taking in the fact that these are God's words to you.

Being **expectant**

1 Chron. 4:9–10;
John 16:23–28

'Oh, that you
would bless me …'
(1 Chron 4:10)

A while back, the 'Prayer of Jabez' seemed to be everywhere! Books, cards, plaques … it seemed inescapable. It challenged me and, I am sure, many others. It's worth thinking about here as we consider the whole subject of 'rest'. Jabez didn't ask God to bless him and 'enlarge [his] territory' and then tell God why He should do so. He just asked. And what happened? God gave.

We ask God for all sorts of things and yet often we seem to hit a wall. So what might be the difference between the way we are asking and the way Jabez asked? I think it's to do with expectancy. Jabez asked God, and expected Him to do it. And He did.

When Christians come to God, we are privileged in that we can bring our requests in the name of His Son. Let's think what that really means: for when we understand, we will pray with confident expectation.

For prayer and reflection

Lord, help me let go of my anxious striving, allowing You to live Your life in me by Your power. In the name of Jesus, who lived the life I could never live and died the death I should have died. Amen.

Jesus lived a life of perfect obedience and then credited it to you and to me. As we come to the Father, knowing that we come clothed in Christ, we ask not because we deserve anything, but because *Christ's completed work means we have God's favour.* Yes, we may ask in Jesus' name; in doing so, we ask for that which we believe Christ Himself would ask for us, and for others, in accordance with His will. When we pray like this, we can be sure that God will answer; we can expect Him to act on our behalf.

Why not take time to surrender your whole life to Jesus afresh today?

Have **confidence!**

After I recovered from my debilitating illness, one glance at my bank balance told me I needed a job. But years of sickness (and writing Christian novels) don't qualify you to actually do anything! I couldn't get any work. I pleaded with God to help me, went to interviews and got nowhere. Then, one day, I went to a Christian meeting and was prayed for. I was 'slain in the Spirit' – that is, I fell down under the presence of God – and shortly afterwards found that I couldn't *ask* any more. All I could do was praise Him! A week later, I was offered work as an editor of Christian books. From that day to this, God has graciously supplied me with enough freelance work to make a living.

Here, I learned a great lesson. There comes a time when *asking* stops and *expectancy* takes over. In my case, I think I would have kept trying to work things out myself, without stopping and listening to God and giving Him room to manoeuvre. But God intervened, stopped me and sorted things out. He had heard my prayer; His plan for my life was in place. He ushered me into it when I ceased striving.

One of the things I like most about Hannah's story is that after she prayed, 'she went her way ... and her face was no longer downcast' (v.18). She *knew* God had heard her. She *expected* Him to act. So she was at peace. In effect, she rested. And God answered her prayer for a child.

It's important to have expectancy – faith that God will come through for us. But there comes a time when the asking stops and we must rest in the knowledge that God has heard us and will act according to His will – and His timing.

1 Samuel 1:1–28

'... may the God of Israel grant you what you have asked of him.' (v.17)

For prayer and reflection

Lord, thank You that You always hear my prayer. I praise You. Help me to let go and trust You to work everything out according to Your perfect will. In Jesus' name. Amen.

But what **if He doesn't …?**

'… the God we serve is able to save us … But even if he does not …' (vv.17–18)

What happens if I let go and let God – and He doesn't do anything?'

That's something we really struggle with, isn't it? We leave our troubles at Jesus' feet but soon we're fretting about them again. Then, before you know it, we've snatched them up and we're nursing them once more.

Jesus told us that we shouldn't worry; we should trust God (see Matt. 6:25–34). In truth, sometimes it is easier to trust God with things we know we can do nothing about. Like the drowning man we thought about earlier in this study, we may find ourselves exhausting our own strength before we let God step in.

I imagine the Israelite lads who were threatened with the furnace hoped that God would step in before they went through their fiery trial. But I am always struck by the fact that although they knew He *could*, they seemed confident that even if He *chose not to*, their faith in Him would stand. As it turned out, they did have to go through the trial – but He was with them, as we see from a 'theophany' appearance of a mysterious fourth man in the flames. And when they came through their ordeal, they were not harmed (v.27).

Although sometimes God spares us, we go through many trials. But we are never alone. And nothing can permanently damage us (Rom. 8:38–39); that is, the trials, problems and hard times cannot separate us from Jesus and our eternal inheritance 'that can never perish, spoil or fade – kept in heaven for [us]' (1 Pet. 1:4). So if you're going through the fire today, trust in His perfect will and timing. Let Him take over, for He cares for you (1 Pet. 5:7).

For prayer and reflection

'We do not make requests of you because we are righteous, but because of your great mercy' (Dan. 9:18). Thank You, Lord, for Your tender mercy. Help me to rest in You, knowing that You are in control.

WEEKEND

It starts with resting

For reflection:
'Trust in the LORD with all your heart …' (Prov. 3:5)

In Watchman Nee's excellent book *Sit, Walk, Stand*, he uses the example of a drowning man to help us understand the concept of letting go and letting God. A drowning man can only be saved once he has stopped struggling, or else he will drag his rescuer under the water too. 'God is waiting for your store of strength to be utterly exhausted before He can deliver you,' says the author. 'Once you have ceased to struggle, He will do everything.'

Do you keep mentally and emotionally beating yourself up because you feel that you always let Jesus down? STOP! Quietly say to yourself, 'He has done it all, and I can enter into it.' Trust Him to live His life in and through you. When it's all Him, and not us, who gets all the glory? Precisely. So let go and let God do what He wants to in Your life. And remember – He really, *really* loves you. Yes, YOU!

Optional further reading

Luke 15:11–32 – Read through the story of 'The Lost Son'. If it helps, imagine that you are the lost child and God is the loving Father.

Luke 23:32–43 – Consider that the criminal being crucified alongside Jesus could not lift a finger or take a step towards his own salvation, and yet Jesus accepted him.

Sing it!

Acts 16:16–34

'About midnight Paul and Silas were praying and singing hymns to God …' (v.25)

There you are in a dark prison cell. You've been beaten, severely flogged, and your feet are fastened in stocks. 'Hey, let's have a praise party!' is probably not the first thing you'd think of saying.

And yet, Paul and Silas must have said something just like that when they were arrested for upsetting the owners of a demon-possessed slave girl. These men praised the Lord. Their focus was on the God who changes impossible situations. And nothing can help focus the mind like praise.

When we get our minds on the Person who can change our situation, instead of the situation itself, we put ourselves in a place where God can act. Like Peter, stepping out of the boat and fixing his eyes on Jesus, we can 'walk on water' if we don't look down (see Matt. 14:25–31). For, just as God can change 'impossible people', He can change 'impossible circumstances'.

I wonder whether Paul and Silas would ever have got out of their predicament if they hadn't praised God. I don't know. But one thing's for sure. If we're in a dark place, with our backs against the wall, and there seems no way out, we must fix our eyes on the One who can help. In effect, stop our striving and praise God. Yes, it's hard. But praise gives us a different perspective. When we are in the middle of our troubles, we can say, along with the Israelites in 2 Chronicles 20:12: 'We do not know what to do, but our eyes are upon you.' The Lord told them 'Do not be afraid or discouraged … the battle is not yours, but God's' (2 Chron. 20:15). Is He saying that to you today?

For prayer and reflection

Are you standing before a closed door? Praise God and trust Him to deliver you. Your times are in His hands. Read aloud Psalm 31:14–15a, making it your prayer for today.

Looking **back**

'**D**o you remember when we were young?' asked my friend. 'Up the disco every Saturday! What fun!'

'Huh!' I muttered. 'I'd like to go back and tell myself to stop wasting time and give my life to Jesus.'

I thought about my 'old' life with great regret. Then it dawned on me. I could see that, even before I knew Jesus, His hand was on my life, bringing me to the point when I finally surrendered to Him. People, places, events ... it was a journey. And I'd had an unknown Companion.

Joseph must have really despaired, especially when he was in prison for his non-assault on Potiphar's wife (Gen. 39:20). He thought he was going to get out at one point, but was again forgotten (Gen. 40:23). Another two years passed before he was released – and wonderfully promoted. Then he looked back and saw that God had been in control all the time, working out every detail of his life. He must have marvelled at the amazing jigsaw puzzle of people and revelations. It all worked together perfectly; the chief cupbearer remembered Joseph's gifts at the right time and, because of that, Joseph's own family did not starve to death.

God really is incredible: He can work out our lives for good – all the mistakes, errors, bad judgments and wrong turns. In fact, He promises to do just that for all who love Him and who are called 'according to his purpose' (Rom. 8:28). That is, according to His plan. As you reflect on this today, allow it to remind you of the importance of resting in the God who is in control of *everything* – even the detail. Trust Him to work things out for your good.

Genesis 50:15–21

'You intended to harm me, but God intended it for good ...' (v.20)

For prayer and reflection

Lord, thank You for your good plans for my life. When I review my past, help me to see Your footsteps accompanying me on my journey. Amen.

'Who are You, Lord?'

Acts 9:1–19;
Colossians
2:6–12

'For in Christ
all the fulness of
the Deity lives in
bodily form …'
(Col. 2:9)

A village near my home has an annual 'Scarecrow Trail'. It's great fun – trying to decide on the best efforts. This year I found one just a little too convincing. It turned out later that he was a 'living scarecrow'! But if I had told my friends, 'I saw that one move' before knowing that, would they have believed me?

We've been talking about resting. Resting, in this context, is connected with trust. If we know someone and trust them, we feel we can believe them even if they tell us something that appears to be unbelievable at first: 'I *know* her. She wouldn't lie.'

When Saul (later Paul) had his encounter with the risen Christ, he asked 'Who are you, Lord?' Saul knew that he was in the presence of the Divine, and Jesus confirmed it. While I believe Damascus-Road-type conversions do happen today, many of us come to an acceptance of who Jesus is by a process of understanding and belief. But we *do* need to come to that point where, like Thomas, we can say 'My Lord and my God' (John 20:28), seeing that Jesus is fully God and fully man, the exact representation of His being (Heb. 1:3); the Word of God, communicating to us what He is truly like. Only a sinless man could pay the price for humanity's sin; only our perfect God could pay that price of infinite worth.

Just as people were fooled by the 'living scarecrow', it's easy to be fooled today into believing Jesus is someone He is not. There are many deceptive beliefs around, telling us of a different Jesus than the one Saul discovered on the Damascus Road. They say He was a good man, a great prophet, even a mighty angel, but not God in the flesh. However, like Saul, we need to meet the true Jesus for ourselves.

For prayer and reflection

You can only really trust someone you know. Do you know Him? Do you know the real Jesus?

Misunderstandings

One day, a young friend of mine asked, 'Can you explain the Trinity?' 'Why not ask me a hard one?' I said. Still, I tried (inadequately) to explain that as water has several manifestations including ice and steam, the Trinity is manifested in three Persons. And yet the three are one in essence.

Some people find it enormously difficult to understand how God could sacrifice His own Son; some think it barbaric. But I suggest this shows a misunderstanding of who God is.

Sin against God needs to be 'expiated' (atoned for). But humankind couldn't do it; all our good works could never make us clean in His sight; we're all sinners. So God Himself provided the way back into His favour, through the appeasing sacrifice of Jesus' death on the cross (propitiation). Essentially, *He* fulfilled what *He* demanded. Why? Love. Our sins separate us from God, but Jesus (who was sinless but took on Himself our sins) is the Bridge. There is no other name given to us by which we can be saved (see Acts 4:12). And He doesn't just promise us 'pie in the sky when we die'; it's about a completely fresh start. He takes our old sinful nature away and nails it to the cross; we are new creations, for the old has gone and the new has come (see 2 Cor. 5:17). We can enter into a living relationship with our Creator here and now, lived in His power. *This* is our God; the God who gives sacrificially because He is love (1 John 3:16). Did you get that? He *is* love. And His actions prove it.

This is the God we are called to know and to rest our load upon. He came in person, taking our sins on the cross. He rose from the dead and equips us with power to live for Him. This is the God of grace, who asks us to trust Him.

Isaiah 53:1–12

'... the punishment that brought us peace was upon him ...' (v.5)

For prayer and reflection

Dear Lord Jesus, please reveal Yourself to me more and more as I surrender my life to You. Help me to rest in Your perfect love today. Amen.

Can't work it up!

Galatians 5:22–23

'… the *fruit* of the Spirit is …' (v.22, my italics)

I've got a big apple tree in my garden. When people come to visit and admire the tree, I don't have to say, 'Yes, it's beautiful. But I don't know what kind of tree it is.' I know what sort it is – because of the abundance of Bramleys every autumn.

The fruit of the Spirit is precisely that. It is the *fruit* of God's *Spirit* living in us. We don't have to work it up; again, we are faced with the principle we have been studying – we have to rest and let Him do the work through us. As soon as we have believed in Christ as our Lord and Saviour and been born again by the Spirit of God (John 3:3), we can rely on the fact that God will begin to produce fruit in keeping with our new nature.

But there's a proviso. Jesus said we must 'remain in Him' (see John 15:1–8). What does that mean? Well, it means we have to stay rested in Him, stay connected, surrendering to Him – sometimes moment by moment. We listen for His voice and obey it, in the power and strength He gives us by His Spirit.

Never think that the fruit of the Spirit is something we can 'work up'. We can all fall into this trap: 'I must try to be nicer and forgiving and Christlike to that person who parks in front of my garage without permission. Oh! He's there again. It's no use. I feel so angry!' We can no more work up compassionate and forgiving feelings than we can work up joy or lasting peace. These things are the *fruit* of the One who lives in us. Trust Him to manifest His fruit in your life as you learn to listen and obey and rest in Him. Don't strive to be a better person. Let Him do the work that is needed.

For prayer and reflection

Lord, thank You that You live in me by Your Spirit. Help me to rest in You, trusting You to bring about the good fruit of Your presence. Amen.

WEEKEND

Challenged?

For reflection:

'Be still and know that I am God; I will be exalted among the nations, I will be exalted in the earth.' (Psa. 46:10)

Thinking about this whole subject of 'rest' is challenging, isn't it? It's tied in with expectancy, trust, faith and thanksgiving. This week, we've looked at various Bible characters; seeing how their faith in God grew during difficult times can help us when we go through our own.

King David, the man after God's own heart (1 Sam. 13:14), made big mistakes but he had a real, trusting relationship with his God. Notice how he asked the king of Moab to take care of his parents 'until I learn what God will do for me' (1 Sam. 22:3). And he wouldn't take his future into his own hands by killing King Saul; no, he let God establish him.

A long time passed between David's anointing and the fulfilment of the promise. Let that thought encourage you. Psalm 46:10 tells us to 'Be still, and know that I am God'. Rest! Be still. God is in control.

Optional further reading

David's life story as it appears in 1 and 2 Samuel (1 Sam. 16 – 2 Sam. 24); and his prayer in 1 Chronicles 29:10–20.

Dodgy **dads**

Luke 11:11–13

'… how much more will your Father in heaven give …' (v.13)

We have thought about who Jesus is and what He has done for us; and the fact that He gives us His Spirit so we can live for Him in His strength, not ours. But the one Person we haven't really thought about is God the Father.

It is enormously difficult for some people to accept the idea of God as a loving father. This is often because of their own family experiences. Dad is sometimes not around, not available, or even known. Even those who have known a father in the home cannot always be sure of a positive experience. And this all affects how we perceive God as Father.

If your father was absent when you were growing up, you may not be able to get your head around a loving Father who wants to be a part of every detail of your life. If your father was largely unavailable, you may think of your heavenly Father as far away and not really interested; maybe you 'don't want to bother Him'. Perhaps your dad was critical and harsh. No prizes awarded for guessing how you may view God. There are even some who might read today's Bible passage and think, '*My* dad gave me the scorpion instead of the egg and expected me to be happy with it.' I hope that's not the case, but if it was, know your heavenly Father is not like that. He is everything you could want in a perfect father.

Previously, we looked at the story of 'The Lost Son'. If you have a problem thinking about God as Father, I urge you to read this story again. God shows us what He is like in the person of that father. This is *your* Father. Trust Him to always do you good.

For prayer and reflection

Father in heaven, thank You for loving me. Help me to rest in the kindness of Your Fatherhood and to know today that I am Your precious child. Amen.

Good gifts

One night, I had a dream. I saw a huge old car being towed by men on foot who were clearly exhausted. The car was also being pushed along by others from behind. As I watched, I thought, 'Why don't they just turn the engine on, jump in and drive?' They weren't using the car's own power at all and it was a desperate struggle.

Hopefully, by now, we are getting the idea that God is the One who saves, equips and empowers. None of this is of us. That is why we must rest in Him. And, as we get to know Him better, we can surrender ourselves all the more, for we are growing in our trust as we grow in our relationship with Him. There will be times when we struggle (and we will look at some of these struggles next week), but let's ensure that the one struggle we never have is trying to live the Christian life in our own power instead of living in the power of the Spirit. Like the people in my dream, we so often struggle when we don't have to; we simply don't tap into the power available for us.

Perhaps you feel that you would love to rest back in God concerning a specific worry or problem, but you just feel you can't. You know Him, you trust Him, but you simply can't let go. Maybe it is time for you to ask God to fill you afresh with His Holy Spirit. The Spirit comes into our lives when we come to know Christ, but we need His continuing infilling. He is like refreshing water; water bubbling up to eternal life (John 4:13–14). He reveals Jesus to our hearts and makes God real to us. If you have never been filled with the Holy Spirit, ask Jesus to do this for you. And trust Your heavenly Father to give you the *good* gift of His Spirit when you ask Him.

Acts 1:1–8; 2:1–4

'All of them were filled with the Holy Spirit …' (2:4)

For prayer and reflection

Lord, thank You that You are good and give good gifts. Please fill me afresh today with Your Holy Spirit. Thank You, Lord. Amen.

In the **dark**

Exodus 13:17–22;
40:36–38

'… the LORD went
ahead of them …
by night in a pillar
of fire to give
them light …'
(13:21)

We've seen that we mustn't strive to work for God, and that we must rest in His finished work on the cross and His equipping power. We can do nothing to make ourselves more Christlike; in fact, we must 'die' to self so that Christ can live His life in and through us (see Col. 3:1–3).

But dying to self every day isn't easy. Surrendering to the Lordship of Christ and resting in Him is challenging, especially when things are dark for us. That's when we find out if our lives are built on rock or sand (Matt. 7:24–27). Can we really 'let go and let God' when times are hard?

The Israelites spent a lot of time wandering in the wilderness. There, God taught them about His daily provision (Exod. 16) but it was not an easy experience for them. He gave them bread every day: Jesus is our daily Bread (John 6:25–59) and we must learn to walk with Him on a daily basis.

One of the pictures I find most helpful during dark times is that of the pillar of cloud and fire which accompanied the Israelites day and night (Exod. 13:21–22). It gives an awesome sense of God's powerful presence not just during daylight hours, but in the dead of (spiritual or actual) night. God never sleeps; there's never a time when He's 'not in'.

Are you going through an especially difficult time? Instead of striving, rest. Roll your burden onto Jesus. He specialises in turning up in the middle of our dark nights (see Matt. 14:25). And to stay in His presence (Exod. 40:36–38) is the secret of living in peace when life is tough, bleak and just plain difficult!

For prayer and reflection

Lord, I praise You that You are the One who turns darkness into light. You promise to be with Your followers forever, and I thank You that You are here with me right now. Amen.

Don't be afraid

A nother thing that can really upset our rest in God is fear. I'm not talking about being slightly nervous. I'm talking about gut-wrenching, panic-inducing, nauseating FEAR.

I was spending time alone with God, when I had a picture of me in a kayak. Now, I love the countryside, I enjoy walking my dog and when I was younger I loved horse riding. But my idea of water sports is glancing into my garden pond. So I was quite surprised to see me in a kayak, being tossed around in a lot of foaming white water. And then I realised that I wasn't alone – Jesus was in the kayak with me and He had the paddle. Soon, we were out of the white water and safe on a placid lake. Of course, the picture was of my present situation, not a prophecy about any future activities (I hope).

When the disciples hit rough times in their boat, we see that Jesus was actually asleep (Luke 8:22–25). But they called on Him, and soon everything was still. The danger was real (see v.23), yet Jesus calmed the storm with a word. How terrifying it must have been for them before He acted on their behalf!

It's hard when we are in a dire situation and are waiting for God to act, especially when time seems to be 'running out'. Is Jesus sleeping? No. Sometimes His delays are for a far greater purpose (see John 11:21–23, 32–44). Even when a situation seems hopeless, He can still intervene (see Mark 5:22–23, 35–43).

Perhaps you need to know that Jesus is in the kayak with you. The danger may be real; it may all seem 'too late'; remember who is in charge – the One who says 'Don't be afraid' (Mark 5:36). Let Him restore your rest. Let go, let God.

Psalm 91

'You will not fear …' (v.5)

For prayer and reflection

Read and reflect on Psalm 91. If you are especially fearful, ask God to minister to you deeply through these powerful words.

The **big picture**

Luke 10:38–42

'... Mary has chosen what is better ...' (v.42)

It's easy to get things out of perspective, isn't it? Particularly when you're feeling especially stressed.

Because I couldn't travel at all one summer due to illness, I cut out pictures from magazines of all the things I liked – windmills, sunsets, hollyhocks, Labradors – and stuck them on a board in a big collage. I'd look at it to cheer myself up. I looked at *all* the pictures, not just one. If I looked at just the picture of windmills, and never bothered to look at the rest, the whole board might just as well have been one big picture of windmills. But it wasn't: windmills were just one small part of the whole.

When we focus on one thing, our immediate worry or whatever it is, everything (and everyone) else in our lives tends to get ignored or shoved to one side. Our concern looms larger and larger, completely out of perspective, because that's all we are really 'seeing'. That's when we have to step back and make an effort to look at the whole – and put everything into the right perspective again.

I'm sure we can understand how frustrating it was for Martha, rushing around to get the dinner, watching her sister at Jesus' feet – apparently doing nothing! No wonder Martha asked Jesus to tell Mary to help her. I don't suppose she expected Jesus to reply as He did: essentially, 'No, it's OK. Leave her where she is. What she's chosen to do is better.'

God's kingdom has rightly been called God's 'upside-down' kingdom. He turns things on their heads and says and does things we don't expect. His perspective is different to ours. He sees a *much* bigger picture.

For prayer and reflection

Do you focus on what you think are important things? Stand back and ask yourself about the bigger picture. Whatever is robbing you of your rest ... is it really that important?

WEEKEND

Really knowing

For reflection:

'If you really knew me, you would know my Father as well.'
(John 14:7)

When we have a wrong or incomplete idea of who God is, we cannot fully trust Him. It follows that we will feel unable to rest our cares and burdens on Him and wait in expectancy for Him to work out His good purposes in our lives.

This weekend, try to spend some time studying the character of God. Get a good concordance and see what God says about Himself – Jehovah Jireh, the provider, Jehovah Rapha, the healer, etc. This is the God who became man so we would see what He was like and who then carried out a rescue mission on our behalf. Instead of shouting from glory, He came into our world Himself. How would this challenge someone who did not believe that Jesus was their God in the flesh? How might it change their idea of their own self-worth if they believed that their God wanted a relationship with them *that* much? How does it challenge you?

Optional further reading

Galatians 3:1–4:7; *I Dared to Call Him Father,* by Bilquis Sheikh (Eastbourne: Kingsway, 1984).

When **dreams die**

Psalm 73

'Whom have I in heaven but you?' (v.25)

Recently, I was invited to a football club centenary dinner. Reluctantly, I had to turn down the invitation, but the whole episode made me think. When I was a teenager, my dad was the second-team manager for this little village side and I wrote the match reports for the club. Over twenty years later, I wondered how the guys I'd known had turned out. What had happened to them? Were they rich, poor, married, divorced? Had any of them found Christ?

I took a trip down memory lane, remembering those early days and the happy village existence with my mum and dad, when we were new to country living. My grandparents used to visit; I had a wide circle of friends and life seemed full of excitement. I guess I'd imagined meeting Mr Right and living somewhere beautiful and expensive with an Aga; I'd have children who rode ponies. I certainly didn't imagine that in a few short years my parents would break up, or that I'd find myself called to be single, childless.

For prayer and reflection

I spent some time wallowing in self-pity. Then I realised something important was missing. I don't mean the man, the children and the large bungalow. Something was just *wrong*. I couldn't fathom what. Something was simply *gone*. It took me a while to realise it was God! I repented – and was immediately restored to the sunshine of His presence.

It's easy to slip into envy and the 'If only' of lost dreams. Maybe you know the pain of having a dream die; something you wanted and hoped for *so* much, but it didn't happen. Are you full of resentment about that – or is this something else you can let go of and let God?

Father, thank You that You always know best. I bring my disappointments and broken dreams to You and I trust You to give me Your dream for my life – a fresh and better vision for my days.

Forgive!

L et's consider today something else that may hinder our rest in God. It's a big one: unforgiveness.

Forgiveness isn't easy. The trouble is when we don't or can't forgive, the person who is damaged most is – us. Harbouring unforgiveness has the power to keep us locked in a prison where we replay past hurts, to the detriment of our own happiness, fulfilment and spiritual growth.

If we have suffered badly we may need counselling or ministry to be truly free. But we do *need* to be free *for our own sakes* – regardless of whether the person who has hurt us ever repents. Unfortunately we think forgiveness (where we believe it's undeserved) is like letting someone 'off the hook'. It isn't. Forgiveness lets *us* off the hook – so we are able to look *forward* to all that God has for us, instead of looking *backwards* to the person or event that harmed us.

Jesus demonstrated forgiveness when He forgave His killers (Luke 23:34). His words in the Lord's Prayer are very challenging, for we see that God's forgiveness of us depends on our forgiveness of others. As we know, none of us *deserves* God's forgiveness, so in forgiving those who've hurt us we're only doing what our heavenly Father has done for us. It's hard, however – and you may feel absolutely unable to forgive. Rest in God; ask *Him* to forgive in and through You. Then see what happens.

This prayer may help you: Lord, thank You for Your wonderful gift of forgiveness. I bring [name of person and their offence] to You. I'm sorry I haven't wanted/ been able to forgive them. Lord, please enable me through Your power to forgive [.........] and let go. Help me to rest in You, trusting You to do this. Amen.

Matthew 6:9–15

'… if you forgive … your heavenly Father will also forgive you.' (v.14)

For prayer and reflection

Jesus, I believe You want me to live free – and I really want to. If there's unforgiveness in my heart, please show me, and enable me to forgive, let go, and live in the power of Your love.

Into the **hallway**

'If anyone hears
my voice and
opens the door,
I will come in …'
(v.20)

When I was a child, I lived in a cinema, in a flat made from converted dressing rooms. Our front door (it was actually the fire exit) led into a strange hallway, with only a store room. The first floor held a bedroom and bathroom. The second, my bedroom. The third, the kitchen and living room. The fourth, another bedroom. It was a scary place for a kid, but it was home for two and a half years. In case you're wondering how I managed to have such a weird existence, my dad was the cinema manager.

My family weren't practising Christians, but I remember going to a local church once or twice. The church folk came knocking when we didn't show up again, but they received no reply. They didn't even get into the strange hallway.

When we ask Jesus into our lives, we sometimes unconsciously say, 'You can come in so far, but no further.' In effect, He gets as far as the hallway. Because we haven't opened up all the floors or all the rooms to His presence, we keep Him at bay and wonder then why we aren't able to live in the power and the peace we feel we should have as Christians. We might have asked Jesus to come into all our 'rooms' but one. 'Yes, Lord, You can come in. But not in there.'

If we still struggle to really rest in God, it may be worth investigating whether there are still areas of our lives into which Jesus is *not* allowed to go. Be aware that Jesus will never enter forcibly; He waits to be invited. Spend some time today thinking about any areas in your life you know you haven't fully surrendered to Jesus. Do you feel you can invite Him in or are you still keeping Him out? Why?

**For prayer and
reflection**

**Lord, please show
me if I have any
'locked rooms'
in my life. Will
You give me Your
power to trust You
enough to invite
You in? Thank
You, gentle Lord.
Amen.**

All of **You**

Where did you feel safest when you were a child? For me, it was in the car, when we were travelling back from our holidays. As an adult, I might be more anxious: 'Watch out, Dad! You're too near the car in front. Do you want me to take over?' But as a child I'd fall asleep, just trusting my father to get us home safe. Recently, God spoke to me very clearly, using that picture: 'Just trust Me. Be like that child. Rest.'

As we come to the end of our studies about resting in God, I hope one thing is clear: it's all of Him; the Christian life is not our doing – it's His, from start to finish. We can't make ourselves right with Him and we can't live for Him in our own power. He wants to live His life in and through us, and He will – if we let Him. Then we'll know increasingly His presence, His power and His joy and, as we see Him at work in our lives, our faith in Him will grow.

And there's something else. People will notice when we find our rest in God. When we stop striving, our unsaved family, friends and colleagues will see something 'different' about us. Frankly, they will see less of us and more of Him. And that's the whole point.

So, as a result of our resting, we may find we have 'open doors' to share our faith. People can argue with what we say, but they cannot argue with what we *are*. What we believe and practise in our hearts will certainly shine through in actions. Who knows? Someone might find Christ because you found your rest in Him.

Remember the picture of the child in the car. Let go – your Father is driving. He knows the way. So rest.

Isaiah 64:6;
Romans 3:10–12;
9:16

'It does not …
depend on man's
desire or effort, but
on God's mercy.'
(Rom. 9:16)

For prayer and reflection

Father, help me to trust and rest in You every day, knowing it's all of You. Help me to let go, so that others may see Your Son living in me by His Spirit and be drawn to You. I praise and thank You with all my heart. Amen.

Esther

Celia Bowring

Celia is married to Lyndon, and works alongside him at CARE, which seeks to be a Christian voice in society concerning human life, family and other issues of concern. She is a speaker and writer with a particular interest in prayer, women in leadership, marriage and family matters. Lyndon and Celia have two sons and a daughter and they live in London.

Esther

'... Xerxes who ruled over 127 provinces stretching from India to Cush.' (v.1)

For prayer and reflection

If we are tempted to envy those who seem to 'have it all' let's remember our greatest treasure is found through our knowing Christ.

From 486–464 BC, Xerxes (also known as Ahasuerus) ruled the Persian Empire, a vast collection of states and kingdoms. The scene of this story of how one young woman saved the Jewish people is in the city of Susa, situated in modern-day Iran near the Iraq border. Commentators trace many events and characters in the narrative from historical and archaeological records. Although the book does not mention God, He is clearly at work through the actions of the main characters, especially Esther and her uncle Mordecai. Even when we are not conscious of Him being involved – He is.

The story begins in the splendid setting of Xerxes' palace, at a banquet sumptuous beyond belief thrown for nobles, officials, military leaders and provincial princes. The king has two motives for his ostentatious hospitality: to secure the loyalty of his high-profile visitors meeting for a military planning session prior to his campaign against the Greeks, and to show off his wealth and god-like power. The white and violet hangings (the Persian royal colours) in the palace garden, with a dazzling mosaic floor where everyone reclines to savour the feast, are exquisite. The finest wine flows – served in individually designed gold goblets. Meanwhile, hidden away from male eyes, Queen Vashti is instructed to impress the women at her own royal table. The machinations and politicking of the court are about to begin. Behind the showy façade, how solid is the ground beneath Xerxes' royal feet?

Although Xerxes enjoyed great earthly riches and power for a season, he failed to find God's peace and favour. Jesus said, 'For where your treasure is, there your heart will be also' (Luke 12:34).

WEEKEND

Jesus – King of kings

For reflection:

'… Christ Jesus: Who, being in very nature God, did not consider equality with God something to be grasped.' (Phil. 2:5–6)

The grand pomp of King Xerxes and his royal court, who ruled in the days in which the story of Esther is set, could never be compared to the splendour of Christ's eternal kingdom!

The Persian king was fabulously wealthy with a lavish lifestyle, far-reaching authority and powerful armies that made him famous and feared in his time – but today Xerxes is only remembered in museums and history books; his empire has disintegrated into the desert sand.

From before time began, the Son of God, in, through and for whom all things were created – was worshipped and served by angelic beings too blindingly magnificent for human eye to behold. Now He sits in the place of highest honour, at the Father's right hand in the heavenly realms for all eternity.

Spend time reflecting on these glorious truths this weekend.

Optional further reading

Revelation 1:13–16; Colossians 1:15–20; Ephesians 1:20–23

Meekness and Majesty, R.T. Kendall (Christian Focus Publications, 1992)

Queen Vashti's **refusal**

Esther 1:10–22

'… Vashti has done wrong, not only against the king but … the provinces of King Xerxes.' (v.16)

For prayer and reflection

James 1:5 urges us to ask God for wisdom, coming humbly to Him in every circumstance. Father, help me to curb my anger, not to overreact and cause hurt and harm.

Vashti seems to be the Persian name for Queen Amestris, who was referred to by Greek historian Herodotus, writing about 50 years afterwards. She was probably in her thirties by this time and tradition describes her as cruel and jealous. Even in the male-dominated society of that time this queen wielded considerable power and influence behind the scenes; the royal harem would have been rife with vicious intrigues and rivalries. You do not need overt power in order to ruin people's lives.

At the banquet, Xerxes drinks his way through several goblets of alcohol and starts boasting to his guests about Vashti's beauty, demanding she be brought for everyone to admire. The queen's response infuriates her royal husband, sending him into a white-hot rage.

Xerxes overreacts and summons his most distinguished counsellors to consult the law on this matter. Before he knows it, Xerxes has signed, sealed and despatched an irreversible royal decree throughout the empire to warn any other wives who might be tempted to copy Vashti and cause a full-scale feminist uprising against male authority.

What an extraordinary overreaction from a man who clearly considers himself the most powerful and admired person in the known world! In such a male-dominated society why is he so fearful of a mere female's influence? Like many tyrants, beneath the bluster, he is weak and unstable.

Hasty decisions taken in the heat of anger and wounded pride are very dangerous and far-reaching.

The perfect **beauty queen**

Some time later – he probably went off to fight the Greeks in between chapters 1 and 2 – the king reflects on the Vashti episode. However, bound by the 'laws of the Medes and Persians' he has to stick to his decision. Even the mighty Xerxes realises he must submit to a higher authority and, having published his irrevocable royal decree, he cannot reinstate his queen. Now his courtiers come up with the great idea of an exclusive Miss World pageant which will not limit Xerxes just to looking; he is welcome to sleep with them all and keep them as possessions in his palace to use whenever the fancy takes him.

Talent spotters throughout the empire bring the loveliest virgins to Xerxes' harem in Susa so he can choose which one to crown as queen. By contemporary standards, this shows a chillingly matter-of-fact disregard for these young women's welfare. The idea that anyone has the right to abduct children and teenagers to be sexually used and locked away for the rest of their lives is abhorrent. Unfortunately it still happens now – every year thousands are trafficked into the UK, for instance, and along with girls and women living here already, are tricked and coerced into prostitution. 'So God created man in his own image ... male and female he created them' (Gen. 1:27). Jesus cared for women, respecting them as men's equals in a culture which regarded them as inferior. Even though the Church has not always honoured and valued us in this way, women today in most parts of the world are free to be godly influences and serve Him with our whole lives in a myriad of ways, uniquely reflecting and expressing aspects of His character.

Esther 2:1–4

'... let the girl who pleases the king be queen instead of Vashti.' (v.4)

For prayer and reflection

Lord, thank You for creating us in Your image. Please draw near to any woman – or child – today who is regarded as worthless and abused in some way. Amen.

A girl called Hadassah

Esther 2:5–7

'Mordecai had a cousin named Hadassah, whom he had brought up …' (v.7)

The two intriguing characters we meet next do not belong to the pizzazz and hedonism of Xerxes' court but come from a humble Jewish household in the city. Mordecai is a descendant of Kish – probably part of Israel's nobility when his family was carried away years before. He is an exile, uprooted from the home of his ancestors and seeking to maintain his Jewish identity and faith in an alien culture. Mordecai's orphaned niece or cousin is named Hadassah, which means 'myrtle', a common but beautiful plant prized for its fragrant oils, with deep-green scented leaves, delicate white star-shaped flowers and dark berries. It symbolises God's forgiveness and acceptance and is used during the Feast of Tabernacles when the Jews remember His care and protection during the 40 years when the children of Israel wandered in the desert, living in tents.

In the Bible, names almost always carry deep significance and for Hadassah this is no exception. This lovely Jewish girl, although she does not yet know it, will be the fragrance of God's salvation through her great beauty, her marriage and her courage. Hadassah's Persian name, Esther, means 'Star', echoing the shape of the myrtle blossom. It was probably based on 'Ishtar' the powerful goddess of love and war – both important themes in Esther's unfolding story.

Uncle Mordecai, meanwhile, has been given a name connected to the warlike Babylonian god 'Marduk.' God will use him to fight against Haman's genocidal threats to his people. Do you know what your name means? How wonderful it is to know that Jesus has a secret name for each faithful believer that He will reveal to us in heaven (Rev. 2:17).

For prayer and reflection

Thank You, Lord, that You have a special name for me and that I am special to You.

Chosen by the king

Mordecai's household lives within the citadel, so he cannot hide the lovely Esther from the king's talent spotters. Most Persian monarchs kept hundreds of concubines besides their legitimate wives and palace harems were places of jealousy and intrigue. Esther's pious family must have been horrified that she would spend the rest of her life locked away. She is compelled to enter a situation she did not choose – something that may happen to any of us. There are Christian women today forced into relationships that bring shame and isolation from those they love. God weeps with them and is ready to bring them through. There is no situation that can separate us from Him.

Esther bravely accepts her fate, determined that good should come from it. Without this positive attitude Hegai, the eunuch in charge, may not have noticed her. Presumably many girls just as attractive as Esther were delivered to him crying for their mothers, totally disoriented in the grandiose surroundings of Xerxes' palace. Esther's dignity in this situation so impresses Hegai that he decides to fast-track her. He treats her almost as if she were queen already, providing luxury accommodation, special food, the seven best maidservants and an exotic year-long beauty regime.

Meanwhile, Mordecai, who has told Esther to conceal her Jewish background, comes by the harem courtyard daily like a loving father to hear news of her and she submits to his guidance. On the night that Esther is to sleep with the king, she follows Hegai's advice about her clothes and jewels. Xerxes falls in love with her, a fairytale wedding follows and everyone is granted a holiday and gifts.

Esther 2:8–18

'… she won his favour and approval … So he … made her queen instead of Vashti.' (v.17)

For prayer and reflection

Almighty God, please help us, even in hopeless circumstances, to trust You to work everything together for good in our lives. Amen. (Rom. 8:35–38)

Mordecai **uncovers a conspiracy**

Esther 2:19–23

'… Mordecai found out about the plot and told Queen Esther, who … reported it to the king …' (v.22)

Esther's royal position now seems secure. All the other young women who were potentially her rivals join Xerxes' concubines in the harem but still Esther does not disclose her Jewish origins, just as Mordecai has instructed – still obeying him as a daughter despite her exalted rank. By this time Mordecai is a palace official, 'sitting at the King's gate' (vv.19,21), although he too keeps quiet about his close relationship with the queen. If we are in a position to push ourselves forward but choose to act humbly, this pleases the Lord very much. He favours the humble. 'So humble yourselves under the mighty power of God, and at the right time he will lift you up in honor' (1 Pet. 5:6, NLT).

One day, Mordecai overhears two of the king's guards planning to assassinate Xerxes. To kill a king was a terrible crime, however tyrannical he might be; years before, David had had two opportunities to take the life of his enemy Saul the anointed king, but he refused, believing that God would reward him for not doing such an evil deed. Mordecai tells Esther about the plot and as a result the traitors are condemned to a grisly death. Neither Mordecai nor Esther look for reward but demonstrate remarkable humility. Both have influence in the court and yet do not abuse their positions. Mordecai might have been tempted to exploit his niece's rank for his own ends to gain further promotion. Esther could have turned away from her duty to honour her adoptive father and fallen into the ethos of the palace – becoming a backbiting, ambitious and corrupt schemer, seeking to exert control and further her own interests. Justice – brutal though it appears to us – was done thanks to their integrity and loyalty.

For prayer and reflection

Lord, help us to seek only to serve You and not look for any reward except to know we are doing Your will. Amen.

WEEKEND

Jesus – suffering Servant

For reflection:

'[Christ Jesus] … made himself nothing, taking the very nature of a servant, being made in human likeness. And being found in appearance as a man, he humbled himself and became obedient to death – even death on a cross!' (Phil. 2:7–8)

Jesus' entire life was spent giving Himself to others; whether through healing, teaching or humbly washing the disciples' dirty feet.

His last earthly service to the human race was to climb the hill of Calvary and die there for our sake. On the cross He gave up His reputation, laid down His life and faced the pain of separation from His Father so we can be part of His family, receive eternal life and be together with God for eternity.

Take time alone with God this weekend praising Him and asking Him to help you understand more of what He did for you on the cross. Revisit the awful cruelty and rejection of the crucifixion and anticipate the triumphant resurrection three days later; when death, sin and Satan are utterly defeated.

Optional further reading

Isaiah 53:1–12; Psalm 22:1–19; Acts 2:22–24

Haman plots **to kill the Jews**

Esther 3:1–15

'... Haman looked for a way to destroy all ... the Jews, throughout the whole kingdom of Xerxes.' (v.6)

A few years pass and Haman enters the story, evidently a descendant of Agag, king of the Amalekites – Israel's enemies in King Saul's time (read more in 1 Samuel 15:1–33). Xerxes appoints Haman as prime minister, who clearly relishes this elevation.

Everyone follows protocol, obsequiously bowing before Haman – except Mordecai. Haman is so furious he plots revenge by seeking not just Mordecai's death but that of every Jew in the empire. A superstitious man, Haman asks the court sages to draw lots ('*pûr*') for the most auspicious date. March 7, a year hence, is chosen – which happens to be Passover marking God's miraculous rescue of Israel from Pharaoh! Now Haman persuades Xerxes, maligning the Jews without actually identifying who they are. Some of what he says is factual; they keep themselves apart and have their own customs, but then he twists the truth, accusing them of flouting the king's authority. Haman offers a huge sum of money to the king if he will allow the slaughter to go ahead. Incredibly, Xerxes does not even bother to ask who these people are but lets Haman do whatever he likes, offering his signet ring to authorise the plan.

For prayer and reflection

Haman's extreme hatred for God's chosen people has been repeated throughout history. Pray for those being persecuted for their faith.

Today many laws that challenge God's laws of goodness and grace are brought to our parliaments. 'Evil triumphs when good men do nothing' (Edmund Burke). If we know about any issues of concern to Christians we can contact our MP or other political representative or write to a local paper – and pray. Haman sends the order all over the empire to plunder and kill all Jews on the appointed day. The news causes panic in Susa while Xerxes and Haman relax over a drink.

Mordecai **in mourning**

Throughout the Bible, wearing sackcloth and covering the head with ashes signifies mourning: for someone who has died, in response to a personal or national disaster, when praying for deliverance, or repenting of sin. And it's a tradition some continue today as well. On Ash Wednesday, which marks the beginning of the season of Lent, Christians may use black ashes to mark a cross on the forehead as a visible sign of their repentance and need for forgiveness. It is a time of fasting and prayer before the subsequent triumph of Easter.

Back in Esther's story, learning of Haman's planned genocide, Mordecai and his fellow Jews throw themselves into a state of deep mourning. Perhaps they turn to the Psalms in their prayers – such a comfort in trouble (eg Psalms 31, 86, 91 and 121). Locked away from the outside world, Queen Esther is unaware of all that is happening, but when she hears about Mordecai's demonstration of grief, she initially fails to understand. It is possible to become cut off from what is happening in society – we need to keep alert to what goes on. She learns that she must go to her royal husband, who alone has the authority to rescue her people, and beg him to save them from their fate. Although Mordecai asks Esther to appeal to Xerxes, he knows that ultimately it is God who is in control. And today, as we reflect on his example, we too recognise that although we bear responsibility for how we lead our lives and the choices we make, only the King of kings can save *us* from the consequences of *our* sin – without His grace we are lost.

Esther 4:1–8

'… Mordecai … tore his clothes … and went out … wailing loudly and bitterly.' (v.1)

For prayer and reflection

Lord, help me to grasp the true significance of the cross; what it means for the world and how it has the power to transform our lives the more we trust in You. Amen.

Esther makes **her choice**

Esther 4:9–17

'… I will go to the king, even though it is against the law. And if I perish, I perish.' (v.16)

W e have seen Esther's strength of character. When she first came to the harem she was not intimidated by the pagan practices and immorality there but held her head high and excelled in everything that was asked of her. She could easily have drifted away from the teachings and values of her childhood and become absorbed into her new surroundings – where she was to stay for the rest of her life. But now we read of Esther's faithfulness to her uncle and the faith they share. So far this has cost her nothing, but now if she stands by her people, she may be put to death.

Esther is not allowed just to swan into the throne room as she pleases. To protect Xerxes from unwanted intruders or irritating courtiers, ceremony dictates that on pain of death, nobody, not even the queen, may enter the king's presence without his permission. Unless he deigns to hold out his gold sceptre as a symbol of his acceptance of her, all is lost. Esther is afraid, especially as for the last month he seems to have lost interest in her. And even if she survives entering his presence, can she persuade him to reverse Haman's murderous plan?

Mordecai makes it plain: this is a moment of destiny. If Esther does not act, some other way to rescue their people will be found. If the slaughter goes ahead she, a Jewess, will die with everyone else anyway. But who knows? Esther may well have 'come to royal position for such a time as this'. The queen agrees to do what she can. What if you had been in Esther's shoes? Is there a situation you are aware God may have placed you in for 'such a time as this'? Call upon Him 'who is able, through his mighty power at work within us' (Eph. 3:20, NLT) for help and hope today!

For prayer and reflection

Is my faith in God's wisdom, power and love strong enough to trust Him even in the most fearful circumstances?

Esther and the king

W hat do Esther, her maids and the Jews in Susa ask of God? I imagine Esther prays for wisdom, courage, to find favour with Xerxes and for God to act in this impossible situation. When she faces the king, Esther looks absolutely stunning in her royal robes. The Persians were experts at beauty treatments but Esther's charm is more than skin deep. In 1 Peter 3:3–4 we read: 'Your beauty should not come from outward adornment ... braided hair and the wearing of gold jewellery and fine clothes. Instead, it should be that of your inner self, the unfading beauty of a gentle and quiet spirit, which is of great worth in God's sight.'

Xerxes extends the royal sceptre to bid her to come near. This golden staff symbolises arrogance, power, cruelty, lack of integrity and selfish ambition. Esther has risked her life to enter the king's presence. Compare this with our wonderful privilege – welcome to enter the throne room of God Almighty at any time without fear. '... we have confidence to enter the Most Holy Place by the blood of Jesus, by a new and living way opened for us ... let us draw near to God with a sincere heart in full assurance of faith ...' (Heb. 10:19–22). Although we come in rags, He considers us clean and holy because of what Jesus has done. Esther's request to the king feels like an anticlimax! Even though he promises her whatever she desires, Esther merely invites him and Haman to dine with her.

They eat and drink together and when Xerxes asks her a second time she insists her heart's desire is to host them both again the following evening. In difficult and uncertain situations are we as wise, or do we sometimes rush ahead of God?

....

Esther 5:1–8

....

'... he ... held out to her the gold sceptre that was in his hand. So Esther approached ...' (v.2)

....

For prayer and reflection

....

Loving God, thank You that Jesus holds out His wooden cross, splintered, pierced with nails, blood-stained. When we touch it we live. Amen.

Haman's **boastfulness**

Esther 5:9–14

'Haman boasted
… about his vast
wealth … and all
the ways the king
had honoured
him …' (v.11)

Haman's attitude and behaviour are outrageous. Someone once said 'power tends to corrupt, and absolute power corrupts absolutely', and here is a shameful example of how wicked and deluded someone can be. Thrilled to be asked to the queen's soirée, Haman is rushing home to show off to his family and friends when he crosses paths with Mordecai, who again refuses to kowtow to him. Haman is furious – his nice day is ruined. Even boasting to his wife and friends cannot take away Haman's indignation.

Mordecai is in double danger; from the threatened genocide and now also from Haman, who with his wife and their cronies hatch the grotesque plan to have Mordecai killed next to Haman's house, then impaled on a pole 50 cubits high. This gallows is about as tall as a modern block of flats of five or six floors! Haman plans to see Xerxes first thing in the morning and get him to sign Mordecai's death warrant. He is 'a proud and haughty man – "Scoffer" is his name; He acts with arrogant pride' (Prov. 21:24, NKJV).

Imagine the rumours spreading throughout the city. Nobody could miss Haman's bizarre construction project – probably carried out through the darkness. If the news reached Mordecai's ears he most likely spent the night on his knees seeking God's salvation. Again, perhaps he used the Psalms – whether we are rejoicing or in trouble, they are a wonderful help in prayer. 'May those who seek my life be disgraced and put to shame; may those who plot my ruin be turned back in dismay … LORD, you have seen this; be not silent' (Psa. 35:4,22). Pray for innocent men, women and children throughout the world whose welfare is threatened by the violence, oppression and greed of evil people.

For prayer and reflection

Lord, we long to see Your justice and mercy extend throughout Your world! Amen.

WEEKEND

Jesus – exalted to the highest place

For reflection:

'Therefore God exalted him to the highest place and gave him the name that is above every name, that at the name of Jesus every knee should bow, in heaven and on earth and under the earth, and every tongue confess that Jesus Christ is Lord, to the glory of God the Father.' (Phil. 2:9–11)

God is the righteous judge of all creation. Although we know of so much injustice in the world, both past and present – the Bible promises repeatedly that in His perfect time God will set everything right.

One day He will come to judge the world and call us all to account. At that time the entire human race will come to acknowledge the authority and glory of the Lord Jesus Christ. The gospel offers us the freedom to choose to follow Him today and escape God's anger at sin on that day of Judgment.

As you meditate on this, pray for those you know who have not made the choice to follow Christ.

Optional further reading

Matthew 25:31–46; 2 Peter 3:8–13; Revelation 4:1–11

Honour for Mordecai

....

Esther 6:1–9

....

"'What honour
and recognition
has Mordecai
received for this?"
the king asked.'
(v.3)

Xerxes cannot sleep – maybe he has eaten too many spicy lamb kebabs for dinner or perhaps he is just restless or anxious. In the small hours he summons the servants to read to him from the royal chronicles and they just happen to select the record of Mordecai's discovery of the plot to kill the king – of which we read in chapter 2.

Xerxes discovers that this loyal subject has not been rewarded and decides to rectify the situation at once. Solomon wrote, 'The king's heart is in the hand of the LORD; he directs it like a watercourse wherever he pleases' (Prov. 21:1). God has surely allowed this.

Meanwhile, Haman arrives, ready to lobby the king about Mordecai's death sentence and finds himself immediately called to attend the king in his bedchamber, seemingly a great sign of trust and friendship. The following scene is full of dramatic irony as Haman assumes he is the man the king says he intends to reward – 'What should be done for the man the king delights to honour?' He cannot believe his luck and, with self-important presumption, makes grandiose suggestions, involving the king's robes, horse and even a modest crown, for the man of the moment to process through Susa and receive the people's adulation.

Prayer has been offered up, humbly and sacrificially, pleading for the Lord's intervention, mercy and grace, and now the answers are cascading down like a river bursting through a dam, to silence wrongdoers and fulfil the will of God! William Temple, Archbishop of Canterbury during World War II said: 'When I pray, coincidences happen, and when I don't pray, they don't.' Do we really believe that God hears and answers prayer?

For prayer and reflection

....

Today could be a good opportunity to renew our trust in Him and pray specifically about something that troubles us and that we know concerns Him too.

Humiliation for Haman

I magine Haman's rage at having to show honour personally to the person he hates so intensely that he has already erected the massive scaffold on which to execute him! Xerxes, completely unaware of the animosity between Haman and Mordecai, directs his prime minister to parade the very enemy he wants to destroy around the city. This must have been an extraordinary experience for the Jew – but when it is all over Mordecai quietly returns to his normal duties. Once this excruciating exercise is over, Haman too goes home feeling utterly humiliated. His friends and Zeresh his wife – who previously encouraged Haman in his ambitions and plans of revenge – now change their tune, predicting Haman's downfall.

Do we encourage those we claim to love, helping them to do better and sticking by them through thick and thin – or do we turn on them when things get tough?

The Bible consistently denounces the sin of pride. Proverbs 16:18 warns, 'Pride goes before destruction, a haughty spirit before a fall.' Isaiah 14:4–5 describes the ultimate destiny of rulers who set themselves against God's people and challenge His rule and authority, proclaiming, 'How the oppressor has come to an end! How his fury has ended! The LORD has broken the rod of the wicked ...'

We begin to see that the balance of power has shifted. Haman's previously unquestioned authority has suffered a serious blow – maybe his days are numbered.

An old proverb says, 'Night is always darkest just before the dawn.' When hope has almost gone we can put our trust in God to intervene. There are many living in countries governed by capricious rulers who indulge in violence and self-seeking corruption. Pray for them.

Esther 6:10–14

'... Haman rushed home, with his head covered, in grief ...' (v.12)

For prayer and reflection

'O God, declare them guilty ... Drive them away ... for they have rebelled against you' (Psa. 5:10, NLT).

The villain **unmasked**

....
Esther 7:1–10
....

'Esther said,
"The adversary
and enemy is this
vile Haman."' (v.6)

As Esther serenely welcomes her guests to a second banquet, her mind must be in turmoil, given all the events of the last few days. Presumably Mordecai has communicated with her via Hathach or another trusted eunuch attendant so she knows both about Haman's menacing behaviour and Xerxes ordering Haman to honour Mordecai's loyalty by parading him throughout Susa.

This time Queen Esther bravely admits to her Jewish identity and entreats the king to save her and her people from the slaughter to come. If, she adds, the Jews had merely been sold as slaves she wouldn't have bothered him. Esther wisely attaches no blame to the king – although without his royal seal Haman's letter would have had no authority. Full of his renewed affection for her, Xerxes demands with furious indignation to know who is responsible and Esther dramatically denounces Haman. Xerxes storms into the garden to calm his fury while Haman literally throws himself on Esther's mercy – landing on the couch where she is reclining! At this moment the king comes back and, seeing this supposed sexual assault, immediately condemns Haman to death on the sharpened pole the traitor has prepared for Mordecai. Proverbs 26:27 says: 'If a man digs a pit, he will fall into it; if a man rolls a stone, it will roll back on him.'

....
For prayer and reflection
....

Lord, help me to live according to Your ways of truth and love and to keep my steps from wrong paths. Amen.

This extraordinary drama reveals Esther's qualities of courage, wisdom and discernment. But, unmistakably, behind the scenes we see God graciously allowing people and events to come together in response to the prayers of His people. Do you need to ask God for the kind of courage, wisdom and discernment Esther had?

Esther pleads with the king

Haman has lost his life and all that he had now belongs to his enemies. However, the Jews are still in danger because Haman's edict still holds and time is running out. Once more the queen approaches Xerxes for help, this time not using the courtly arts of charm and persuasion. Throwing dignity aside she weeps before the king, which is very courageous. As individuals, Esther and Mordecai would probably be safe now – but she willingly risks her neck for the sake of her people. Xerxes was apparently a strict follower of the Zoroastrian religion and history tells us that he was intolerant of other beliefs, destroying many pagan temples. There is no guarantee that this capricious man will look favourably upon his queen's request for mercy towards the Jewish people, especially as he would then lose out financially. And besides, just as at the beginning of the story, he cannot reverse his decision. Xerxes is totally bound by what is written and sealed with his signet ring. Although he has so much power the king must abide by the 'law of the Medes and Persians'.

Perhaps Xerxes is still so enraged with Haman's infamy that he agrees, glad to do anything to dishonour his name. He reminds Esther that he has already avenged her by giving her Haman's estate and impaled him on the sharpened pole that had been meant for Mordecai. He now goes even further and gives permission for a new letter to be sent, sealed with his signet ring.

Is God asking us to speak and act on His behalf about anything? Proverbs 24:10 says: 'If you falter in times of trouble, how small is your strength! Rescue those being led away to death; hold back those staggering towards slaughter.'

Esther 8:1–8

'Esther … pleaded … falling at his feet … She begged him to put an end to the evil plan …' (v.3)

For prayer and reflection

Are there people we should pray for – for example our brothers and sisters in the persecuted Church?

Operation **Rescue**

Esther 8:9–14

'The king's edict granted the Jews in every city the right to … protect themselves …' (v.11)

God is at work in both Xerxes and Mordecai who, like his niece, has been brought to a place of authority 'for such a time as this'. Xerxes allows Mordecai to write a new royal decree giving the Jews the right to defend themselves against any who might attack and plunder them on that fateful day. He uses the signet ring representing Xerxes' absolute authority and immediately sends it throughout the empire by messengers on the king's speediest horses.

What an amazing turn of events! Days earlier Haman had sat in Mordecai's position, choosing to unleash untold misery on the Jews – but now he is dead, disgraced and replaced by the man he most hated. God has answered prayer and also shown Mordecai what to do. This decree cannot guarantee the Jews total protection from evil but it counteracts it, and as Christians we are in a similar position. On the eve of His crucifixion Jesus said; 'My prayer is not that you take them out of the world but that you protect them from the evil one' (John 17:15).

We are not immune to suffering and pain but we do have the royal promise of God's presence, provision and peace. The gospel – sent out to every corner of the world in every language – brings the life-giving news of God's forgiveness, healing and grace through the cross and resurrection of Jesus. It too is an unalterable edict, sealed by the King of kings, bringing release from the law that says 'the wages of sin are death'. We too are called as 'the Church militant' where necessary to lay down our lives in the service of God's truth and for the love of His people. As Augustine said, 'Pray as if everything depended on God and act as if everything depended on oneself.'

For prayer and reflection

Pray for Christians known to you who face fearful or seemingly impossible situations and are in need of God's help.

WEEKEND

Jesus – overcame sin, death and Satan

For reflection:

'… he raised him from the dead and seated him at his right hand in the heavenly realms, far above all rule and authority, power and dominion, and every title that can be given, not only in the present age but also in the one to come. And God placed all things under his feet and appointed him to be head over everything for the church, which is his body, the fulness of him who fills everything in every way.' (Eph. 1:20–23)

Life consists of far more than what we can see, hear, taste, smell and touch. There is also a spiritual dimension which is far more real because it goes on forever. We believe that Jesus Christ has won the right to rule over every spiritual and earthly authority because although the devil plotted to destroy Him, God reversed the verdict and raised Him up to take His rightful place as Head of the Church, reigning throughout eternity.

Remember the spiritual reality that lies behind what we can see. Jesus reigns over all!

Optional further reading

Psalm 68; Revelation 12:10–11

The Lamb Wins!, Richard Bewes (Christian Focus Publications, 2006)

The **triumph of the Jews**

Esther 8:15–17

'For the Jews it was a time of happiness and joy, gladness and honour.' (v.16)

For prayer and reflection

Father God, You have placed us all in positions of influence. Help us always to walk humbly before You, ready to stand up for truth and love. Amen.

Haman's demise has caused rejoicing everywhere – he probably ill-treated others as well as the Jews. In Susa, Xerxes presents his new prime minister to the crowds, decked out with a golden crown and royal blue, white and purple robes demonstrating his authority. Mordecai joins the ranks of other great Old Testament leaders like Joseph and Daniel; powerful politicians serving alien cultures in foreign lands.

In today's society we urgently need more men and women of faith and integrity to be assigned to positions of influence – in Parliament, local government, business, industry, medicine, education, arts and the media – contributing their godly wisdom and moral values. Perhaps God is leading us – or someone we know – to be involved in public life. We need to pray for Christians in key roles and also remember that in God's eyes 'important' people are no more special than the rest of us. He particularly loves to work through those the world considers insignificant! Remember that we are all 'the salt of the earth ... the light of the world' – strategically placed by God to demonstrate His goodness and to share the good news about His Son – here to make a difference. We may not *always* need to express our Christian beliefs publicly but some occasions will require us to put our allegiance to God's kingdom before every other loyalty.

Micah 6:8 says: 'He has showed you, O man, what is good. And what does the LORD require of you? To act justly and to love mercy and to walk humbly with your God.'

Remember, we have the Holy Spirit within, encouraging and equipping us to do God's work wherever we find ourselves.

The reputation of Mordecai

The fateful day arrives but Haman's plan of ethnic cleansing has been so effectively countered that instead of the Jews cringing in fear of those who are authorised to attack them, almost everyone is frightened of them – especially of Mordecai!

Proverbs 11:10 says: 'Through the blessing of the upright a city is exalted, but by the mouth of the wicked it is destroyed.' When we hear of countries disintegrating into disorder and despair as a result of evil government let us take every opportunity to pray for Christians there and help practically if we can. Jubilation spills onto a city's streets when an oppressive regime is overthrown by those who love freedom and care about people. In 2004 we witnessed the Ukraine's bloodless 'Orange Revolution' when, despite strong external opposition, devout Orthodox Christian Viktor Yushchenko was voted President. His wife Katya said, 'We're strong believers in God, and we strongly believe He put us in this place for a reason.'

God is at work in many nations today – frequently we find it is the Church opposing evil totalitarianism alongside fulfilling Christ's commission to preach the gospel. East German Christians believe the Berlin Wall's collapse in 1989 was a result of many years of prayer vigils. Filipino believers attribute the end of the corrupt and repressive Marcos regime 'to prayer power'. The churches in Romania and South Africa affirm that the greatest factor leading to the overthrow of the Communist leader Ceausescu and the ending of apartheid was concerted, fervent prayer. But every new generation needs its own Esthers and Mordecais; bringing the rule of God and spreading joy and gladness to more and more people.

Esther 9:1–4

'… all the nobles … helped the Jews, because fear of Mordecai had seized them.' (v.3)

For prayer and reflection

O Lord, please send Your people to bring new life, freedom and truth to countries in desperate need today. Amen.

Destroying the enemy

Esther 9:5–19

'The Jews struck
down all their
enemies with the
sword, killing
and destroying
them …' (v.5)

The Jews still have enemies even with Haman out of the way, not least his ten sons who want to avenge their father's death. Anti-Semitism goes back a long way; the Jews have suffered so much: discrimination, exile and violent pogroms, sometimes at the hands of those who claim to be Christians. When the day comes, battle is fierce and the Jews stand together to face the many attacks launched against them. In Susa, 500 (including Haman's sons) are killed, and throughout the empire the death toll comes to 75,000.

The reputation of the Jews spreads everywhere and many are so awed at their victory and accepting of Mordecai's growing authority that they convert to Judaism themselves. Note that the Jews refuse to confiscate their enemies' possessions. One commentator observes, 'the deliberate decision not to enrich themselves at the expense of their enemies would not go unnoticed in a culture where victors were expected to take the spoil. The very novelty of such self-denial would be remarked upon and remembered and taken as proof of the upright motivation of the Jewish communities.'* God's people need to be distinctive and not tempted to imitate what others do. Greed and wanting what others have are temptations we all face; let us ask for the desire and integrity to do right.

**For prayer and
reflection**

'**Courage is an
inner resolution
to go forward in
spite of obstacles
and frightening
situations**'
(**Dr Martin
Luther King Jr).
Do you need to
ask God for that
courage now?**

Who and what are our enemies today? Paul reminded us that 'our struggle is not against flesh and blood, but … against the spiritual forces of evil in the heavenly realms' (Eph. 6:12), encouraging us to take up the 'full armour of God' (v.11) in our fight against evil and to 'pray in the Spirit on all occasions with all kinds of prayers and requests' (v.18).

*Joyce G. Baldwin, *Esther*, Tyndale Old Testament Commentaries series (IVP, 1984).

The celebration of Purim

Mordecai is determined that this victory should never be forgotten so he commands the Jews to celebrate it for two days every year with 'feasting and joy and giving presents'. This has been an important event in the Jewish calendar to this day – Purim is celebrated every springtime. The word 'Purim' means 'lots', reminding us of how Haman cast lots to select the most auspicious date for destroying the Jews. As this fell on a date one year distant, there was a long delay between the announcement of the attack on the Jews and it actually happening, giving Esther and Mordecai time to fast, pray and act.

The Jews had the opportunity to prepare for the threatened attack and Purim is a significant reminder that God is at work even through the seemingly random circumstances of life. Purim is one of the most high-spirited celebrations in the Jewish year and always includes four elements:
1) The book of Esther (called the Megilah) is read publicly;
2) Food gifts are sent to friends;
3) Charitable gifts are made to the poor;
4) Everyone enjoys a festive meal. During the public service in many congregations, every time Haman's name is mentioned (ie 54 times!) everyone makes a loud noise, hissing, stamping and rattling disapproval of this ancient enemy.

Jesus would have celebrated Purim from His childhood. I wonder what He thought about the story – for He also was brought to the kingdom for a special purpose: to rescue His people. Celebrations remind us of God's goodness so we can thank Him for all He has done. Do we give time and energy to make the most of Christian festivals for ourselves and our families?

Esther 9:20–28

'... their sorrow was turned into joy and their mourning into a day of celebration.' (v.22)

For prayer and reflection

Thank You, Lord, for special times in the year when we focus on particular events and aspects of Your character. Help us to make the most of them. Amen.

Queen **Esther's decree**

Esther 9:29–32

'… Esther … along with Mordecai the Jew, wrote with full authority … concerning Purim.' (v.29)

We might have expected Mordecai, now in such an unassailable position of authority, to decide he no longer needs Esther – who after all is only a woman – and send her back to the harem. But no, this passage makes it quite clear that she continues to be regarded as an important public figure – at least for the Jewish community – and remains in the spotlight alongside him 'with full authority'. The letter sent across the empire is known as Queen Esther's decree. She has come a long way since the day she left her life as Hadassah, the daughter of Abihail who had died and left her in the care of her uncle. Ephesians 2:10 says 'we are God's workmanship, created in Christ Jesus to do good works, which God prepared in advance for us to do.' He loves us and as the psalmist so beautifully puts it: 'even the darkness will not be dark to you; the night will shine like the day, for darkness is as light to you. For you created my inmost being; you knit me together in my mother's womb. I praise you because I am fearfully and wonderfully made … When I was woven together in the depths of the earth, your eyes saw my unformed body' (Psa. 139:12–16).

For prayer and reflection

Jesus, take me as I am and fill me with Your Spirit. I will serve You in whatever ways You choose, trusting in Your love. Amen.

We have always been precious to God and intimately known by Him. He has so many plans for our lives that He longs to bring about. As we've seen, although the book of Esther never mentions Him by name, God is clearly at work behind the scenes and through the people involved, bringing His plan of salvation to fruition. Perhaps we fail sometimes to recognise God's imprint on our lives, but I hope that reading the story of Queen Esther has inspired us all to reach out in faith to the One who loves us, believing He has prepared a unique destiny for us.

WEEKEND

Jesus – our heavenly King

For reflection:

'And all [King Xerxes] acts of power and might, together with a full account of the greatness of Mordecai to which the king had raised him, are they not written in the book of the annals of the kings of Media and Persia? Mordecai was ... pre-eminent ... and held in high esteem ... because he worked for the good of his people and spoke up for the welfare of all the Jews.' (Esth. 10: 2–3)

The story ends. Xerxes stays on his throne for many years, helped by the wisdom of his prime minister, Mordecai. But how can we begin to compare this proud ruler's reign with the kingship of Christ? Xerxes was a mighty emperor: Jesus washed His followers' feet as a slave. Xerxes chose Esther for her exquisite beauty: Jesus gave His life in love for us who came to Him with nothing but the filthy rags of our sinfulness. Xerxes did not know or understand the people of his empire: Jesus sees into our hearts and loves us. Xerxes carelessly used a piece of wax to seal an edict of death: Jesus guaranteed His promise of eternal life with His own blood. Xerxes throne room was very dangerous: through Jesus we enter God's presence without fear, confident that He hears our requests. When he died, Xerxes sank into obscurity: Jesus' name lives forever and His kingdom will last for eternity!

The book of Esther encourages us to live with renewed confidence in God's faithfulness and the loving support of His people. We too need to be strong and courageous in the face of hostility and testing.

Suffering for
the gospel

Beryl Adamsbaum

Beryl Adamsbaum, wife, mother and grandmother, a
former language teacher living on the border of France and
Switzerland, has ministry opportunities in both countries. She
has had five books published. She is a regular contributor to *Day
by Day with God* (BRF). She also writes a monthly meditation (in
French) entitled 'Méditations mensuelles' for her church website
– see www.eebg.ch

Suffering **for the gospel**

2 Timothy 1:1–3

'Grace, mercy and peace from God the Father and Christ Jesus our Lord.' (v.2)

I came to know the Lord thanks to missionaries in Zambia where I spent my childhood. When I left Lusaka at age eighteen to travel to France for my studies, the missionaries made sure they wrote to me in order to encourage me in my walk with the Lord.

Many of the apostle Paul's letters were written to churches. Some, however, were to individual Christians. This particular letter is a very personal one. Written to Timothy, it includes many expressions of affection, for Paul had a close relationship with him. Here he calls Timothy his 'dear son' (v.2); elsewhere he refers to him as 'my son whom I love' (1 Cor. 4:17). It would seem that Paul had been instrumental in his conversion. Timothy may have come to faith in Christ when Paul preached the gospel in Lystra on his first missionary journey (Acts 14:6–7). Timothy's mother and grandmother were both believers (v.5) and had surely taught him the rudiments of the faith as he was growing up.

Paul begins his letter, as was customary, by introducing himself. He is 'an apostle of Christ Jesus by the will of God, according to the promise of life that is in Christ Jesus' (v.1). An apostle was an eyewitness of the risen Christ. Paul's Damascus Road experience (Acts 9:3–6) gave him this qualification. He acknowledged that it was by God's will that he had become an apostle. God had given him a message of life for those who were dead in their sins.

Even though the 'grace ... and peace' (v.2) greeting was usual (and Paul adds 'mercy' in both of his letters to Timothy), they are not empty words. In accepting Christ, we are all beneficiaries of His grace and mercy and we experience the peace of sins forgiven and of reconciliation with Him.

For prayer and reflection

Read Acts 16:1–3 to learn a bit more about Timothy and his family, and to see how and where Paul first came into contact with him.

Fan **the flame**

Timothy was young (1 Tim. 4:12), not in very good health (1 Tim. 5:23) and timid. If you are shy, no doubt you will sympathise with him. You may also be encouraged by Paul's words to him. Paul points out that, rather than giving Timothy 'a spirit of timidity', God has given him gifts, gifts that he is to put to good use. And these gifts are not given exclusively to Timothy, but to every believer. Timothy is a leader in the church at Ephesus (1 Tim. 1:3). It would seem that he had been placed in a position of leadership almost in spite of himself and certainly beyond his natural gifts and capabilities.

We may not all be leaders, but if we belong to Jesus, we are all called to be His witnesses. God has given to us, as well as to Timothy, 'a spirit of power, of love and of self-discipline'. How are we to exercise these gifts? We can count on God's power to live the Christian life, to serve Him and to testify to saving faith in Christ. As God has given us a spirit of love, we must show love to those around us by being patient and kind, generous, humble and sincere. Basically, we must show forth the fruit of the Spirit: 'love, joy, peace, patience, kindness, goodness, faithfulness, gentleness and self-control' (Gal. 5:22).

The poignancy of this letter lies particularly in the fact that it is the last recorded letter of the apostle Paul that we possess. He is in prison about to die for his faith. Aware that the end is near, he writes with a sense of urgency to instruct, exhort and encourage Timothy to carry on the good work of faithfully preaching the gospel. And we know that he constantly prayed for Timothy (v.3). Let us too be faithful in praying for one another.

2 Timothy 1:5–7

'For God did not give us a spirit of timidity, but ... of power, of love and of self-discipline.' (v.7)

For prayer and reflection

Lord, thank You that I can count on Your power as I witness to people. Thank You that I love because You first loved me (1 John 4:19). Help me to be self-controlled.

Not **ashamed**

2 Timothy 1:8–12

'So do not be ashamed to testify about our Lord, or ashamed of me his prisoner.' (v.8)

For prayer and reflection

Lord, please encourage and uphold those Christians who today are suffering persecution because they believe in You. Strengthen them, Lord, and keep them faithful.

Are you ashamed of the gospel in the face of opposition? Do you sometimes feel you want to hide the fact that you are a Christian? None of us relishes the thought of being persecuted, but as a Christian I must be prepared at the very least to meet mockery and misunderstanding. In many parts of the world today believers are facing persecution and even martyrdom. In the same way, the apostle Paul was heading for death because of his proclamation of the gospel. For that reason he exhorts Timothy not to be ashamed of him or of the gospel, just as he himself is 'not ashamed' (v.12). 'Join with me in suffering for the gospel', he says (v.8). To the Corinthians Paul writes in more detail of the sufferings he had had to endure: he had been imprisoned, flogged, exposed to death, beaten, stoned, shipwrecked, in danger from many different sources, hungry, thirsty, cold and naked (2 Cor. 11:23–27). Weak and timid though he is, Timothy must make a stand. He too must be prepared to suffer for what he believes.

Are you prepared to suffer for the gospel? Paul assures Timothy that his suffering will be 'by the power of God' (v.8). It will not have to be undertaken or endured in his own strength. You too can count on God's strength and power if called upon to suffer for the sake of the gospel. The apostle Paul explains that this gospel is a gospel of grace and salvation given to us in Jesus, according to God's purpose. Whoever believes in Jesus has eternal life. 'I am not ashamed of the gospel', writes Paul to the Romans, 'because it is the power of God for the salvation of everyone who believes' (Rom. 1:16). May we never be ashamed of the gospel. Surely such a gospel is worth suffering for!

Sound teaching

How would you describe the gospel? In today's passage, Paul uses two different expressions in referring to it. It is a 'sound teaching' (v.13) and a 'good deposit' (v.14). He refers to the sound teaching again in chapter 4, where he says that '... the time will come when men will not put up with sound doctrine' (4:3). What do we understand by 'sound teaching' or 'sound doctrine'? Surely it is teaching that is true, reliable, correct. Paul encourages Timothy to follow his example – his 'pattern of sound teaching' – and teach in the same way. But the teaching, even though done with conviction, must not be aggressive. It must be characterised by the faith and love that stem from a close relationship with Jesus.

What does Paul mean by the 'good deposit'? Other Bible versions paraphrase this expression as: 'this precious thing' (*The Message*), 'the good treasure' (NRSV), 'the truth of the good news' (NIrV). This precious truth has been given to Timothy to look after; he is to 'guard' it. As we will see later in this letter there were false teachers around, particularly in and near Ephesus where Timothy was a church leader. They tried to distort the truth of God's Word. Timothy was to be on his guard, so that this would not happen. He was to preserve the gospel, to keep it pure. But how can weak, timid Timothy do this alone? Ah! but he is not alone. Paul says he is to do this 'with the help of the Holy Spirit' (v.14). How wonderful to be indwelt by God's Spirit, who helps us and strengthens us, enables us and equips us as we seek to be faithful and true to God in the face of distorted truth and opposition. Timothy could count on the power of God's Spirit. So can you!

**2 Timothy
1:13–14**

'What you heard from me, keep as the pattern of sound teaching, with faith and love in Christ Jesus.'
(v.13)

For prayer and reflection

Thank You, Lord, for those who have given me sound teaching. Help me to guard the gospel and live out the truth of Your Word. Thank You for Your Spirit within me.

Mercy

**2 Timothy
1:15–18**

'May the Lord
show mercy to
the household
of Onesiphorus,
because he often
refreshed
me …' (v.16)

**For prayer and
reflection**

**Thank the Lord for
friends who are an
encouragement to
you. Pray that you
too might have
the opportunity
of reaching out to
those in need and
showing love to
them.**

How good it is, when we are going through a difficult time, to have the help and support and encouragement of a Christian friend. I'm sure you can testify to that! This is what Paul experienced with Onesiphorus, who had already been a great help to him in many ways in Ephesus during the years he had preached the gospel there. In fact Paul says that Onesiphorus often 'refreshed' him (v.16).

When Paul had been put in prison in Rome, Onesiphorus 'searched hard' for him (v.17). He persevered in looking for him, even though – during such a time of persecution – Rome would not have been a very safe place for a Christian to be, and prisoners not easy to find. Eventually he found Paul and encouraged him and showed him kindness. And Paul certainly needed cheering up at that time! Not only was he in prison, facing martyrdom, but he had also been abandoned by 'everyone in the province of Asia' (v.15), of which Ephesus was the capital. This must have caused him much pain, as we know from Luke's account that, thanks to Paul's ministry there a few years earlier, '… all the Jews and Greeks who lived in the province of Asia heard the word of the Lord … and the name of the Lord Jesus was held in high honour' (Acts 19:10,17). But, even though others in Asia had deserted Paul, Onesiphorus remained faithful to him. He at least was 'not ashamed' of Paul's chains (v.16), even if others were.

Paul must have felt betrayed and rejected. How lonely he would have been without the support of Onesiphorus – a good friend, faithful and true. And so Paul prayed for him and his family, that the Lord would show them mercy, just as Onesiphorus had shown mercy to Paul in his deep need.

WEEKEND

Filled with joy

For reflection: 2 Timothy 1:4
'Recalling your tears, I long to see you,
so that I may be filled with joy.'

Can you rejoice in your salvation even in the midst of trials? Are you able to look beyond the sufferings of this life to the joy of spending eternity in the Lord's presence?

In the Scriptures, tears and joy are often closely associated, as in the above words of the apostle Paul. The apostle Peter also writes, almost in the same breath as it were, of rejoicing and grief: 'In this [all that is included in salvation] you greatly rejoice, though now for a little while you may have had to suffer grief in all kinds of trials' (1 Pet. 1:6). He continues, '… do not be surprised at the painful trial you are suffering … But rejoice that you participate in the sufferings of Christ, so that you may be overjoyed when his glory is revealed' (1 Pet. 4:12–13). James also says something similar: 'Consider it pure joy … whenever you face trials of many kinds, because you know that the testing of your faith develops perseverance' (James 1:2–3).

Optional further reading
2 Corinthians 4:16–17; 1 Peter 1:3–7; Revelation 21:4
The call to joy and pain, Ajith Fernando (Crossway, 2007).
You could read the whole letter of 2 Timothy to get an overview of it.

Be **strong**

....

2 Timothy 2:1–2

....

'… be strong in
the grace that is in
Christ Jesus.' (v.1)

....

**For prayer and
reflection**

....

**Read
2 Corinthians
12:7–10 to see
how, in his own
weakness, the
apostle Paul was
able to find his
strength in God.
'When I am weak,
then I am strong',
he said (v.10).**

H ow would you feel if, conscious of your own
weakness, you were told to 'be strong'?
Strength is not something you can drum up.
We have already referred to the fact that Timothy is
weak and timid. Now Paul is telling him to 'be strong'.
However, he is not telling him to be strong in himself. He
is to 'be strong in the grace that is in Christ Jesus'. That
makes all the difference! With God's help, Timothy is to
make a firm stand and faithfully proclaim God's Word
in the midst of what sounds like widespread apostasy.
It is very tempting, in the face of opposition, to water
down the gospel and distort the truth in order to make
it more palatable. It is in the midst of such confusion
and rejection of God's Word that Timothy is to persist in
teaching sound doctrine and make a stand for the truth.

You may not be a church leader like Timothy, but if
you profess to love and serve the Lord, you will want to
remain faithful to Him and to the teaching of His Word.
You will want to live in a way that honours Him. If you
do have responsibilities in your church, you will aim to
carry them out, with the Lord's help, to the best of your
ability. Whatever your role and even in the most humble
of tasks, you can count on God's strength to enable you
to do this work to His glory.

Just as Paul trained Timothy to teach God's Word, so
Timothy in turn was to train others – faithful, reliable,
trustworthy people – to carry on this ministry. We can
follow his example. And we can count on God to give
us His strength. We can also pray for those who are
involved in Christian ministry – all kinds of ministry –
that they will 'be strong in the grace that is in Christ
Jesus'.

Chained like a criminal

A friend of mine who wrote to tell me she had been diagnosed with terminal cancer said, 'I may have cancer, but cancer doesn't have me. God alone has me!'

God is sovereign. He is in control. He knows best. We can trust Him. Surely the apostle Paul's thinking is much along the same lines in today's passage. In the verses we looked at over the weekend, Paul exhorted Timothy to 'endure hardship' (v.3). Now he shares something more of the hardship he himself is enduring, but with very positive effects and results. He is in prison – 'chained like a criminal' (v.9) – for preaching the gospel. 'But God's word is not chained' (v.9), he exclaims. And the fact is the gospel has often spread far and wide during times of persecution. Many people have turned to Christ when believers have suffered for their faith. That is what Paul expresses in these verses. Through his suffering as a result of proclaiming the Word of God, others will come to faith in Christ. They will 'obtain the salvation that is in Christ Jesus, with eternal glory' (v.10). Salvation in Christ finds its fulfilment and consummation in 'eternal glory'. We know from what he wrote to the Corinthians that Paul's sufferings too would give way to 'eternal glory' and so will ours: '... our light and momentary troubles', he says, 'are achieving for us an eternal glory that far outweighs them all' (2 Cor. 4:17). The 'troubles' may in fact be very deep and serious, but Paul qualifies them as 'light and momentary' only in comparison to the 'eternal glory'.

So whatever hardship we may be enduring, whatever troubles we may be going through, we can focus on that 'eternal glory' which is an integral part of our salvation in Christ.

---

2 Timothy 2:8–10

'... God's word is not chained.' (v.9)

For prayer and reflection

Thank You, Lord, for the salvation You have given me in Jesus. In times of trouble, help me to focus on the eternal glory to which I can already look forward.

He is **faithful**

**2 Timothy
2:11–13**

'… if we are
faithless, he will
remain faithful …'
(v.13)

I don't know about you, but I am very aware of inconsistencies within myself. I don't want to be inconsistent, but because of my sinful nature it is not always easy for me to follow through perfectly on what I claim to believe, or to keep promises I may have made. I think most of us have probably failed in this respect. Jesus is the one exception, and we will see from what Paul writes to Timothy in the part of his letter we are looking at today, how consistent Jesus is. That is because He is 'without blemish or defect' (1 Pet. 1:19).

It would seem as if Paul is quoting from a poem or hymn that Timothy might easily have recognised at the time. The first half of the quote refers to our dying to self and enduring in order to follow Jesus. Remember that Jesus Himself said, 'If anyone would come after me, he must deny himself and take up his cross daily and follow me' (Luke 9:23). If we do this, we can rejoice at the prospect of living and reigning with Jesus. The apostle Paul underlines this thought in his letter to the Romans: 'Now if we died with Christ, we believe that we will also live with him' (Rom. 6:8).

The second half of the verse has a mainly negative connotation, and refers to those who might disown or deny Christ and who are faithless. Again, these words echo what Jesus Himself said: '… whoever disowns me before men, I will disown him before my Father in heaven' (Matt. 10:33). But however inconsistent we may be, Jesus will always be consistent. He will keep His promises. 'He will remain faithful, for he cannot disown himself' (v.13). He will always remain true to His own sinless nature and character, for Jesus is the perfect Son of God.

For prayer and reflection

Thank You, Lord, that even though You have not promised us an easy life here on earth, we can already rejoice at the prospect of living and reigning with You.

Approved and unashamed

**2 Timothy
2:14–15**

'Do your best to
present yourself
to God as … a
workman who
does not need to be
ashamed …' (v.15)

aybe you're good at DIY; you don't need to get workmen in from outside. However, as we all know, there are good workmen and bad. We once had a disastrous experience with one who came to do a job in our home. He created a flood and ruined a carpet! I think he was probably a bit ashamed of himself! Paul tells Timothy how important it is to teach God's Word correctly. He is to be 'as one approved, a workman who does not need to be ashamed and who correctly handles the word of truth' (v.15). The literal meaning of the expression 'correctly handles' (v.15), is the verb to 'cut straight'. John Stott gives the illustration of 'a motorway … cut straight through the countryside'.* As one commentator puts it, 'Timothy must be scrupulously straightforward in dealing with the *word of truth*, in strong contrast to the crooked methods of false teachers'.**

When did you last quarrel with someone? What was the dispute about? How easy it is to fall into the trap of 'quarrelling about words' (v.14)! Misunderstandings and disagreements can often engender arguments. So can false teaching. How would you respond to false teaching? Basically Paul says, 'What's the use of quarrelling?' It only has negative results. 'It is of no value, and only ruins those who listen' (v.14).

We will want to do our best in anything we do for God. We want to please Him. We will study and prepare well if – like Timothy – we have any teaching responsibilities. Paul points out the value of self-discipline. Rather than getting embroiled in controversy with false teachers, we need to focus on the truth of God's Word, 'the word of truth' (v.15), and we should seek God's approval.

* John Stott, *Guard the Gospel* (Nottingham: IVP, 1973) p.67.
**Donald Guthrie, *The Pastoral Epistles* (Tyndale Press, 1967) p.148.

For prayer and reflection

Lord, I know that 'your word is truth' (John 17:17). Help me to focus on the truth of Your Word and live it out faithfully. I want to please You and do my best for You.

A solid **foundation**

**2 Timothy
2:16–19**

'… God's solid
foundation stands
firm …' (v.19)

When I was a teacher, I used to work on the principle that repetition is a good teaching tool! The apostle Paul, in both his letters to Timothy, repeats things that are important. And what is most important? The gospel. Paul wants to make sure that after his own imminent death Timothy would 'guard' the gospel and continue to faithfully proclaim it. The Roman authorities as well as heretics and false teachers were trying to distort and destroy it. Paul mentions by name two of the false teachers: Hymenaeus and Philetus. How sad to read that they 'have wandered away from the truth' (v.18). Presumably they had once seemed to be true believers, but had got caught up in some false doctrine that they began propagating. Their teaching had done a lot of harm, destroying the faith of some. False teaching spreads very quickly, 'like gangrene' (v.17).

Paul tells Timothy to 'avoid godless chatter' (v.16). He uses almost the same expression in his first letter: 'Turn away from godless chatter' (1 Tim. 6:20). I wonder how you would define 'godless chatter'? Empty words? Futile speech? I think it must mean more than that. It has to include saying things that are contrary to the teaching of God's Word and that would lead people away from God. It has harmful results, as '… those who indulge in it will become more and more ungodly' (v.16). In contrast, 'God's solid foundation stands firm' (v.19). What is 'God's solid foundation'? The Church. It is 'solid' – immovable and sure. And it 'stands firm'. The adverb 'firm' immediately conveys a sense of security and permanence. 'The Lord knows those who are His' (v.19). God knows who the true believers are. And He continues to build His Church.

**For prayer and
reflection**

**Pray for your
own church.
Bring before God
the members,
the teachers,
the leaders, the
services and
activities. Thank
the Lord that He
continues to build
His Church.**

WEEKEND

What is your aim in life?

For reflection: 2 Timothy 2:3–7

'Endure hardship wit h us like a good soldier of Christ Jesus. No-one serving as a soldier gets involved in civilian affairs – he wants to please his commanding officer.' (v.3)

W hen our children were young, we spent some happy family holidays on a farm in Somerset. As we relaxed, work on the farm went on as usual. And farmers work hard!

Paul uses three illustrations – the soldier, the athlete and the farmer – to describe aspects of the Christian life. Like a soldier, we will have to 'endure hardship' (v.3). Just as 'a good soldier … wants to please his commanding officer' (vv.3–4), so the Christian's aim is to please Jesus Christ.

In order to receive the wreath or the crown, the athlete must compete according to the rules. Similarly, in order to receive our reward in heaven, Christians must live in a way that is pleasing to God and consistent with the teaching of His Word.

Just as 'the hardworking farmer should be the first to receive a share of the crops' (v.6), so those who have sown spiritual seed will receive fruit from their labours.

Optional further reading

John 4:35–38; 1 Corinthians 9:7–11,24–27; 2 Timothy 4:7–8

Useful to the Master

2 Timothy
2:20–21

'In a large house
there are articles
not only of gold
and silver, but
also of wood
and clay ...' (v.20)

aul now changes metaphors as he carries on basically with the same teaching. A few verses earlier he used the picture of good and bad workmen (v.15) to illustrate true and false teachers of God's Word. Now he refers to different utensils, some of which 'are for noble purposes and some for ignoble' (v.20). In yesterday's reading we saw that the Church was referred to as 'God's solid foundation' (v.19). In today's passage the Church is depicted as 'a large house' (v.20). It is in this 'large house' that these different articles are found.

What is particularly encouraging in these verses is the discovery that cleansing and purifying are possible. And what a transformation this will bring about! Those used for 'ignoble' purposes will become instruments 'for noble purposes' (v.21). Surely that means we can all be used of God to accomplish His purposes. There is just one condition: that we are purified. Our minds must be cleansed of any wrong teaching and our hearts and lives must be free from evil.

Jesus told His disciples that, 'What comes out of a man is what makes him "unclean". For from within, out of men's hearts, come evil thoughts, sexual immorality, theft, murder, adultery, greed, malice, deceit, lewdness, envy, slander, arrogance and folly. All these evils come from inside and make a man "unclean"' (Mark 7:20–23). That doesn't seem to leave much hope for anyone, does it? But that is reckoning without God's cleansing work through Jesus on the cross. The Bible says that, 'If we confess our sins, he is faithful and just and will forgive us our sins and purify us from all unrighteousness' (1 John 1:9). Then, and only then, will we be 'useful to the Master' (v.21).

For prayer and reflection

What kind of 'instrument' are you? Do you want to be 'an instrument for noble purposes, made holy, useful to the Master and prepared to do any good work' (v.21)?

Terrible times

As you read Paul's description of these 'terrible times', I wonder if any of it rings a bell? Is any of it true to your own experience? Does any of it correspond to what you hear on the news or read in the papers? Do you know any people like this? It is frightening to think that people who have been made in the image of God (Gen. 1:27) can be influenced to such a degree by the devil (see 2 Tim. 2:26).

Just as Paul made sure Timothy knew that opposition to the gospel would continue, so too must we be prepared to meet hostility, heresy, perversion, corruption, unholiness and godlessness. Forewarned is forearmed. Just as the people to whom Paul refers had 'a form of godliness', so too did the Pharisees in the time of Jesus, and so too do certain people today. Outwardly they may seem religious. They might go to church and make all the right noises, but their religiosity goes no further than that. They have not put their trust in Christ. They are not real believers in Jesus. The 'power' (v.5) is lacking. Paul says, 'Have nothing to do with them' (v.5). We need wisdom and discernment to recognise those who have 'a form of godliness' (v.5) but who lack its power.

Paul does not want Timothy to leave open any door for false teaching or heresy within the Church. We must see his words in that context. He is not saying that we must avoid all contact with sinners. Otherwise how would anyone hear the gospel and come to repentance and faith in Christ? And we know that we are all sinners, 'for all have sinned and fall short of the glory of God' (Rom. 3:23). In his first letter to Timothy, Paul wrote: 'Christ Jesus came into the world to save sinners – of whom I am the worst' (1 Tim. 1:15).

2 Timothy 3:1–5

'There will be terrible times in the last days.' (v.1)

For prayer and reflection

Thank You, Lord, for salvation in Christ. Please give me the wisdom and discernment to recognise those who have 'a form of godliness' but who lack its power.

Folly

'… their folly will be clear to everyone.' (v.9)

Following on closely from the verses we looked at yesterday, today's passage continues describing the kind of people Timothy is to 'have nothing to do with' (v.5). The actions and falsehood of these heretics will finally betray them and eventually they will all be recognised for what they really are – depraved and immoral. 'Their folly will be clear to everyone', says Paul (v.9).

False teachers are still around today. Representatives of false sects still knock on doors and try to 'worm their way into homes' (v.6) in order to propagate error. The problem is, such people often come across as credible and successful. Let's just make sure we are not among those 'weak-willed women' (v.6) who fall for their spurious remarks and deceitful approaches. Let us beware of their cunning, sly devices! The apostle John says, 'Many deceivers, who do not acknowledge Jesus Christ as coming in the flesh, have gone out into the world … If anyone comes to you and does not bring this teaching, do not take him into your house or welcome him' (2 John 7,10).

Jannes and Jambres (v.8) are not mentioned anywhere else in the Bible. Legend has it that they were Pharaoh's magicians who sought to oppose Moses and failed in the attempt. In the same way, in the long run, these dishonest, heretical teachers, who are in opposition to the truth of God's Word, will fail. So let us take heart. Today's false teachers will not be able to do any lasting damage to the Church. The truth of God's Word will prevail.

We ought to pray for people we know who could be easy prey for false teachers and people from false sects. Pray that they may be grounded in the truth of God's Word and that they will not be taken in by heresy.

For prayer and reflection

Lord, help me to recognise error and to stand firm on the truth of Your Word. I pray for those who are easily taken in, that You will open their eyes and protect them.

Sufferings **and persecution**

Paul wants to be sure that Timothy will remain strong amid the apostasy and false teaching. He must be faithful to God's Word, even if such a stand causes him sufferings and persecution. As we mentioned earlier, Paul himself was writing from prison in Rome. He would soon face martyrdom due to his faithful proclamation of the gospel. In order to encourage Timothy, Paul uses some of his own experiences as an example of God's faithfulness.

Timothy came from Lystra and had maybe witnessed the brutality to which Paul refers in verse 11. Luke tells us in the Book of Acts that Jews from Antioch and Iconium went to Lystra and 'won the crowd over. They stoned Paul and dragged him outside the city, thinking he was dead' (Acts 14:19). That was in the first century. In the twenty-first century, sufferings and persecution continue. In Eritrea, not only key evangelical leaders but also ordinary believers are arrested. Beatings and agonising torture in prison cripple many and some die. The trial drags on in Turkey of those suspected of brutally murdering three Christians in 2007; church leaders uncover murder plots and congregations live with the threat of gunfire or mobbing. Some young Christian girls are abducted and forcibly married into other faiths. Believers who attend house churches in China are always at risk of facing interrogation and even imprisonment. These examples could be multiplied many times over.

We too must make a stand. We must 'be strong in the Lord' (Eph. 6:10). We are not to be conformed to this world; we are to be transformed by the renewing of our minds (see Romans 12:2). We must be prepared to suffer for our faith. Yet, like Paul, we can count on God's faithfulness.

2 Timothy 3:10–11

'You … know all about … my purpose, faith, patience, love, endurance, persecutions, sufferings …' (vv.10–11)

For prayer and reflection

Pray for the families of those who have been imprisoned or martyred for their faith, that the Lord will comfort them and strengthen them and meet them in their need.

A godly life

**2 Timothy
3:12–13**

'… everyone who
wants to live a
godly life in Christ
Jesus will be
persecuted.' (v.12)

I wonder how you would define 'a godly life'?
Surely a person 'who wants to live a godly life …'
is someone who puts God first. Paul implies that
a godly life can only be lived 'in Christ Jesus'. Jesus
Himself says: '… apart from me you can do nothing'
(John 15:5). Doing God's will and living for Him, rather
than pleasing oneself, is what counts most. A godly
person will reflect those qualities already mentioned by
Paul in this letter: 'righteousness, faith, love and peace'
(2 Tim. 2:22). Basically, godliness amounts to being like
Jesus. Paul wanted to live a godly life. So did Timothy.
Do you?

If you want to live a godly life in Christ Jesus then be
sure you will suffer for it sooner or later. Maybe you can
already give examples of times when you faced ridicule
or antagonism because of your Christian commitment.
Where are you likely to meet this most? At home? At
work? In some other setting? Paul's teaching here
concurs with that of Jesus Himself, who often warned
His disciples that they would be persecuted. 'If the
world hates you,' He said, 'keep in mind that it hated me
first … I have chosen you out of the world. That is why
the world hates you … If they persecuted me, they will
persecute you also' (John 15:18–20). If we do not seem
to be suffering in any way because of our faith, then
maybe we should examine ourselves to see if we really
are living 'a godly life in Christ Jesus'.

Paul says that things will get worse and, like Timothy,
we must be prepared. But whatever happens, we can be
encouraged, because did not Jesus say to His disciples,
'In this world you will have trouble. But take heart! I
have overcome the world' (John 16:33)?

**For prayer and
reflection**

**Lord, make me
more like Jesus.
May I be prepared
to face trouble
and persecution.
Strengthen
me, Lord. I take
courage from the
fact that You have
'overcome the
world'.**

WEEKEND

A pure heart

For reflection: 2 Timothy 2:22–26

'… pursue righteousness, faith, love and peace, along with those who call on the Lord out of a pure heart.' (v.22)

Think of someone you know who in your estimation most resembles Jesus. How would you describe that person? What essential qualities does he or she possess?

In 2 Timothy 2:22 Paul tells Timothy to 'pursue righteousness, faith, love and peace'. In his first letter, Paul tells him to 'pursue righteousness, godliness, faith, love, endurance and gentleness' (1 Tim. 6:11). There we have the main characteristics of a Christian. Surely that is something for us all to work towards, something for us all to pursue. And we are not alone in our pursuit; we are in it together, with other like-minded Christians, other sincere believers. Like Timothy, we are to 'pursue righteousness, faith, love and peace, along with those who call on the Lord out of a pure heart'. Let's make sure we encourage one another as together we focus on becoming more like Jesus.

As you pursue these Christ-like qualities, are there any negative influences you need to get rid of or avoid?

Optional further reading
Matthew 5:8; Galatians 5:22; 1 Timothy 1:5

Wise for salvation

**2 Timothy
3:14–15**

'… from infancy
you have
known the holy
Scriptures, which
are able to make
you wise for
salvation …' (v.15)

**For prayer and
reflection**

**Thank You, Lord,
for those who
first taught me
the Bible. Help
me to 'continue
in what [I] have
learned and have
become convinced
of'. Equip me and
enable me to
teach others.**

Mothers and grandmothers are obviously Very Important People! If Timothy knew the Scriptures 'from infancy' (v.15), it was thanks to his mother, Eunice, and his grandmother, Lois (see 2 Tim. 1:5 and Acts 16:1). They were believers; they taught him the Scriptures and lived out their faith before him. If you are a mother – and maybe a grandmother – how privileged you are to be able to teach your children and grandchildren the fundamentals of the faith. Do they see Christ in you? We have a responsibility to make sure that our children have a solid foundation of Bible teaching.

Not everyone has the advantage that Timothy had of being taught Bible truths from early childhood. My grandmother gave me my first book of Bible stories, which I treasured for many years. I am also grateful to missionaries in Zambia who started a Sunday School when I was still a child. They faithfully taught me the Scriptures and I came to know Jesus at an early age. Even if you did not have such a privilege, take heart: the very fact that you are reading these notes shows your desire to understand and apply Bible truths and to grow in the knowledge of the Scriptures.

Later, Paul himself also taught Timothy. He encouraged him to share his knowledge: '… the things you have heard me say … entrust to reliable men who will also be qualified to teach others' (2 Tim. 2:2). We too are to pass on what we have been taught; he was to 'continue' (v.14) in what he had learned. We too must 'continue in what [we] have learned and have become convinced of' (v.14). We need to stand firm on the truth of God's Word, grow in our knowledge of it and live it out in practice moment by moment.

Be **prepared**

2 Timothy 4:1–2

'Preach the Word;
be prepared in
season and out of
season; correct,
rebuke and
encourage …' (v.2)

Paul's words, though addressed to Timothy, are valid for all Christians who desire to serve God faithfully and who long to see others come to a knowledge of the truth. It is 'the Word' (v.2) that Timothy is to preach and proclaim, not his own ideas, and certainly not the watered down, heretical philosophy of the false teachers. God's Word is the gospel that everyone needs to hear. The message is so crucial, so incredibly important, that we must be prepared at any time to share it with others, even when it might not seem particularly convenient for us. Paul tells Timothy to 'proclaim the message; be persistent whether the time is favourable or unfavourable' (v.2, NRSV). This does not mean we are to thrust the gospel down people's throats or bash them over the head with a Bible. We need discernment, sensitivity and respect, as well as love and 'great patience' (v.2), as we look for ways to communicate the good news of salvation in Jesus Christ. We must get alongside people and show them that the gospel is relevant to them in whatever situation they find themselves.

Depending on the person and on the circumstances, we may have to 'correct, rebuke [or] encourage' (v.2). We must not pressurise people into making a decision. Our responsibility is to make the Word known. It is God – through His Holy Spirit – who convicts people and saves them. Then they will need that 'careful instruction' (v.2) that Paul tells Timothy to give.

Verse 1 adds solemnity to the charge in verse 2. It is 'in the presence of God and of Christ Jesus' that Paul lays this responsibility upon Timothy. One day Jesus 'will judge the living and the dead' (v.1) so there is a certain urgency about preaching the gospel.

For prayer and reflection

Lord, thank You for those who first shared the gospel with me. May I be ready at all times to proclaim to others the message of Your love and salvation in Jesus Christ.

Itching ears

2 Timothy 4:3–5

'For the time
will come when
men will not put
up with sound
doctrine.' (v.3)

Paul tells Timothy to 'keep [his] head in all situations' (v.5). That is probably good advice for all of us at all times! Don't let's get off track, caught up with 'spiritual junk food – catchy opinions that tickle our fancy' (v.3, *The Message*). There are many people with 'itching ears' (v.3) around today, those who 'will turn their ears away from the truth and turn aside to myths' (v.4). They will find teachers 'to suit their own desires' (v.3) – people who will tell them just what they want to hear.

A slogan some years ago in one of our local supermarkets was: 'Feel good'. Products bought in that shop were supposed to make the customer 'feel good'. To 'feel good' is what many people long for and aim at today. That is what counts the most for them. In some circles this seems to have become the criterion in the spiritual realm too. It no longer matters whether a particular teaching is true, but whether it makes people 'feel good'. How subjective and dangerous! Notice that these people to whom Paul refers actually selected their teachers to suit their fancy. They chose people who would tell them exactly what they wanted to hear. Once again, shy, timid Timothy is not to be put off and discouraged by this. He is to make a stand and be different. Unlike these other teachers, Timothy is instructed to impart 'sound doctrine' (v.3). He must continue to teach the truth. We need discernment and we need to be well grounded in the Scriptures in order to recognise and reject fables and 'myths' (v.4) and to remain faithful to the truth of God's Word.

So, what will it be for you – 'sound doctrine' and truth or 'spiritual junk food' and 'myths'? To obey God or to 'feel good'?

For prayer and reflection

Thank You, Lord, for faithful, competent Bible teachers, who teach sound doctrine. Give me the wisdom and discernment to recognise fables and myths and to reject them.

Crown of righteousness

2 Timothy 4:6–8

'I have fought the good fight, I have finished the race, I have kept the faith.' (v.7)

While writing these notes, I met up one day with a 93-year-old Christian woman, a member of our church. She no longer gets out to church services. In fact, she doesn't get out much at all, apart from her brief daily walk when she is well enough. Each afternoon, when she can, leaning on her stick she walks down the road to a café. She sits in there – always in the same seat by the window – for three hours. It is her moment of ministry. On her way there, she asks the Lord to bring across her path people to whom she can witness. And there she sits each afternoon, quietly and discreetly evangelising the people around her.

When I met up with her – in the café – she told me that she wanted to do what she could to serve the Lord while peacefully awaiting that moment when He will take her to be with Himself. Then I'm sure she will echo the words of the apostle Paul: '... the time has come for my departure' (v.6). Like Paul, she has a sense of fulfilment and accomplishment. Paul wrote: 'I have fought the good fight, I have finished the race, I have kept the faith. Now there is in store for me the crown of righteousness which the Lord ... will award to me on that day – and not only to me but also to all who have longed for his appearing' (vv.7–8). Paul has struggled, endured and been faithful to the end. He is looking forward to his reward. This 'crown' awaits all true believers, justified through the blood of Christ. It is something to which we can all look forward.

Meanwhile, 'we who are still alive and are left' (1 Thess. 4:17) have a responsibility to carry on the good work.

For prayer and reflection

Lord, bring across my path people to whom You want me to witness. Inspire me in what I say to them. Convict them of sin and draw them to Yourself. Save them I pray.

Deserted

2 Timothy 1:15;
4:9–16

'At my first defence, no one came to my support, but everyone deserted me.' (4:16)

This last letter of the apostle Paul is very poignant and personal. Like us, he has physical and emotional needs. He is very conscious of having been abandoned. He uses the word 'deserted' three times (1:15; 4:10,16). He wants Timothy, his 'dear son' (1:2), to 'come to [him] quickly' (v.9). He had already said, at the beginning of his letter, how much he longed to see him (1:4). He sounds sad, lonely and cold. He wants companionship. 'Only Luke is with [him]' (v.11), probably – as a doctor – to care for his physical needs. Crescens and Titus had moved on elsewhere. Timothy is to bring Mark with him, as he could be helpful to Paul. He also asks for his cloak and his scrolls. He warns Timothy about 'Alexander the metal worker' (v.14), who could be one of the false teachers Paul referred to earlier in this letter. 'He strongly opposed our message', says Paul (v.15). He had also done Paul 'a great deal of harm' (v.14) personally. No wonder he sounds so discouraged.

No one likes to feel abandoned or deserted or friendless and alone. It was not God's intention that a person should be lonely. Having created man in his own image, God said that it was not 'good' that he should be alone. He made 'a helper' for him (Gen. 2:18). This was the beginning of community, of togetherness, reflecting the oneness existing from all time within the three Persons of the Trinity and the oneness that should exist in the Church. May we 'love each another' (1 Pet. 4:8), 'offer hospitality to one another' (1 Pet. 4:9), 'carry each other's burdens' (Gal. 6:2), 'encourage one another' (1 Thess. 5:11) , 'pray for each other' (1 Thess. 5:15) and 'be kind to each other' (James 5:16).

For prayer and reflection

Lord, thank You for the precious gift of friendship. Help us to truly love each other and to reach out to people who are lonely or in need.

WEEKEND

Why read the Bible?

For reflection: 2 Timothy 3:16–17
'All Scripture is God-breathed and is useful for teaching, rebuking, correcting and training ...' (v.16)

Have you ever stopped to think why you read the Bible? Do you read it for pleasure? For entertainment? For intellectual stimulation? As a means of acquiring knowledge? Or for some other reason?

Paul tells Timothy that all Scripture is 'useful' or profitable. Why is it useful? It is useful because it is 'God-breathed' (inspired by God). It is God's Word and it is true. And Paul says that it is useful, both intellectually and practically, in a positive and a negative sense. It tells us what to do and what not to do. We need to understand it with our minds, but it must also impact the way we live. As James says, 'Do not merely listen to the word ... Do what it says' (James 1:22). If we assimilate and appropriate the Scriptures, we will grow in our faith. If we live out the teaching of God's Word, it will gradually transform us and lead us on to Christian growth and maturity.

Optional further reading
Hebrews 4:12; James 1:22–25

Delivered

**2 Timothy
4:17–22**

'The Lord will
rescue me from
every evil attack
and will bring
me safely to
his heavenly
kingdom.' (v.18)

**For prayer and
reflection**

**If you have time,
read through
the whole of this
letter again in
order to see more
clearly Paul's
preoccupation
with the gospel
and the need to
'guard' it and
proclaim it.**

Even though Paul was deserted at his first defence, and 'no one came to [his] support' (v.16), he was conscious of the Lord's presence (v.17). His main concern was that 'the message might be fully proclaimed' (v.17). He wanted the Gentiles to hear it too. Now, his work completed, he is looking forward to being taken safely into the Lord's heavenly kingdom.

He ends his letter, as was customary, with greetings. He mentions Aquila and Priscilla whom he had first met in Corinth (Acts 18:2) and with whom he travelled to Ephesus (Acts 18:19). He also refers to Onesiphorus again (2 Tim. 4:19; 1:16), as well as to other key figures in the Early Church. Amid the greetings is one urgent phrase, pregnant with meaning: 'Do your best to get here before winter' (v.21). Paul knows that he has very little time left, and he very much wants to see his 'dear son' (1:2) again before he dies, so Timothy needs to hurry. Also, winter is on the way and he is in a damp, cold prison cell. He needs his cloak to give him some warmth. It appears too that ships did not sail during the winter months, so Timothy had to arrive before the winter set in. I wonder how long it would take him to get from Ephesus to Rome?

What a fantastic letter! It is so intense, so inspiring, so personal, so moving and of such great importance. It is also relevant to the 21st-century Church. We too must be on our guard against false teachers and those who water down the gospel. Like Timothy, we must 'guard' the gospel, be prepared to suffer for it, 'continue' in it and proclaim it. Like Timothy, we must be faithful. And – like Paul and Timothy – we can count on the Lord to give us strength.

Joy in disappointment

Abidemi Sanusi

Abidemi Sanusi (www.abidemisanusi.co.uk) is an author
of several books. Her book, *Eyo*, was nominated for the
Commonwealth Writers' Prize. Abidemi runs her own
copywriting company, www.thereadywriter.co.uk, which
delivers corporate content to commercial companies. She
is also the editor of www.readywritermag.com, an online
magazine for Christians who write. She enjoys cooking,
photography and running, although not necessarily in that
order, and certainly not all at the same time!

Joy in disappointment

Psalm 30

'… weeping may remain for a night, but rejoicing comes in the morning.' (v.5)

As I write, I've just been speaking to a friend who's going through a difficult time and is disappointed with many people – not least herself. *'When I became a Christian,'* she said, *'I thought I would sail through trials and tribulations full of the joy of the Holy Ghost. Instead, I'm worn out, angry and, dare I say it, bitter about many things.'*

It seems obvious, but bitter and disappointed people do not become like that overnight. A series of incidents and experiences have made them that way. A woman may have been waiting on God, believing He had promised her a husband. Time has passed. She's now 60 and is wondering where her life has gone. At first, she was hopeful, but, as time went by, her disappointments piled up. One day, she woke up and realised that her heart had hardened – without her knowing it.

We'll look at how to retain our joy in the midst of disappointment. We'll start by examining the lives of several biblical characters to see how they retained their joy whilst enduring difficulties and disappointments. From there, we'll look at practical steps to retaining our joy: nurturing our relationship with the Holy Spirit, learning how to discern the times and seasons of our lives and discovering how to rest in the Lord in a season of disappointment. We'll conclude by looking at ways to develop a lifestyle of worship to enable us to retain our joy in *all* seasons.

If you can, keep a prayer journal. The point of this exercise is to develop and monitor your spiritual growth, and to witness it first-hand through your own handwritten observations.

For prayer and reflection

Lord, I pray for an open heart to receive all I have to learn about joy in the midst of disappointment. Amen.

Defining **true joy**

The primary difference between a Christian and those in the world is our faith in Jesus Christ. This faith makes all the difference to the way we live and handle our challenges here on earth.

Today's reading is rather like a handbook for handling trials. The exhortation that: 'Perseverance must finish its work so that you may be mature and complete, not lacking anything' (v.4), ought to give us some relief because it reassures us that there is indeed an end to our trials. But how do we get to the end – with our faith and joy in the Lord intact?

Joy is frequently cited as a 'fruit of the Spirit'. In other words, it is a natural outpouring of a born-again, Spirit-filled Christian. The apostle Paul explains to the Galatian Christians: 'But the fruit of the Spirit is love, joy, peace, patience, kindness, goodness, faithfulness, gentleness and self-control ... Since we live by the Spirit, let us keep in step with the Spirit' (Gal. 5:22,25). Thus, it is clear that joy is not something we can manufacture ourselves. It is God's gift to us and only available through the Holy Spirit.

A lot of the Bible 'Greats' (the apostle Paul comes to mind) found and expressed immense joy in the midst of great disappointment. They did not tap into their 'inner human strength' nor did they have to manufacture this joy. Their joy was a natural fruit of their submission to the Holy Spirit. And this same joy is available to you today, as you go about your daily business. Why don't you ask the Holy Spirit to fill you with it?

James 1:1–18

'Consider it pure joy, my brothers, whenever you face trials of many kinds ...' (v.2)

For prayer and reflection

Are your emotions dictated by your trials or by the Holy Spirit? If it is the former, how do you think you can reverse this habit?

The 'Greats' – not always great

Genesis 18:1–15

'After I am worn out and my master is old, will I now have this pleasure?' (v.12)

Picture the scene: a married couple, devoted God worshippers and, to all intents and purposes, unable to have children. They know God's voice and, intermittently, over the course of 25 years, He reassures them that they will indeed have children.

In ancient times, women were measured by two things: marital status and children. Imagine the years rolling by for Sarah and her shame, humiliation and anger each month as the red spots appear. Imagine the silences when the women gather round the campfire with expectant faces. Imagine the expectancy fading away to pitying smiles whenever Sarah walked into a gathering. God's visits, meant to increase her faith, must have chafed her instead – reminding her of what she didn't have instead of what He promised. Seen from this light, it is easy to see how disappointed she must have been. Yet, her name is mentioned alongside Abraham's in Hebrews 11:11–12 as one of the great men and women of faith. Looking down on earth today, I'm sure Sarah would never have imagined that she would one day be used as an example of a great woman of faith of the Bible.

How did she retain her joy? Who did she turn to when her faith seemed weak? The answer lies in her husband, Abraham, who 'considered him [God] faithful who had made the promise' (Heb. 11:11). The Christian life is not meant to be lived in isolation. We all need someone to bring joy into our lives in our moments of weakness. If you do not have such a person, ask God to bring them into your life. He's done this for me before. I know He can do the same for you.

For prayer and reflection

Lord, I ask You to send a friend I can trust into my life today. Amen.

Great **expectations**

avid was anointed by God to lead Israel during a time of great change. He slew Goliath, a Philistine giant, with one stone. He proved himself an able soldier on the battleground and was also an accomplished musician. In short, he was a modern-day all-round celebrity. In time, he also proved to be a murderer and an adulterer and, towards the end of his reign, was forced to abdicate his throne for his son Absalom – the same son who slept with his (David's) concubines on the palace rooftop, in plain view of all Israel.

1 Samuel 16:1–23

'Rise and anoint him; he is the one.'
(v.12)

As a ruddy teenage shepherd, the future must have indeed looked bright to David. When Samuel anointed him as God's chosen king over Israel, I wonder whether David thought to himself: *It can't really get much better than this!* But it did get better. He slew Goliath. He became famous throughout the land and beyond for his prowess, winning battles against Israel's enemies and then bringing the ark back to Jerusalem to restore worship.

However, David then started to make unwise decisions. He committed adultery with Bathsheba and had her husband killed. The son Bathsheba bore him died as an infant. I'm sure that David would be the first to admit that his life, with its many twists and turns, did not turn out the way he'd expected. But, and this is key, even though some of his actions had devastating consequences, throughout all the disappointments, anger and pain he always maintained his relationship with God.

For prayer and reflection

What can we learn from David? That sometimes, in the midst of trying situations – sometimes of our making – the easiest and best thing to do is simply to cry out to the Lord, like David: *'Restore to me the joy of your salvation ...'* (Psa. 51:12).

In your journal, write about a situation that robbed you of your joy and how the Lord restored your joy to you.

WEEKEND

Springs in desert places

For reflection: Psalm 84

'Blessed are those whose strength is in you, who have set their hearts on pilgrimage' (v.5).

The psalmist makes a declaration: when those whose strength is in God pass through hard times (the Valley of Baca meaning weeping) they will find, even as they journey through them, that the place of despair becomes transformed into a place of springs and refreshment. This is a promise for everybody who puts their faith in Jesus Christ.

The psalmist does not brush over the fact that there will be hard times. In fact, he confirms that we *will* all go through them (the 'Valley of Weeping'), but reassures us, the readers, that there will be rest on the other side. Indeed, the first step to getting and retaining our joy in the midst of disappointment can be something as simple as a whispered prayer:

Lord, I cannot see my way out of the pain of this disappointment but You can. Help me to deal with it. In Jesus' name, I ask. Amen.

Optional further reading

Isaiah 40:27–31; Psalm 27:4–5

Read Sarah's story in *God has daughters too* – a 'fictionalised non-fiction' account of ten Old Testament women – to get a personalised account of how Sarah persevered. Abidemi Sanusi, *God has daughters too* (Oxford: BRF, 2006).

You made me this way

The first time I read this story as a young Christian, I didn't understand it. Naomi told Ruth to uncover Boaz's feet and wait for his reaction. *How on earth*, I thought, *is that meant to redeem her situation as a penniless widow living with her equally penniless mother-in-law?*

Now, with a better understanding of the levirate law, what seemed obscure is infinitely clearer. By uncovering Boaz's feet then asking him to cover her with the corner of his garment, Ruth was making a request for marriage. In ancient times, the practice of marrying a widow in the family was to ensure that a childless widow would have a son who would inherit her late husband's estate and, in turn, care for her. This law was enshrined in Deuteronomy 25:5–10. Thus, Boaz, as a close relative of Naomi's husband's family, was obliged to marry Mahlon's widow, Ruth, to preserve the family line.

Naomi was wise, recognising that Boaz needed to be 'pushed' to honour his duty to Ruth. In those days, widows ran the risk of economic penury without husbands to provide for them. Naomi recognised this and wisely advised Ruth of what needed to be done.

Are you like Ruth, in that through no fault of your own you find yourself in a seemingly hopeless situation? Perhaps you feel disempowered and disappointed with yourself, wondering about the next step to take. Take heart and learn from Ruth and Naomi. They found themselves in a situation not of their own making and sought to do something about it – all within the framework of God's law. If you are going through some form of disappointment right now, ask God: *Lord, what godly action can I take to redeem the situation?*

Ruth 3:1–15

'When he lies down, note the place where he is lying. Then go and uncover his feet and lie down …' (v.4)

For prayer and reflection

Lord, help me to take my life back in my hands by giving me godly plans to redeem my current trials. In Jesus' name. Amen.

The truth about **expectations**

Jeremiah 1

'... before you were born, I set you apart; I appointed you as a prophet to the nations.' (v.5)

It is certainly not always easy to choose to obey and serve God. Living a Christian life in a fallen world that chafes against everything we know to be true is a constant battle. God calls people to do different things, and some might not bring visible rewards in themselves. For such things, I would argue that the reward is simply doing God's will.

When God calls us to do something, we have to be truthful about our reasons for obeying Him. You may believe that God has called you to be a writer, but you're disappointed because you haven't obtained a publishing deal (or you have, but the sales are disappointing). You might need to factor in that just because He's called you to write for Him may not mean that you will immediately be catapulted into the 0.5 per cent of writers who earn untold millions for their work. You might simply be called to write articles that will encourage others for your church magazine or a blog.

Disappointment with God is one of the major ills of the Church today and I strongly believe that we should encourage more people to talk about it. Be honest with yourself about the real reason you're disappointed with the outcome of your following God. Only then will you be free to release the joy of your salvation.

Think about the times you've obeyed God and the results weren't quite what you expected. Were you honest with yourself about your disappointment with God? If not, why not? Remember, God does not condemn you. Being truthful about the way you feel is probably one of the most practical and important steps in the healing process. If you do not face up to your disappointments, how can you be set free from them?

For prayer and reflection

Father, help me be honest with myself and You about my disappointments. Give me the strength to face up to them and to be set free. In Jesus' name. Amen.

The **yielding**

I n preparation for writing these notes, I asked a friend how she retained her joy in the midst of disappointment. Her answer encouraged me so much I'm repeating it verbatim.

'It was my second year in Bible school. I had not paid the fees because I didn't have the money. I didn't have the money for rent either so I was in danger of being made homeless. To top it all off, I had no money, no food and no job. I had exactly nine pence in my bank account.

'One day, after Bible school, I took a walk down the street. I thought about my situation. On the surface, it looked hopeless. But I had to come to a decision: either I could leave everything to God or I could drive myself mad, worrying about my situation. I made the decision to trust God and, when I did, a weight seemed to lift off my shoulders. I started smiling and laughing to myself because I was so happy. I know everyone else on the street thought I was mad, laughing to myself – but I didn't care. On the face of it, nothing in my life had changed, but I had, *inside*. I had resolved to trust God. I made a decision to yield to Him and that made *all* the difference.'

Having handed her worries over to God, my friend eventually got a job as a live-in nanny, which enabled her to save money towards her Bible school fees.

Living a life anchored and rooted in God means yielding to Him. However, we have to make the initial decision to yield (ie submit) and that is the 'difficult bit'. Yet, it's not something we're expected to do in our own strength. God's promise of the Holy Spirit is available to all who trust in Him for salvation. Today, ask the Holy Spirit to help you yield to God and release His joy to you.

John 14:1–20

'… the Father … will give you another Counsellor to be with you for ever – the Spirit of truth.' (vv.16–17)

For prayer and reflection

Holy Spirit, visit me afresh this week to help me gain a better understanding of who You are. In Jesus' name I pray. Amen.

Hearing **voices**

John 16:1–15

'… the Spirit will take from what is mine and make it known to you.' (v.15)

I was a young Christian. One day, after a church service, I sensed an urging to speak with the pastor so I went to see him. I told him what I thought and he said, 'Well, let's see what the Lord has to say.' He cocked his head to one side as if he were listening to something. I asked him what he was doing. He said he was listening for the voice of the Holy Spirit. 'You mean you can hear Him?' 'Yes,' he replied. I asked him if I could do the same. He replied, 'When you go back home today, lock yourself in a quiet room and just wait in the silence. You'll hear Him and you will know when you hear Him.' I flew home and did exactly as he said. It took about 10–15 minutes for my wired emotions to calm down but then I finally heard a still small voice: 'Abidemi, my child.'

That day was a turning point in my Christian life and I have learnt much more about the Person and work of the Holy Spirit. He does speak: through the Bible, through His voice speaking into my heart and, at other times, through a strong, pressing urging within me (an 'unction'). As today's verse says, the Holy Spirit will make known to us the things of God. He can help us prepare for the dark times and rely on His gifts to help us through them. Listen hard: is the Holy Spirit warning you to prepare for challenging times ahead?

Have you ever heard His voice? Try this. Go somewhere quiet, sit still and invite the Holy Spirit to make Himself known to you. (Alternatively, some may prefer to go for a leisurely walk somewhere quiet, beautiful and peaceful.) What can you hear? If you are nervous and fearful about hearing from God, remember: He is your Father. He longs to reveal Himself to you even more than you want to hear His voice.

For prayer and reflection

Lord, help me to discern all the different ways in which You want to speak to me. May I recognise Your voice. Amen.

Free means **free**

I do not recall a time in my Christian life when I haven't thirsted for spiritual gifts. Even as a young Christian, I took the Bible at face value. If spiritual gifts were available to all Christians as the Bible said, then surely, I figured, it was my right to have them. Having been taught that they would also make our lives easier, I told the Lord, 'I want them!'

There is a certain mysticism about spiritual gifts in Christian circles today that shouldn't be there. The apostle Paul, writing to the Corinthians, said, 'There are different kinds of working, but the same God works all of them in all men' (v.6). This means that these gifts are to help us as part of the Body, the Church, and they are free – courtesy of the Holy Spirit.

It is entirely possible that we will demonstrate one or more of these giftings at different points in our lives. This year I went through a season of heightened prophetic gifting. At a prayer meeting, the leader of the session told me that my season of prophetic gifting was in preparation for the future, to get me through what would eventually be tough times ahead. Three months later, I understood what she meant. I found myself referring to my journal to draw strength from the prophetic utterances I'd received earlier in the year. If I hadn't nurtured those spiritual gifts, I don't know how I would have managed in what was, quite possibly, the most challenging time in my life to date.

If you are going through disappointing, challenging times today, ask God for spiritual gifts that will help you endure them and will bring the joy back into your life.

1 Corinthians 12:1–11

'There are different kinds of gifts, but the same Spirit.' (v.4)

For prayer and reflection

Have you ever thought that spiritual gifts were for superstars and not for the likes of you? Why not ask the Holy Spirit for the gift(s) you need at this moment in time?

WEEKEND

Love – the message of grace

For reflection: 1 Corinthians 13:1–13
'And now these three remain: faith, hope and love.
But the greatest of these is love.' (v.13)

It might seem strange to talk about love when dealing with disappointment, but I believe that this chapter of the Bible is a fitting one on which to base our reflections on the Person of the Holy Spirit. To know God is to know love. However, when we are going through hard times, love for ourselves and for others is often what we feel least.

To know and experience a relationship with the Holy Spirit is to know the liberating love of Jesus Christ. You might not feel able to accept that love currently, but this is what the Holy Spirit offers us: 'Love never gives up, never loses faith, is always hopeful, and endures through every circumstance' (1 Cor. 13:7, NLT). Truly knowing and receiving this love will help to restore the peace and joy to our Christian walk.

Whereas before you were weary, disappointed and, perhaps, even bitter about certain things, you'll find yourself giving Spirit-directed love to others. Receive the love of the Holy Spirit today – and give love in return.

Optional further reading
1 John 3

Ask not, **want not**

Today we continue our study on the Holy Spirit and turn, once again, to the first chapter of James. He exhorts us that we should consider it pure joy when we face trials, because the testing of our faith develops perseverance – and this exhortation couldn't have come at a better time. At closer look, it seems like a tall, even hateful, order. Consider it joy when we're hurting or suffering the pain of disappointment? Surely that is not an exhortation from a loving Father!

We've often heard the adage, *'Life is tough'*. God knows this, which is why He's given us the Holy Spirit to enable us to respond to these challenges in a way that will strengthen our character and give glory to Him. Sounds impossible? Not really.

When I look back on my spiritual journey, I can see how I've evolved as a person, grown as a Christian and developed as a writer. Undoubtedly, the greatest growth has come from the lessons I've learnt in my most difficult times. And now, just as I realised then, I know that I would not have made it through without the Holy Spirit.

You might be going through a season of disappointments because people have let you down. Perhaps you've made unwise decisions and are now living with the consequences of those decisions. Or, maybe, you've grown weary of doing good. You've lost the joy of your salvation and you do not understand why or what happened. Ask God to show you the 'reason for your season'. Remember: 'If any of you lacks wisdom, he should ask God, who gives generously to all without finding fault, and it will be given to him' (v.5).

What are you waiting for? Ask!

James 1:1–8, 19–27

'… you know that the testing of your faith develops perseverance.' (v.3)

For prayer and reflection

Lord, I ask You today to give me discernment regarding issues I'm facing right now. In Jesus' name. Amen.

Resting – it's not a crime!

Matthew 14:6–23

'… he went up on a mountainside by himself to pray.' (v.23)

Last week, we looked at spiritual gifts and the Holy Spirit. One of the 'curses' of Christian women is the 'To Do' list. We hear the messages of restoration, joy and peace from the pulpit, but they don't always filter down to the life we live from Monday to Saturday.

Jesus understood the need for rest. The Bible recalls that He often went into the mountains to pray. He didn't allow the demands of His vigorous ministry to get in the way of His physical and spiritual refreshing.

A friend of mine works as a consultant. After the project he was working on finished he struggled to find an employment contract with another company. He finally got one – three months later. When I spoke to him, he said that, in retrospect, it was probably good that he hadn't found a contract straight after his previous one finished. He had been able to spend time with his family and get some physical rest which he badly needed – but hadn't realised.

We are all familiar with the words, 'Be still, and know that I am God' (Psa. 46:10). This idea of stillness is repeated again in Psalm 37:7. The Amplified Bible phrases it this way: 'Be still *and* rest in the Lord; wait for Him *and* patiently lean yourself upon Him'. Also, in Psalm 131 the psalmist notes, 'But I have stilled and quietened my soul; like a weaned child with its mother …' (v.2).

So you didn't get the job you wanted. Perhaps you were passed over for promotion or even, maybe, a relationship didn't work out. In your disappointment, take note of the fact that God may be calling you to rest.

For prayer and reflection

Thank You, Lord, for showing me that I can indeed rest in You. Grant me the wisdom to see when God-ordained rest is what I need. Amen.

The woman **at the well**

H er story is probably one of the most famous in the Bible; that of the woman at the well who encounters Jesus and is changed forever. Today, I would like to focus on another part of her story. Scripture records that the woman had five husbands and that the man she was living with was not her husband. What was she looking for?

It seems to me that we women are constantly in search of fulfilment. Some women do this through men. So they go through them, one after the other, convinced that the men will love them and give them what they really need. When painful disappointment comes – which it surely does – disillusionment comes with it. I do not know the woman at the well's story but, surely, the reason she kept on remarrying is because in ancient society widowed or previously-married women stood in danger of being impoverished, as men held the purse strings. Thus, the lady at the well needed a man for economic reasons. Whatever her story, it was clear that she felt the need to plough through men for her economic survival.

Are you, like the woman at the well, still searching for things that have disappointed you? Do you find yourself doing the same things over and again and having the same disappointing results? Maybe this is the time for you to take stock, look back and discern why this particular disappointment is occurring. Perhaps you'll need counselling. Or, maybe, you'll need to take practical steps to reverse those bad habits and start afresh.

We've talked earlier about the Holy Spirit. Why don't you ask Him to show you what needs correcting in your life?

John 4:4–26

'… but whoever drinks the water I give him will never thirst.' (v.14)

For prayer and reflection

In your journal, list those things you believe the Holy Spirit is asking you to change about yourself and ask Him to help you do so.

God's appointment

Genesis 37:1–28

'... my sheaf rose and stood upright, while your sheaves gathered round mine and bowed down to it.' (v.7)

I do not remember a time when I didn't want to be a writer. From an early age, I read and wrote voraciously. Today, I write full-time, whether it's writing as a consultant for a global company, writing fiction novels or preparing devotionals such as this to encourage God's people around the world.

My publishing journey has sometimes been hair-raising and has not correlated in any way to some 'prophecies' I've received. But I am beginning to see a pattern in the way God operates and it is simply this: He never operates in the way we expect Him to – because He's God. He sees the overall picture and we see our limited earthly picture.

Today, I want to reassure you that just as God had a plan for Joseph, so He has a plan for you. God needed Joseph in Egypt. The brothers' sale of Joseph to the Midianite merchants happened to be the means by which Joseph could get there. As we read on in his story (Gen 37:36; 39:1–23) we see that, even in jail, Joseph maintained his integrity.

God may not have ordained everything that happened to Joseph but He used it to build his character. Your current disappointment might not be the way you envisaged your life to be, but today I want to encourage you to draw strength from Joseph's life. Each disappointment brought him closer to God's destiny for his life and shaped his character – so that when Joseph did eventually become the Prime Minister of Egypt, the wisdom, integrity, foresight and other character traits he had learned in his years of disappointments stood him in good stead.

So rejoice! Your disappointment might be God's appointment!

For prayer and reflection

Thank You, God, that while every disappointment might not come from You, my journey will nonetheless take me to my appointed destination.

One rest – many ways

Resting in the Lord means different things to different people. In the case of the friend I wrote about earlier, although being out of work for three months was financially challenging, his body got a physical rest. Additionally, he was able to spend time with his family which his previously demanding job hadn't permitted.

For another friend, resting in the Lord meant something else entirely. Her father passed away. My friend didn't go to church for a few months but she attended our weekly Bible-study home groups. The weekly meetings were small and intimate enough to give her the close support and help she needed at that particular time.

For some, resting is sleeping. For others, it can be something as simple as stopping and assessing our next step after things haven't gone as we'd hoped. We all need thinking time – but somehow, in today's 24-hour culture, it's seen as a luxury and, at times, counter-productive if it is backed up with little action. In today's reading, Elijah has just slain 450 false prophets. On the run from Jezebel, Ahab's wife, he is fearful and disappointed: 'Take my life; I am no better than my ancestors' (v.4). Knowing the physically demanding journey ahead of Elijah, God fortified him with food and drink. He also revealed Himself to Elijah in a way that would encourage him.

What is God saying to you in your season of disappointment? Is He using this time to fortify you for the journey ahead? Look around you: who is God using to bring you rest? Is it possible that you are shunning those whom God wants to use to bless you? Don't miss your blessing because it doesn't fit in with your expectation of how you believe God ought to be working in this season.

---

1 Kings 19:1–21

'Get up and eat, for the journey is too much for you.'
(v.7)

For prayer and reflection

Lord, help me to see that this season of disappointment is also a time of rest. In Jesus' name. Amen.

WEEKEND

A new clarity

For reflection: Psalm 147
Great is our Lord and mighty in power; his understanding has
no limit.' (v.5)

While He was on earth Jesus went through many of the same trials we do. This knowledge should be reassuring for us. During this week we will ask God to show us how to rest in Him and see that rest means very different things to different people.

For some, it's physical rest. For others, it might be stepping back from a situation to see it more clearly. And for another group of people, rest might just be a hiatus in the grand plan of whatever God has in store for them. Whichever category you fit, knowing where you are in your current situation should release some joy for you. Jesus understands – 'He heals the broken-hearted and binds up their wounds' (v.3).

This weekend, in the midst of the housekeeping, shopping and church activities, remember to keep God at the centre. Spare a thought for those still going through their season of disappointment – and try to be the vehicle God uses to bring joy into their lives.

Optional further reading

Hebrews 13:2; Exodus 18:13–26
Not everyone has seen angels, but we can all be an angel to someone.
This weekend, ask God to show you the people He wants you to bless.

He redeems it all

I'm writing this at the British Library in London, surrounded by students, researchers, journalists, scientists, authors – all of us ploughing through books which enable us to do our work. As for me, one dogged thought is constantly going through my mind: *When I finish these devotional notes and my next book, I'll go on holiday and be refreshed.*

I hope the previous week has helped you to think about which season you are currently in with the Lord. Nobody likes trials. Nobody likes dealing with the pain of disappointment but, as Christians, we know that in partnership with God He can work for the good in any situation (Rom. 8:28).

I've often joked that I sometimes cannot see the point of the trials God allows me to endure. That is not strictly true. I do see the point – eventually. (Usually after it is over and I have the benefit of hindsight.) A look through the Bible will reveal this to be true for every believer. From Noah (who had to endure the mockery of his neighbours – and possibly even his family – for years while building the ark) to the first Christians. They laid down their lives (as some are still laying down their lives today) so that we can enjoy the freedom of the gospel. As Christians and children of God, we have the assurance that God can and does redeem every trial we go through.

During the past three weeks we've looked at skills in dealing with disappointment, nurturing our relationship with the Holy Spirit and knowing how to extract joy from disappointment. This week, we'll be considering how to develop a lifestyle of worship that will keep us through all the seasons of life – yes, even challenging ones.

Romans 8:28–39

'... we are more than conquerors through him who loved us.' (v.37)

For prayer and reflection

Look through your journal. What have you learnt about yourself and how you handle disappointment? Have you found this journey refreshing?

Dealing **with the roots**

Proverbs 31:10–31

'Many women do noble things but you surpass them all.' (v.29)

I've been to many Christian weddings where Proverbs 31 was recited to the dewy-eyed bride. In fact, I believe that Proverbs 31 was the forerunner to 'Superwoman'!

There was a time in my life when I looked up to certain women. They had everything I could possibly ever want: a seemingly profound relationship with Jesus Christ, a high-flying career, an active church life, a dashing husband and beautiful kids to boot. In comparison, my own life seemed drab. The more I looked at these women, the more disgruntled I became. It didn't take long for disappointment to take a hold and for jealousy to sink its evil claws into me. I started railing at God. *'It isn't fair. Why do they have it so easy when I'm striving so hard and everything is pear-shaped?'* I didn't want to admit it to myself, but in truth I was jealous of my friends and their seemingly perfect lives – even if I continually told myself that I looked up to them because they epitomised the living ideal of the woman of Proverbs 31.

I soon realised that my blinkered view of these women was negatively impacting my relationship with God – and other people. It took a lot of Spirit-led spiritual reconstructive surgery before I could finally be free of jealousy's poisonous claws.

Cain killed his brother, Abel, because he was envious of him. Jacob stole from his twin, Esau, because he wanted what Esau had. What is at the root of your disappointment? Be honest with yourself. Let the Holy Spirit work on your heart, as He did mine, and set you free. Only then can you embrace the joy He willingly gives.

For prayer and reflection

Lord, I lay my heart and everything within it before You. I ask You to reveal the root of my disappointment and set me free from it. In Jesus' name. Amen.

Freedom of information

At the beginning of Job's trials, his confidence and faith in God is unshaken. As matters get progressively worse, his cry becomes, 'Why?' God does answer Job (chapter 38) but doesn't tell him the reason for his trials. It's interesting to know that Job never does find out why. Only we, the readers, know – because we've been given heavenly insight.

We should draw strength from Job's example. When we're going through trials, we ask God questions; we want to know, 'Why?' It's as if knowing will enable us to bear our present circumstances much better. When heaven is silent, it's not because God is withholding that information in order to lord it over us. He is God, omniscient, while we are human – looking at things from an earthly, fleshly perspective.

When we don't get the answers we want, we must not allow our disappointment (at not receiving the answers) to drive us even further away from God. As hard as it is, we should work at leaving our pain and disappointment at God's door, knowing that, as God and Saviour, He knows best. We should also try to be content with not knowing. When we release our disappointment to God, the joy we seek will be released into our hearts – and our disappointment (at not knowing) will not be turned into something (such as bitterness) the devil can use against us.

If you are able, list in your journal everything that has ever happened to you which you never understood. When you finish, read this list through and declare to yourself: *Lord, I leave all this with You and I ask You, Holy Spirit, to flood me with the peace that surpasses all understanding so that I can leave these disappointments of not knowing where they are – in the past.*

***

Job 1:1–22

***

'There is no-one on earth like him; he is blameless and upright, a man who fears God and shuns evil.' (v.8)

***

For prayer and reflection

***

Thank You, Holy Spirit, for giving me the grace to leave the past behind and the joy to look to the future. In Jesus' name. Amen.

Being **happy**

'I will betroth you in faithfulness, and you will acknowledge the LORD.' (v.20)

For prayer and reflection

Think back over your Christian life. Can you see a correlation between the times you've followed the world and being disappointed in the results? Why do you think that is?

How do you stay happy? A valid question. From time immemorial, people have sought to find the key to happiness. And today, selling happiness is a lucrative business. Lifestyle movements abound, promising peace, prosperity and happiness.

In comparison, the Christian life, seen from the outside, may not seem to offer much. Biblical economics, such as tithing ten per cent of our income, defy worldly economic principles. Other dearly-held values, such as not having sex before marriage, may even seem archaic today. God's laws, designed to bring liberty of mind, soul and spirit, have become a stumbling block to some.

Gomer was Hosea's promiscuous wife, who had several illicit affairs. Each time, Hosea went after her to bring her back to their marital home. Like Gomer, some Christians have chased after the same things as the world, applying worldly principles to Christian living only to find themselves disappointed with the results.

The 'Scarlet Thread' is the story of redemption given to humans by the shedding of Jesus' blood. It runs through the Bible as a constant reminder that we are not of the world. If we profess to love God and follow Christ, we cannot live as the world does because, inevitably, we will suffer the pain of disappointment along the way. We can only be truly happy, joyful and fulfilled when at the centre of God's will for our lives, following biblical principles.

Are you chasing after worldly goals and getting disappointed? Decide to live as God wants you to live. This will not always protect you from disappointment, but will enable you to live through it in the peace and joy the Holy Spirit gives freely to all God's children.

Spiritual truths – **total freedom**

ome Christians don't like ascribing spiritual meanings to certain things. If you are one of those people, you might actually wonder what your current disappointment has to do with putting on the whole armour of God and my answer is this: many things.

We might try to ignore the fact – perhaps out of fear – but the truth is that there are spiritual undercurrents to everything we do. I am reminded of a very challenging period of my life. The only way I could describe that period, indeed that year, was black. At times I could barely get out of bed. When I looked at my life, all I could see was everything that had gone wrong. I knew there was something going on, but I couldn't put my finger on what it was.

It wasn't long before I could barely hear or say Jesus' name without flinching. After a while, I stopped going to church and avoided my Christian friends. To cut the long story short, five female intercessors (and noted house group leaders) in my church were told by the Lord in a prayer meeting that I was under spiritual attack. This was the reason I was depressed and having difficulty with anything to do with Jesus or church. These women prayed on my behalf and, within days, the joy of my salvation was restored.

The apostle Paul tells us to, 'be alert and always keep on praying for all the saints' (v.18). A spiritual giant himself, he knew what he was talking about. Ask the Holy Spirit to reveal the root of your disappointment to you. If it is an attack from the evil one, ensure that you receive prayer ministry either at your church or by praying with other close, trusted Christian friends. Endeavour to get the joy of your salvation back.

Ephesians 6:10–20

'Put on the full armour of God so that you can take your stand against the devil's schemes.' (v.11)

For prayer and reflection

Heavenly Father, I pray for spiritual gifts to enable me to triumph over every situation in my life that is contrary to Your plans for me. In Jesus' name. Amen.

WEEKEND

Looking ahead

For reflection: Habakkuk 2:2
'Then the LORD replied: "Write down the revelation and make it plain on tablets so that a herald may run with it."'

T his weekend's reading reminds us of the importance of keeping written records of spiritual developments in our Christian life. These developments can range from answered prayers and prophecies given to us to something as simple as keeping a journal – as we've done this month – to monitor our spiritual journey over a particular season or, even, a lifetime.

This weekend I would like us to reflect and look back on what we've learnt. Take a look at your journal and read through it: How have you grown personally and spiritually as a result of these devotionals?

In the future, how do you see yourself? What processes are you putting (or have you already put) in place to ensure that you do not fall prey to the same things that held you captive in the dark grip of disappointment before?

Optional further reading

Meditate on 2 Timothy 1:6–7. How do Paul's words apply to your life? Clare Blake's book, *(Extra) Ordinary women: Reflections for women on Bible-based living* (Oxford: BRF, 2004), takes a fresh look at the stories of female Bible characters through Bible reflections and explores God's calling for each of us.

Sustainable steps **to a life of joy**

I f we want to retain our joy in the midst of disappointment it means developing and maintaining certain habits. A popular saying states: 'What you feed on is what will come out of your mouth.' The same goes for our Christian life. If we want to sustain a lifetime of experiencing Spirit-filled joy, the kind that will steer us through challenges, then we have to develop a spiritually healthy lifestyle. This starts with reading the Bible.

Some people struggle with reading the Bible. If that's the case for you, why not purchase a Bible-reading plan or find a free downloadable one on the internet? I follow CWR's bimonthly *Cover to Cover* study notes because they break the daily Bible readings into chunks and, most importantly, keep me grounded in the Word of God.

Other people talk about time. Nowadays, the Bible is available in many formats: cassette, CD, mp3, PDA, mobile phone – you name it, you can have it. In some countries you can even arrange to have daily Bible verses texted to you.

If you're wondering how reading the Bible every day can set you on the road to joy-filled living, even in the midst of disappointment, the reason is it will keep you rooted in the Word of God which brings guidance, comfort and peace. You'll be focused on God instead of your pain during tough times. Also the Holy Spirit will often use Bible verses to bring your attention to something – for example, a relevant verse may flash into your mind at the opportune moment.

Endeavour to lead a life of discipleship. Read the Bible and root yourself in God's Word. Discover what the psalmist had always known: 'How sweet are your words to my taste, sweeter than honey to my mouth!' (Psa. 119:103).

Psalm 119: 97–112

'Your word is a lamp to my feet and a light for my path.' (v.105)

For prayer and reflection

Do you struggle with finding time to read your Bible every day? What changes can you make in your daily life to enable you to do this?

The fellowship of **the saints**

Hebrews 10:19–25

'Let us not give up meeting together …' (v.25)

During hard times the easiest thing to do is to draw back from people. This tendency manifests itself in different ways: 'I just need time out from church'; 'I need to be alone.' While there is a time and a place for solitude, self-imposed isolation is the easiest way to leave ourselves vulnerable to the attacks of the devil.

There is a lot to be gained from fellowshipping with other saints. The Bible says that there is nothing new under the sun (Eccl. 1:9). How true! When we're disappointed with life or people, or when difficult situations arise, it's a well-known fact that the simple process of sharing these things with trusted friends or family makes us feel better.

No man is an island. It is said that 'a problem shared is a problem halved'. Whatever has brought about your season of disappointment, don't be surprised if when you share your situation with trusted members of your congregation, they begin to tell you their own experiences. You can often learn from them.

God uses different people to bless us at different times. In a Christian fellowship, the gathering of the saints, God will use certain people to bring relief to your disappointed soul and to bless you. It may be the pastor, whose teaching will suddenly have new relevance for your own life. And, finally, there's strength in numbers. Anchored in a Bible-believing church, with loving Christians around you, you can draw strength from the multiple prayers offered on your behalf.

If you have locked yourself away because a church has disappointed you, take heart. Ask God to show you another church where you can worship. Whatever you decide, don't forsake the fellowship of the saints.

For prayer and reflection

Heavenly Father, grant me the grace to trust and help me to reach out to those You've sent to help me in this season. In Jesus' name. Amen.

Songs of **praise**

'm a bit of a scholar at heart so, in difficult times or whenever I needed a lift, I would reach for my Bible and read. But lately, this has changed. I find myself singing worship songs more than ever before. Perhaps it's because my understanding of God and my Christian life has changed as well.

I'd heard all the sermons on worship and the release of power and joy it brings into one's life but, until I started doing it myself with an ease brought about by the Holy Spirit, I neither grasped nor understood it.

Worship brings freedom. When we sing praises to God, it takes our mind off our situation and turns our attention back to God. Today's psalm tells us that God's 'faithfulness continues through all generations' (v.5). It reminds us of His faithfulness by saying that we are God's people and that He has made us – so it stands to reason that He is and will be faithful to us.

Developing a lifestyle of praise doesn't necessarily mean singing 24/7. Indeed, that is neither practical nor advisable! It could be something as simple as a two-line prayer, as you prepare dinner or wait at the bus stop: 'Thank You, God, for the joy You have brought into my life.' Even such simple prayers, if from the heart, are very precious to God. However, the best way to worship is quite simply to live a life that's consistently yielded to His will. And it can be done – with the Holy Spirit's help.

Today, as we finish our devotions on joy in the midst of disappointment, make a commitment not to allow disappointment to drag you down and rule your emotions. Develop a lifestyle of praise, re-engage with the Bible, ensure you remain rooted in a Christ-centred church and retain the joy of your salvation.

Psalm 100

'Worship the Lord with gladness; come before him with joyful songs.'
(v.2)

For prayer and reflection

Thank You, God, for the joy of my salvation. I commit my life to You and place myself in the centre of Your will by yielding to You today. In Jesus' name, I pray. Amen.

Old Testament Prayers

Christine Orme

'As a child, Chris had two ambitions – to write and to teach. An Anglican lay-reader, she works with her husband, Eddie, in a South Reading parish. Chris faced a major life-challenge when she was profoundly deafened suddenly in 1986, but a cochlear implant in 2013 brought a huge improvement in her hearing and her new goal is to grow older graciously, prayerfully and with an undiminished sense of humour.'

Old Testament **Prayers**

Genesis 18:1–2, 16–33

'… Abraham remained standing before the LORD.' (v.22)

We begin this month's study of Old Testament prayers with an unusual one – a bargaining prayer. It seems that Abraham is speaking to 'a man' who is in fact the Lord. Abraham's visitors (v.2) tell him that within a year he will have a longed-for heir. He courteously accompanies them on the first part of their onward journey towards Sodom, an evil city where Abraham's nephew lives. Abraham pleads with God to spare the city if there are 50 'righteous' (God-fearing) people there, gradually lowering the number until God agrees to withhold judgment if just ten righteous people can be found.

I have heard sermons based on this passage claiming that we cannot 'bargain' with God. I think this is true in the sense that we cannot dictate conditions to God, but the example of Abraham is slightly different. Firstly, bargaining was part and parcel of Abraham's culture – it was the normal way of transacting business – and secondly, his pleading for Sodom has nothing to do with self-interest, simply with concern that the godly should not share in God's judgment of the wicked. Also, Abraham's plea is based on God's nature (v.25). He knows that the 'Judge of all the earth' will 'do right', and pleads accordingly.

However, I find that the most striking aspect of this is that Abraham waits for God's response each time before he reduces the number. How often do we rush into God's presence, give Him a 'shopping list' of requests and rush out again into 'real' life?

Let's follow Abraham's example: standing (or sitting) before God; expecting to hold a conversation with Him; basing our requests on what we know of His character; then waiting and listening for His response before we continue.

For prayer and reflection

Father, teach me to wait in Your presence when I come to pray, expecting You to speak to me and hearing what You say. Amen.

A prayer **for guidance**

Abraham demonstrated his faith in his chief servant (probably Eliezer of Damascus) by giving him the huge responsibility of finding a wife for Isaac. He demonstrated his faith in God by assuring Eliezer that God would go before him and guide him.

On reaching his destination, Eliezer adds his own prayer – a very simple one: give me success and show kindness to my master. He asks for a sign from God – that the girl who is to be Isaac's wife will go the extra mile when asked for a drink and offer water to the camels too.

And God hears and answers. The answer comes swiftly – while Eliezer is still praying (see Matt. 6:7–8; Isa. 65:24). Eliezer quickly recognises that God has abundantly answered his prayer for guidance: he has been led directly to the family of Abraham's brother! His response (v.26) is to bow down in worship and give thanks.

We, too, can pray for, and expect, guidance from God in big things and small, both spiritual and practical. God is interested in the details of our lives and He will guide us if we ask Him. (While I was writing these notes our ancient washing machine died. We prayed for guidance about a new one. I did some research, and the very model I felt could be the best to buy was reduced by more than 25 per cent in the shop – the only washing machine marked down!) Should we ask for 'a sign' as Eliezer did? We must remember that the people in the Old Testament who asked for signs had neither the Bible as we know it nor the continual indwelling of the Holy Spirit to guide them. I didn't specifically ask for a sign about the washing machine but when I found that model reduced in price I had a strong sense of God's confirmation to me that I'd made a good choice.

Genesis 24:1–27

'Before he had finished praying, Rebekah came out with her jar on her shoulder.' (v.15)

For prayer and reflection

Lord, thank You for the many promises in Your Word about guidance. Help me not to rely on my own wisdom, but to trust You to guide me in all I do. Amen.

WEEKEND

The wrestling match

For reflection: Genesis 32:6–13,21–32
'I will not let you go unless you bless me.' (v.26)

Our weekend meditations this month look at four Old Testament 'pictures' of prayer.

In today's passage, Jacob, who some years earlier had fled for his life from the twin brother he had wronged, now returns home with his household. The night before he is to meet Esau, whose birthright he'd usurped, Jacob sends his entire household ahead of him. He spends the night alone – yet not alone, because 'a man wrestled with him till daybreak'. Despite being injured, Jacob refuses to let his opponent go.

In some mysterious way, Jacob was wrestling with God. Because he had 'struggled' with God (v.28) he was given a new name indicating his new status: no longer is he Jacob ('deceiver') but Israel ('he struggles with God').

Here is an amazing picture of 'wrestling' in prayer – of persisting in our praying until we're sure that we have prevailed with God. For Jacob the struggle was a painful one – any dislocation is agonising – but he refused to give up.

How much do we know of this kind of costly prayer?

Optional further reading

Ephesians 6:10–18 – Paul encourages believers to engage in spiritual warfare.
Colossians 4:2–15 – Epaphras's example of wrestling in prayer for fellow believers.

A prayer **for information**

Genesis 25:19–27

'Why is this happening to me?' (v.22)

Rebekah – the beautiful girl of Friday's reading – becomes Isaac's wife. Naturally they expect that soon she will have a baby – for had God not promised that Abraham's descendants would be innumerable? For 20 long years, however, Rebekah remains barren. Isaac prays and she becomes pregnant – we can imagine their joy and excitement.

But Rebekah is a long way from her family and there are no antenatal clinics or regular checkups. Those of us who have had children can doubtless remember the feeling described in verse 22 – the 'jostling' within her. Even one baby can feel like an entire football team – and Rebekah is carrying two! She decides to ask God what is going on. He tells her that she will bear twins and outlines their future. That information seems to settle the matter satisfactorily for Rebekah.

During my sixth pregnancy, having lost two babies and with three little girls already, I really wanted to know if I was having a boy this time and kept asking God – to no avail. In the end, my husband said, 'I don't think God will tell you'. I asked indignantly, 'Why not?' My husband replied that God doesn't give us information we don't need just to satisfy our curiosity!

Nethertheless, I believe that, like Rebekah, we can ask God, 'Why is this happening to me?', especially when we find ourselves in a difficult or perplexing situation. However, we need to be prepared for a tough answer. Rebekah was given the information she requested – but it wasn't particularly comforting. Nevertheless, it's always easier to face any situation with the assurance that God knows why 'this' is happening and that He will bring us through it as we trust Him.

For prayer and reflection

Father, help me not to be afraid to ask, 'Why?' when things are difficult. You know the problems I face at present; help me to trust You with them and through them.

173

A 'what if …?' prayer

Exodus 3:11–14;
4:1–17

'What if they do
not believe me or
listen to me …?'
(4:1)

I f, like me, you have a vivid imagination, you may sometimes find yourself suffering a bad attack of the 'what ifs …?' 'What if so and so happens/doesn't happen?' 'What if I can't …?' 'What if they don't …?'

Here, after his experience of the burning bush and his commissioning by God to lead the Israelites out of slavery in Egypt, Moses is beset by doubts. 'Who am I …?' (3:11); 'Suppose I go and … they ask me …?' (3:13); 'What if they do not believe me …?' (4:1). God deals graciously with Moses, answering him point by point, even using miraculous signs, until finally He says, 'Now go … I will help you' (4:12). At which point Moses blurts out what has clearly been at the back of his mind all along: 'O Lord, please send someone else!' Have you ever done that?

I'm sure we can all sympathise with Moses. God demolishes all his 'What ifs …?' and Moses is forced to confess that, actually, he just doesn't want to do what God has called him to do – because he feels inadequate. And God, exasperated as a parent can be with a child who 'plays up', tells him that He knows Moses is not an eloquent speaker (herding sheep in the desert for 40 years isn't an ideal preparation for freedom fighting) and has already prompted Aaron, his brother, to come to meet him.

On the face of it, Moses doesn't emerge from this incident looking too good, does he? But … he was honest with God; he told God his anxieties (excuses?); he conversed with God – and God met him 'where he was at' and reassured him. In the end, Moses obeyed, albeit reluctantly. It's OK to feel anxious and inadequate – but the best way to deal with such feelings is to talk to God honestly about them, and to wait for His response.

For prayer and reflection

Lord, help me not to let my feelings of inadequacy or my fear of unknown situations prevent me from doing what You have called and commissioned me to do.

A prayer **of challenge**

The Old Testament characters we are considering at the moment certainly didn't mince their words in prayer. They may not have known as much about God as we do today, but they were honest with Him when they prayed. Here a disgruntled Moses challenges God: 'I did what You told me to do and things have just got worse!'

Following God's instructions to the letter, Moses and Aaron ask Pharaoh to allow the Israelites to go into the desert for a festival. Pharaoh not only refuses but vents his anger on the Israelite slaves, especially the foremen, who complain bitterly to Moses and Aaron.

When people blame or accuse us, how do we react? Do we defend ourselves? Do we attempt to justify our actions or words? Do we respond with a counter-accusation? Or, like Moses, do we take it to God and ask Him to deal with it – and us?

Moses' final point in this prayer of challenge is: 'You haven't done what You promised!' How does God respond? 'I am the Lord' (Exod. 6:2). This is a sort of Bible shorthand for, 'I am the One who has always been, the omnipotent Creator, the covenant-making God; I am true to My word; I keep My promises; I cannot be untrue to Myself and My character. So trust Me!'

In the first eight verses of Exodus chapter 6, God says 'I am' or 'I will' no fewer than 12 times! He is the God who acts and the God who is ever-faithful to His word and His character. He can handle our questions and our challenges. So, let's be honest with God and tell Him how we feel about the things that seem to be a total mess: our 'I did what You said but it's all gone pear-shaped'! He is God. He can handle it. And if we wait, we'll hear His response, as Moses did.

Exodus 5:1–6:2

'O Lord, why have you brought trouble upon this people? Is this why you sent me?'
(5:22)

For prayer and reflection

Lord, when I'm blamed for something that isn't entirely my fault, or others accuse me or complain, may I respond graciously and be honest with You about the situation.

A prayer **of sacrifice**

Exodus 32:1–4,
7–8,15–24,30–35

'… please forgive
their sin – but if
not, then blot me
out of the book
you have written.'
(v.32)

**For prayer and
reflection**

**Father, help me,
like Moses, to
spend time in Your
presence so that
I grow more like
You. Teach me to
see people with
the eyes of Jesus,
and to love them
with His love.**

After the initial excitement of leaving Egypt, the Israelites complained constantly, making Moses' life difficult. Whilst Moses was absent on Mount Sinai, receiving the Commandments from God, the people tired of waiting for him and asked Aaron to make them 'gods'. The golden calf was set up in the very place where God had just made a covenant with them, instructing them not to make 'gods of gold' (Exod. 20:23).

God told Moses what he was about to find, offering to wipe out the rebels and start afresh with Moses' own family (v.9), but Moses pleaded for the Israelites. However, on seeing the extent of their idolatry he angrily hurled down the tablets on which the Commandments were engraved, shattering them. His anger vented, Moses punished the people – but realised that even this wouldn't be enough. 'Perhaps,' he said, 'I can make atonement …' He asked God to forgive the people – or to blot him out of God's book: a sacrificial prayer.

Moses did not want this leadership role and had often 'sounded off' to God about the grumbling Israelites. Yet this Moses, whom God had offered to make into a great nation, now offers his life to atone for the people's sin! What had happened? Moses had spent 40 days and nights in God's presence. Some of God's anger at sin had rubbed off on him – but so also had God's mercy and compassion. Moses loved this complaining, unruly, covenant-breaking bunch and was willing to sacrifice himself for them.

As we spend time with Jesus, we grow more like Him. We begin to view situations and people from God's perspective, so we see not troublemakers but people in need of God's love – and we become more willing to make sacrifices to bring them into the kingdom.

A prayer **for companionship**

At the beginning of our reading God instructs Moses to continue with the Israelites' journey to the promised land; only this time there's a very big 'but': 'But I will not go with you ...' (v.3). God's endless patience, it seems, is exhausted because of the people's rebelliousness. In the short aside that follows (vv.7–11), Moses' astonishingly intimate relationship with God is described – God speaks to Moses 'as a man speaks with his friend'.

Understandably, Moses cannot face the prospect of leading the Israelites without the comforting, sustaining companionship of the Lord whom he has come to know so intimately. He pleads with God, firstly for an even deeper relationship with Him, and secondly that God will remember His promises and continue to accompany them. Specifically, Moses appeals to the honour of God's name, asking how any non-Israelites will know that this group enjoys God's favour unless He is seen to be accompanying them. And God grants Moses' requests.

Even though Moses enjoyed an amazing friendship with God, his first request was to know Him better. How much do we long to know God better and actively request His presence in our daily lives? How much do we desire people to know that we have been 'with Jesus' (see Matt. 26:69)? Or are we still trying to 'go it alone', just paying lip service to 'God with us'? Of course we know that, in one sense, God is always with us, but how much do we acknowledge His presence and talk to Him as we go about our day-to-day business? Like Moses, the more we acknowledge God's presence in our lives, the more we shall know of His 'glory' (vv.10–23) – His goodness, the power of His name, His mercy and His compassion.

Exodus 33:1–3, 7–23

'If your Presence does not go with us, do not send us up from here.' (v.15)

For prayer and reflection

Lord, 'teach me your ways so I may know you and continue to find favour with you'. Let me actively welcome You as my companion on today's journey, wherever it takes me.

WEEKEND

The first prayer triplet!

For reflection: Exodus 17:8–16

'Aaron and Hur held his hands up – one on one side, one on the other – so that his hands remained steady till sunset.' (v.12)

Here we have another story which gives us a picture of prayer. The Amalekites attack the Israelites on their journey. Moses' response is both practical (a fighting force) and spiritual (raising to heaven his staff, the symbol of his commissioning and authority under God). As long as Moses holds up his hands, the Israelites have the advantage in the battle. Whenever Moses lowers his hands, the battle goes against them. Inevitably, Moses grows tired so Aaron and Hur assist him, holding up his arms when he can no longer do so himself.

As Christians we are called to 'hold up our hands' in intercessory prayer – for our families and friends, for God's people worldwide, for those serving God in places hostile to the gospel, for fellow-believers persecuted or imprisoned for His name's sake. If we 'lower our hands' (ie if we don't pray when we should), then the enemy gains an advantage. Like Moses, we shall sometimes grow weary, but often others will join us, assisting and encouraging us in prayer.

Optional further reading

Job 16:16–21 – Job, who has lost everything except his faith in God and whose 'comforters' just add to his misery, expresses his belief that Someone is interceding for him in heaven. Compare this with Romans 8:31–39 and Hebrews 7:24–25, both of which speak of Jesus interceding for us!

A prayer **of exhaustion**

The Israelites were at it again – complaining because they were missing the fish, fruit and vegetables they'd had in Egypt! Moses hears 'every family wailing' and suddenly it's all too much – this is the proverbial 'last straw'. By this stage we should be able to anticipate what Moses will do next: he goes straight to God with the problem, pouring his heart out in a string of six questions: 'Why?' 'What?' 'Did I ...?' 'Did I ...?' 'Why?' 'Where?' (vv.11–13), before getting to the heart of the matter, 'the burden is too heavy for me'.

Moses is physically, mentally, emotionally and spiritually exhausted – even with God's help he can no longer 'go it alone'. He is feeling sorry for himself too – look at verse 15 – because self-pity often goes hand in hand with exhaustion. Of course, as soon as Moses expresses his need, God offers a solution: 70 elders, equipped, like Moses, with God's Spirit, to assist him in the day-to-day task of leadership. Moses immediately accepts God's offer.

We all feel exhausted from time to time, and sometimes it's unavoidable. But, too often, especially if we are exhausted as a result of some form of Christian leadership or other high-profile activity, we can take a kind of perverse pride in being 'exhausted' – exhibiting a martyred attitude, instead of asking God, and perhaps other people, for help. We can 'wallow in self-pity', as my father used to say, whilst simultaneously refusing offers of assistance! This is actually a deeply unattractive attitude and does nothing to further the cause of the gospel. Moses was honest enough to admit his exhaustion, cry out to God for help and graciously accept God's solution to the problem. Are we?

Numbers 11:10–30

'I cannot carry all these people by myself; the burden is too heavy for me' (v.14)

For prayer and reflection

Lord, help me humbly to acknowledge areas of my service for You where I need to accept help instead of battling on, alone and self-pitying, for all the wrong reasons!

A prayer **of anguish**

1 Samuel 1:1–20

'In bitterness of soul Hannah wept much and prayed to the LORD.' (v.10)

Scattered throughout our reading today are expressions which give us a vivid picture of one woman's unhappiness: 'she wept and would not eat', 'downhearted', 'misery', 'deeply troubled', 'great anguish and grief', 'bitterness of soul'. Hannah's childlessness was the cause of this inner pain – a pain shared by many today – but, in her culture, not having children was also considered a disgrace.

The household of which Hannah was a part was God-fearing, each year making a pilgrimage to worship at Shiloh. It should have been a festive occasion but Hannah's distress was worsened by the taunts and provocation of Elkanah's second wife. In the incident recorded here, Hannah, weeping, pours out her heart to God.

Her honesty is as striking as the shortness of her prayer. She addresses God as the 'Lord Almighty' – the One who can do anything He chooses – pleading for Him to 'look', 'remember' and 'not forget'. She asks for a son, vowing to give him to God if her request is granted. The old priest, Eli, at first totally misjudges her and speaks harshly, before accepting her explanation and adding his prayers to hers. And God gave her the longed-for son, Samuel, whose name sounds like the Hebrew for 'heard by God'.

In her 'great anguish and grief' Hannah prayed silently. God hears our voiceless prayers, those cries of anguish arising from deep in our innermost beings when we are in such distress that we cannot even form words with which to express ourselves. He 'hears' our pain – we don't necessarily have to put it into words. Although Hannah was deeply unhappy, she didn't consider that a barrier to praying. She came to God just as she was, in desperation. So can we.

For prayer and reflection

'Out of the depths I cry to you, O Lord; O Lord, hear my voice. Let your ears be attentive to my cry for mercy.' (Psa. 130:1–2)

A prayer **of rejoicing**

Hannah's prayer of joyful thanksgiving reminds us that prayer is not only about asking, but also about receiving, thanking and worshipping. When Samuel is weaned Hannah takes him to Shiloh in fulfilment of her vow. There, in a male-dominated society, an apparently insignificant woman, Hannah, prays aloud, rejoicing in the God who has so wonderfully granted her request.

1 Samuel 1:21–2:11

'There is no-one holy like the LORD ... there is no Rock like our God.' (2:2)

There is little about Hannah herself in this prayer. After the personal assertions in the first verse: 'My heart ... my horn ... My mouth ... I delight ...', it's entirely focused on God and His faithfulness. Verse 2 sums it up: There is no one, but no one, like the Lord! The rest of the prayer expands and illustrates that central truth – our God is great and good and mighty!

Hannah's prayer anticipates the Sermon on the Mount and other teachings of Jesus, highlighting, in vivid picture-language, the many ways in which God turns human values topsy-turvy: the weak are made strong; the barren give birth; God 'raises the poor from the dust and lifts the needy from the ash heap'! We can have confidence in our God, asserts Hannah, since '... the foundations of the earth are the LORD's' (v.8). Because God is omnipotent and sovereign, mere 'strength' – human power – whether it arises from wealth, family status or military might, will ultimately be irrelevant. God, the righteous Judge, will have the final word.

We would do well to take hold of these truths as we look around at our damaged, confused societies and a world which seems to be hurtling towards destruction. Hannah's God is our God. He has not lost control. He is still sovereign. He still answers prayer.

For prayer and reflection

'... lead me to the rock that is higher than I. For you have been my refuge ... you have given me the heritage of those who fear your name.' (Psa. 61:2–3,5)

A prayer **of relinquishment**

....
**1 Chronicles
17:1–4,7–27**
....

'Then King David
went in and sat
before the
LORD …' (v.16)

....
**For prayer and
reflection**
....

**Lord, give me
grace to trust You
as David did, even
when You say 'No'
to something I
really desire. Help
me to know that
Your way for me
is best.**

King David had a wonderful idea: he would build a permanent house for the ark of the covenant, the sign of God's presence. The prophet Nathan encouraged him to proceed ... And then God said, 'No'. Nathan had to backtrack and tell David that his 'good idea' was not in fact a 'God idea' (sometimes we confuse the two!). God would build David 'a house' (ie a family line), but one of his sons, not David himself, would build God's house. This must have been a huge disappointment. David's motives had been entirely right – he didn't want to live in a beautiful palace while God was 'living' in a tent. But God said, 'No'.

We can learn so much from David's reaction, expressed in this prayer. He did two things: firstly, he 'sat before the Lord'. He came into God's presence and reflected on what Nathan had just told him. He didn't argue or rant. He just sat before God. Secondly, David prayed. And what an example he set! There is no 'whingeing', no questioning of God's decision. We see a calm relinquishing of his cherished dream, total acceptance of God's 'No' and a positive, thankful, humble spirit – rejoicing in God's blessings to him in the past and joyfully anticipating the fulfilment of God's promises for the future.

David's attitude may be summed up in five words from verse 26: 'O LORD, you are God!' In that one sentence David acknowledges God's greatness, His sovereignty, His loving-kindness. How do we respond when God says 'No' to some cherished hope or plan of our own; or when He says 'No' to something we've asked for in prayer? Do we sulk and get angry, or do we, like David, relinquish our own ideas, knowing that God's way is perfect and that He is silently planning for us in love?

A prayer **of penitence**

The verses in 2 Samuel provide the background to today's main reading. David had not only committed adultery but had also had Bathsheba's husband murdered: a sordid episode. Again Nathan had the unenviable task of confronting David with God's message. David's deep remorse is recorded for us in Psalm 51 – a psalm often used as a confession – and its varied elements can teach us so much about praying for forgiveness.

Coming to God in repentance, David begins with God's character – His mercy, unfailing love and compassion (vv.1–2) – because he realises it is the source of God's forgiveness. He is totally honest with God, recognising that although he has grievously abused Bathsheba and killed Uriah, his worst offence is against God Himself. David doesn't attempt to make excuses, blame someone else or justify his actions. He asks not just for forgiveness, but for cleansing and renewal (vv.7–12), longing to be brought back into a right relationship with God so that he can help others find that too (v.13).

Under the Old Testament system of worship, sacrifices were offered by the priest to obtain forgiveness of sins, but here David expresses his understanding that what God really requires is a repentant (contrite) heart – a right inner attitude – rather than an external sacrifice (vv.16–17). David recognises too that, however badly we've failed God, when we repent and confess He always forgives and accepts us.

We may not have sinned as dramatically or publicly as David, but all sin (however 'minor' or 'insignificant' in our eyes) is still sin in God's eyes. We all need to come to God to confess our failings and find forgiveness and renewal. This psalm is a good pattern.

**2 Samuel 11:2–5;
Psalm 51:1–17**

'The sacrifices of God are a broken spirit; a ... contrite heart, O God, you will not despise.'
(v.17)

For prayer and reflection

'Create in me a pure heart, O God, and renew a steadfast spirit within me ... Restore to me the joy of your salvation and grant me a willing spirit, to sustain me.'

WEEKEND

Prayer that is costly

For reflection: 2 Samuel 24:2–4,10–25
'I will not sacrifice to the Lord my God … offerings that cost me nothing.' (v.24)

Today's reading contains another story which sounds strange to modern ears. David provokes God's judgment by taking a census of the army, despite advice to the contrary. Deeply conscience-stricken at the consequences of his action, he sets out, at God's command, to offer a sacrifice at the place where the plague ended – the threshing-floor belonging to a man named Araunah.

David declines Araunah's generous offer to give him the threshing-floor and the wherewithal for the burnt offering, in the words of our focus verse. He recognises that sacrifices, by their very nature, are costly and refuses to offer to God something for which he has not paid the full price.

David's statement has always seemed to me to be a picture of sacrificial, costly prayer – the prayer we offer instead of watching TV, relaxing or eating a meal: the prayer-sacrifice that costs us more than simply waving a credit card or writing a cheque for an appeal or mission.

Ask God this weekend what He wants to say to you about sacrificial prayer.

Optional further reading
Daniel 6:1–28 – Daniel continued to pray even though it could have cost him his life.
Luke 2:36–38 – Anna devoted her life to fasting and prayer.

An 'umbrella' prayer

....

Psalm 86:1–17

....

'... give me an undivided heart, that I may fear your name.' (v.11)

My sister gave me a very useful garment from Africa. She calls it a 'God's love' because 'it covers everything'! I've called today's passage an 'umbrella' prayer because it covers so much – in fact I rewrote these notes twice because there are such riches here I hardly knew where to begin.

The prayer opens with David's heartfelt, honest, humble cry for God to hear him, 'for I am poor and needy'. I'm sure many of us can identify with that – a sort of spiritual 'bad hair day'. A plea for God to guard his life anticipates verse 14 – he needs God's protection and His mercy (v.3). As he prays, David's low mood begins to lift and he recognises that true joy comes from relationship with the God who forgives and who answers our prayers.

In verses 8–10 David's prayer moves away from his needs towards God's incomparable greatness, and this lifts the prayer to a different plane as he asks, '... give me an undivided heart ...' For me, this is the key phrase of the psalm, for I know how easily I am distracted and diverted from God, often by things that are neither bad nor unspiritual in themselves. As we saw yesterday, David knew from his own experience the bitterness of soul that can be a consequence of having a 'divided' heart – not wholeheartedly following God's ways and not turning away from evil.

David's prayer for protection in verse 2 is expanded in verse 14 – but the extra dimension here is that these men are godless; they have no 'regard' for God. (How like many in our societies today!) David's prayer for a mark of God's goodness (rooted in his deep awareness of God's unchanging, merciful nature) is so that those who are his enemies – and therefore God's – may be put to shame.

....

For prayer and reflection

....

Pray this psalm as an 'umbrella' prayer for yourself today and, as you do so, ask God to 'underline' in your heart some part of it for you personally.

185

A public prayer

2 Chronicles
6:12,14,20–33,
40–7:3

'Hear from heaven
… and when you
hear, forgive.'
(v.21: cf
vv.25,27,30)

**For prayer and
reflection**

**'I will bow down
towards your holy
temple and will
praise your name
for your love and
your faithfulness,
for you have
exalted … your
name and your
word.' (Psa. 138:2)**

Here, in King Solomon's prayer at the dedication of the Temple, we have a pattern for public prayer by a figure representing a local community of God's people. What are the hallmarks of such a prayer? Firstly, although he was a great and famous king, Solomon's posture – kneeling before the altar with his hands spread out to heaven – suggests both humility and expectancy. I find our Western 'hands together and eyes closed' posture less helpful: praying with my hands open helps me to be more aware of God's presence.

Then, throughout the prayer, there are patterns we may find helpful. For example, we see a repeated acknowledgement of God's promises and an expectation that He will make good those promises – because He is God and He is faithful. There is also the recurrent formula: 'When … hear from heaven and forgive …' (eg vv.24– 25, 29–30), where the king realistically imagines situations in which God's people might be led astray and begs God, for the glory of His name, to forgive and restore.

These situations include both individual (v.22) and corporate (v.24) sin and natural disasters (vv.26,28). The main part of our reading ends with an encouragement for those of us who are not of Jewish descent. Solomon specifically asks God to hear the prayer of 'the foreigner' (v.32), underlining the fact that the Temple is to be 'a house of prayer for all nations' (Isa. 56:7) and that the God of Israel wants 'all the peoples of the earth' to 'know [His] name and fear' Him (v.33).

Solomon's prayer ends with a request for God to manifest Himself in that place so that His people may rejoice. God's glory then fills the Temple, so that the spectators, like Solomon, kneel down and worship.

A prayer **for restored life**

King Ahab was actively promoting Baal worship. Elijah dramatically announces a three-year drought that inevitably affects him too. God directs Elijah into (pagan) Phoenician territory, where a poverty-stricken widow looks after him, trusting 'the God of Israel' to meet her material needs. God miraculously provides for the household (vv.15–16), but disaster strikes: the widow's son (young enough to be carried by his mother and Elijah) falls ill and dies.

The distraught mother turns on Elijah, who takes the lad to his room and cries out to God for the boy's life to be restored. In contrast to Solomon's formal, carefully-structured public prayer we considered yesterday, this prayer is a simple cry from Elijah's heart. Again, as we have noted so often this month, its keynote is honesty. There is no beating about the bush, just a desperate appeal for a miracle. God's response is equally straightforward: 'The Lord heard ... and the boy's life returned ...' (v.22). This second miracle (after the unending supply of flour and oil) convinces the woman of Elijah's credentials and the truth of what he speaks.

Elijah's faith in, and honesty with, God were rewarded with an outcome that brought further glory to God's name. I think there are two ways in which we can apply this incident to our own lives. Firstly, how do we react when tragedy befalls a non-Christian friend or neighbour? Do we offer to pray? Or are we too afraid to do so, in case it 'doesn't work'? Secondly, let's acknowledge that God can bring new life to people who are spiritually dead – maybe He's just waiting for our heartfelt prayers before He acts!

1 Kings 17:1,7–24

'O LORD my God,
let this boy's life
return to him!'
(v.21)

For prayer and reflection

'O for a thousand tongues to sing, My great Redeemer's praise ... He speaks and listening to His voice, New life the dead receive ...'
(Charles Wesley)

A prayer **for sight/blindness**

2 Kings 6:8–23

'And Elisha prayed, "O LORD, open his eyes so that he may see."' (v.17)

For prayer and reflection

'I pray also that the eyes of your heart may be enlightened ... that you may know ... his incomparably great power for us who believe.' (Eph. 1:18–19)

An enemy king has been attacking Israel, planning to ambush their king, but has been repeatedly thwarted because the prophet Elisha accurately predicts where the ambushes will be. Once Elisha has been identified as the culprit, the enemy king sends troops to surround the city where Elisha is living. His servant is appalled and fearful, but Elisha is unperturbed – he knows that his security lies in God Himself and that nothing and no one can touch him without God's permission. He prays that his faithful servant's eyes may be opened to spiritual realities. His prayer is answered: the servant sees the forces of heaven ('chariots of fire') ranged in the hills around them.

Having prayed for spiritual vision for his servant, Elisha then prays the opposite for the enemy soldiers, asking God to render them temporarily sightless. Again, Elisha's prayer is answered, enabling him to conduct them to the court of the Israelite king, where he hands them over and their sight is restored. Elisha instructs the king to treat them generously, so they are feasted and sent on their way.

Here we see that Elisha's prayers are short, on the spot, to the point and precise. In each case, he is granted exactly what he's requested in prayer. God gives specific answers to specific requests. Maybe we are sometimes too vague in our prayers, especially perhaps for those whose spiritual eyes need opening. Perhaps we need to pray that our teenagers' eyes will be closed to things that will ultimately do them harm. We may need to ask God to show us how we should pray in a particular situation. What He shows us may be quite different to what we would naturally have thought of praying – so let's stay tuned to God.

A physical prayer

Hezekiah, king of Judah, was under intense pressure from Assyria, a leading world power of the time. He had 'paid off' Sennacherib, king of Assyria, once (18:14) but the Assyrians are now advancing on Jerusalem. Their spokesmen publicly challenge Hezekiah's negotiators, using Hebrew to demoralise the citizens. They urge them to ignore Hezekiah and defect to Assyria, claiming that God is powerless to help them since no other nation's gods have been able to withstand Assyria's might.

The prophet Isaiah encourages Hezekiah to stand firm, trusting God, so when Sennacherib sends another letter urging surrender, Hezekiah takes it into the Temple and spreads it out, before praying his prayer (vv.15–19). Interestingly, Hezekiah's spoken prayer is not just about being rescued from Assyria – it also expresses concern for the glory of God's name.

Hezekiah's action speaks volumes! Our prayers don't have to be spoken. Here, it seems to me, the very act of spreading out the letter for God to see was in itself a prayer. Hezekiah was wordlessly saying, 'Look, Lord! Look at what this man, this mere mortal, is saying ... about You!'

When young children hurt themselves or break some treasured possession, they often come to us in tears, pointing to the bit that hurts or holding the broken toy. They don't have to spell out what the problem is or why they're crying: we don't wait for them to explain; we take them in our arms and comfort them. Similarly, whilst we can – and usually do – use words when we pray, sometimes a symbolic action is as effective and may also be very helpful for us. God saw Hezekiah's 'action' prayer and heard his spoken one – and answered both (v.20).

**2 Kings
18:17,28–37;
19:9–20**

'Hezekiah received the letter ... and spread it out before the LORD.' (19:14)

For prayer and reflection

Father, when problems loom, help me to bring them to You – perhaps literally, as Hezekiah did – with the trust and expectation of a little child.

WEEKEND

Fragrant prayers

For reflection: Psalm 141
'May my prayer be … like incense; may the lifting up of my hands be like the evening sacrifice.' (v.2)

I f you have ever visited a place where incense is regularly used, for example an Orthodox church in Greece or Eastern Europe, you will know how the fragrance of that incense permeates the whole building. Perhaps too, like me, you have experienced in some ancient place of worship a sense that the whole place is 'soaked' in prayer – the prayer offered there for hundreds of years.

In this 'prayer picture', David asks that his prayers may be like incense. He also wants the lifting of his hands as he prays to be like the regular sacrifices in the Temple.

Incense was a prominent feature of Old Testament worship. It was costly to prepare, being made from fine and rare ingredients; the sweet aroma and clouds of smoke given off as it burned would have been a very vivid visual (and sensuous) aid to worship. So our prayers rising to God, especially those of adoration or contemplation, are a sweet offering to Him – a precious part of our worship.

Optional further reading
Revelation 5:6–14; 8:3–5 – the golden bowls of incense in heaven are 'the prayers of the saints'.
2 Corinthians 2:14–17 – Paul speaks of Christians spreading the fragrance of Christ, with a picture taken from a Roman 'triumph' where sweet spices were burned in the streets.

A prayer **of powerlessness**

2 Chronicles 20:1–22

A 'vast' enemy army is approaching (v.2). 'Alarmed', King Jehoshaphat chooses to pray rather than panic – always better! He asks his subjects to pray with him and proclaims a fast. The fact that they fast as they pray suggests they mean business with God. Maybe we need to take fasting more seriously. Perhaps, too, we should pray together more, especially when there is a threat to an entire community.

Jehoshaphat's appeal for God's aid is based on two things. The first is God's nature and His covenant. God has given Israel the land and now godless men threaten to take it from them – God's honour is therefore at stake. Secondly, Jehoshaphat's prayer depends on his own and his people's powerlessness: '... we have no power ... We do not know what to do, but our eyes are upon you.' Here is an honest admission of their need: no false pride, 'I'm sure we can cope – with a bit of help from God', but rather, 'We can't, Lord, but You can!'

God's answer comes, not directly to the king but to one of the men who has assembled to support him. It's an amazing and encouraging one: 'Don't be afraid – just stand back and see God sort this out for you.' They do – using the 'weapons' of praise (v.22)!

Paradoxically, the prayer of powerlessness can be very powerful! 'Let go and let God' may sometimes be inappropriate advice because we need to trust God and act, but at other times admitting our inability to solve a problem, or the impossibility of a situation, is the key to releasing God's power. When we don't know what to do, it's good to turn our eyes to God, admit our powerlessness, remember His past blessings and deliverances – and wait for His answer.

> '... we have no power ... We do not know what to do, but our eyes are upon you.'
> (v.12)

For prayer and reflection

Lord, help me always to choose prayer over panic. Give me discernment to know whether to trust You and act or to stand back and allow You to work things out for me.

24/7 prayer

'… hear the prayer your servant is praying before you day and night …' (v.6)

I n 587 BC the tiny kingdom of Judah was overcome by the Babylonian Empire. Many of its citizens, especially rulers and leaders, were taken captive to Babylon: this is known as 'The Exile'. They remained in Babylon for many years and, eventually, Babylon itself was conquered by Persia. Meanwhile, Jerusalem, once Judah's proud capital, fell into ruins, the Temple destroyed. Cyrus, the Persian king, allowed some exiles, including Ezra, to return to begin rebuilding the Temple.

Nehemiah, a Jew who has attained a position of great importance at court (v.11), hears from a relative that things are going badly in Jerusalem (v.3). The city wall is broken down, leaving the returned exiles defenceless. Nehemiah, shocked and saddened, mourns, fasts and prays constantly – day and night – for four months. His prayer, recorded here, begins not with Nehemiah's concerns, but with God Himself – the great covenant-keeping Lord God of heaven (v.5). It moves on to confession of Israel's sin – with which Nehemiah identifies (vv.6–7: 'we' not 'they') – and reminds God of His promise to forgive and restore (v.8). Nehemiah then asks God to grant success to his plan by giving him favour with the king.

When we're sad or distressed about a situation that's almost too big to know how to pray about (eg the spiritual and moral decline of our society), it's easy to rush into God's presence and pour out our 'ideas' to Him, or to pray about 'them' without identifying ourselves with the problem and its causes. Nehemiah's prayer is a good pattern for us: start with God and His faithfulness; confess sin, including our own; then remind God of His promises … and finally ask Him to help us play our part.

For prayer and reflection

Father, when I pray, help me to start with You and Your greatness and faithfulness, not with me and my problems and sinfulness!

A 'text-message' prayer!

Yesterday, Nehemiah's prayer ended with a tantalising hint that he had in mind a plan involving the Persian king (1:11). But he is waiting for God's time. We can deduce that he prayed 'day and night' for four whole months (I've rarely prayed that long about a course of action). We know this because the time between the month 'Kislev' (1:1) and 'Nisan' (2:1) is four months. So Nehemiah soaks his plan in persistent, regular prayer and awaits God's opportunity.

Cupbearers were close, trusted, personal servants – one of their duties was to taste the wine to ensure that it hadn't been poisoned – and they were expected to maintain a cheerful expression. But Nehemiah's distress about Jerusalem is evident (v.2). When the king asks the reason, Nehemiah is fearful, but cautiously explains why he is sad, testing the king's reaction. Out of the blue, the king asks, 'What do you want?'

Nehemiah, tuned in to God, recognises that his four months of prayer have borne fruit – this is God's opportunity! But before speaking (although it's clear from his answer that he has thought about and planned his response very carefully), Nehemiah prays again (v.4). This time his prayer is not a long, careful, balanced one, it's one of those instant, 'Help, Lord!' prayers we all pray when a sudden need arises and there's no time for anything more – a quick 'text-message' prayer to God. And, as Nehemiah acknowledges (v.8), God hears and answers that brief prayer just as He had the earlier prayers lasting four months.

It's easy to become so busy that our prayer life is reduced and limited to a series of 'text messages' to God rather than real conversations with Him. Nehemiah got the balance right. Have we?

Nehemiah 2:1–20

'Then I prayed to the God of heaven, and I answered the king …' (vv.4–5)

For prayer and reflection

Father, thank You that You graciously answer when we call. Help me to cultivate an ongoing relationship with You day by day so that I don't just call on You in emergencies!

A prayer **of thanksgiving**

Jonah 1:1–4, 10–17; 2:1–10

'In my distress I called to the LORD, and he answered me.' (2:1)

For prayer and reflection

Father, thank You that I can't run away from You and that, even when I try to, Your compassion and forgiveness reach out to me.

Have you ever made such a mess that you've wondered how God and other people can forgive you? If so, take heart – today's passage is for you! God tells the prophet Jonah to preach repentance to the citizens of Nineveh, capital of Assyria. This does not appeal to Jonah one bit. Why? The Assyrians are long-term enemies of Israel – Jonah wants God's judgment on them, not His compassion.

Jonah tries to run away from God (not easy!), boarding a boat headed for Tarshish (possibly in Spain) – ie in the opposite direction from Nineveh! A huge storm arises and it seems the ship and all aboard will go down. Casting lots reveals the culprit to be Jonah, who admits he's running away from the God 'who made the sea and the land' and tells the terrified crew to throw him overboard. Eventually, and reluctantly, they do. However, God hasn't finished with him! A great fish swallows him and 'from inside the fish' Jonah prays today's prayer.

Surprisingly, it's a prayer of thanksgiving! Between being hurled overboard and in danger of drowning (I love the detail of the seaweed wrapped around his head!) and being swallowed alive, Jonah has cried out to God (2:7). He acknowledges that he has been heard (2:2) and trusts God for a happy outcome (2:4), promising to fulfil a vow – perhaps including a determination not to run away from God and His commissions in future!

Many of Jonah's problems were of his own making, as he tried to dodge God's commands, endangering the lives of the ship's crew in the process. But God reached out and rescued him, prompting this prayer of thanksgiving. God's grace covers us even when we disobey and 'mess up'. Are we thankful, as Jonah was?

An 'even if ...' prayer

The first two chapters of Habakkuk consist of a dialogue in which Habakkuk challenges God about why evil appears to prevail. God's answer satisfies him, and the final chapter – our reading today – is Habakkuk's prayerful response. There is just one 'petition' or request, right at the beginning, in verse 2. Habakkuk recalls God's mighty acts and asks God to act in a similar way in his own time. Then, as if remembering that God's past deeds often included judgment, he pleads for God's 'wrath' to be tempered with mercy. God's fearful righteousness goes hand in hand with His compassionate love.

The central part of the prayer (vv.3–15) is a poetic meditation on God's mighty acts – His 'awe-fulness' that is so overwhelming it affects the prophet physically (v.16).

God has warned Habakkuk that Judah will be invaded by Babylon, and the final verses of the prayer are Habakkuk's response to that prospect. He is living in an agricultural society, where flocks and crops are essential for survival. Habakkuk faces squarely the possibility of these things failing as a result of enemy action – the loss of harvests, a dearth of sheep and cattle. His prayerful response is a triumph of faith in a mighty and all-loving God. Even if these calamities come about '... yet,' says Habakkuk, 'I will rejoice in the Lord, I will be joyful in God my Saviour. The Sovereign Lord is my strength ...' (vv.18–19).

Like Habakkuk, we live in sad and uncertain times with terrorism or financial difficulty an ever-present threat. And yet ... as Christians we can pray with Habakkuk for God to act 'in our time' and say, with him, 'Even if the worst happens, I will rejoice in the Lord; I will be joyful in God my Saviour'.

Habakkuk 3:1–19

'... yet I will rejoice in the LORD, I will be joyful in God my Saviour.' (v.18)

For prayer and reflection

'LORD, I have heard of your fame; I stand in awe of your deeds, O LORD. Renew them in our day, in our time make them known; in wrath remember mercy.' (Hab. 3:2)

Reflections
from
Philippians

Heather Coupland

Heather loves working alongside her husband Simon, who is
a vicar in Surrey. She heads up the women's ministry at their
church as well as co-leading three thriving mums and toddlers
groups and leading services. Whilst working at Lee Abbey she
attended a journalling workshop where she discovered a love
of writing. She now writes devotional articles and Bible reading
notes. She enjoys cooking in her spare time as well as walking in
Richmond Park with her daughter Pippa.

WEEKEND

Reflections from Philippians

For reflection: Jeremiah 29:11–13
"'For I know the plans I have for you," declares the Lord,
"… plans to give you hope and a future.'" (v.11)

I wonder what gets you out of bed in the morning? What drives you to do what you do and be who you are? The singer Madonna is quoted as saying 'I won't be happy until I'm as famous as God'! How sad to be driven by something so self-centred! As we read Paul's letter to the Philippians we see that he is motivated firstly by his love for God and then by his love for the people to whom he is writing. If you have time this weekend, why not try reading Paul's letter right through – it's inspiring! He wants to fulfil his potential and to make a difference in the lives of those around him, not so they will point to him and praise him, but so their eyes will be opened and they will see God and praise Him!

I get out of bed each morning because I know God has a plan for my life and because I long for those around me to know that He has one for them too. Why do you get out of bed?

Optional reading

2 Corinthians 5:14–15; Ephesians 5:15–16
Heidi and Rolland Baker, *The Hungry Always Get Fed* (Bognor Regis: New Wine Press, 2007)

Servants **and saints**

I love Philippians because it's one of the most positive and encouraging of all Paul's letters. You can tell that this church, founded during Paul's second missionary journey in about AD 50, is one for which he has great affection. This letter is not written primarily to address a negative situation, as some of Paul's letters are, but to thank the church for their support and care. Inevitably, Paul can't resist taking the opportunity to give advice and guidance, but the underlying tone throughout the letter is one of joy due to their partnership with him and of gratitude to them for their practical help. Paul is writing the letter from prison where, in his day, no meals would have been provided – so we can see why he is so grateful when Epaphroditus comes with money from Philippi.

I love the way Paul starts by referring to the fact that that he and Timothy are servants who are writing to the saints! At first glance you might think that Paul has got it the wrong way round, but not at all! He wants to encourage all the believers in Philippi to take up their spiritual identity as saints in Christ and to understand that the message he, the servant of Christ, brings is for every one of them.

Do you most naturally think of yourself as a saint or a servant? Can you accept the fact that when Paul is writing to the 'saints in Christ Jesus' he could be addressing you? It's easy to feel that the Christian life is solely about being a servant – and nothing else. However, the paradox is that when we give our lives to Jesus in love and service, He raises us up to sit with Him in heavenly places (Eph. 2:6) from where we will ultimately rule and reign with Him (Rev. 5:10).

Philippians 1:1–2

'Paul and Timothy, servants of Christ Jesus, To all the saints in Christ Jesus at Philippi …' (v.1)

For prayer and reflection

Lord, it is strange to think of myself as a saint, but thank You that that is what I am – not because I've earned it, but because of what You have done for me. Amen.

199

God **doesn't give up**

Philippians
1:3–8

'... being confident of this, that he who began a good work in you will carry it on to completion ...' (v.6)

Are you good at completing things? Or do you give up easily? It's so good that God doesn't! I find this verse incredibly reassuring. However small my faith or however many times I have to confess the same weaknesses to my heavenly Father, He will never give up on me. If my heart's desire is to co-operate with Him and to be transformed from 'one degree of glory to another' (2 Cor. 3:18, RSV) then He will always be there for me with the resources I need.

Paul doesn't tell the Philippians that he has confidence in *them* to work out everything *by themselves*. He has learnt to put 'no confidence in the flesh' (Phil. 3:3): his confidence is in God because it is God who is at work in him.

I know I can be too ready to give up and throw in the towel when the going gets tough, but that is often because I am doing everything in my own strength. We need to learn to tap into the resources of joy and peace and wisdom that God longs to give us. In verse 6 we are told that God wants to transform our lives by the power of His Spirit working in us. When Paul uses the term 'good work', he's talking about the 'good work' of salvation God has begun in their hearts: they all now have a responsibility to live this out with the help of the Holy Spirit. Paul is praying that all the believers in Philippi will understand this truth.

Whether preaching out of wrong motives (like those people mentioned later in this first chapter) or quarrelling like Euodia and Syntyche (mentioned at the beginning of chapter 4), Paul wants the believers in Philippi to know that, imperfect as they are, God still has a purpose for their lives and will not give up on the work He has started in their hearts.

For prayer and reflection

Thank You so much, Lord, that You never give up on me. Please teach me to rely on You and not to go my own way, wasting time doing things in my own strength. Amen.

Love that grows

This is a wonderfully heartfelt prayer, similar to Paul's prayer for the Thessalonians, in which he prays that the love of the believers might 'increase and overflow' (1 Thess. 3:12). He knows how important it is that Christians everywhere show a deep and intentional love towards one another and towards God. The sort of love he is talking about reveals God's character to others and is a powerful witness to those who don't believe.

It is a love that wants the best for the one who is loved and expresses itself in actions rather than remaining just a warm emotion in the heart. It's important that this love has the right motives and doesn't cause offence; in other words, it is 'pure' and 'blameless' (v.10). Paul is not accusing the Philippians of being lacking in love: rather, he is encouraging them to continue in what they have already been doing.

We, too, need encouragement to continue in this focused and deliberate love. We need to be reminded to let God's endless supply of unconditional love shine out through us and not to rely on our own limited resources. Without love permeating our service for God and for those around us, our achievements are worth nothing (1 Cor. 13:1–3). How can we cultivate this kind of love in our lives? By growing in our knowledge and understanding of God and by staying close to Him.

When I first became a Christian I always wanted to experience God's love for me before I felt I could pass it on to others. I have learnt that spending time studying God's Word causes that same love to grow within me and brings a new desire to reach out to others with the love God has shown to me.

Philippians 1:9–11

'… this is my prayer: that your love may abound more and more in knowledge and depth of insight …' (v.9)

For prayer and reflection

Think of someone you find it hard to love. Remember that they are incredibly precious to Jesus, and ask Him to pour out His blessing on them today.

Encouraged by chains?

**Philippians
1:12–18**

'Because of my
chains … the
brothers … have
been encouraged
to speak …
courageously …'
(v.14)

I wonder if you know the feeling of disappointment that comes when your plans haven't gone quite as you wanted them to. A new job that didn't work out; a holiday which had to be cancelled; an illness that stops life in its tracks. It's hard, when plans are thwarted, to remember that God is still in control and can nevertheless work in our difficult situation.

Here is Paul, the travelling evangelist, stuck in prison and therefore seemingly unable to carry on with what God has called him to do. Yet Paul sees no reason to be downhearted, because he has learnt to use every opportunity God gives him. He continues to talk about his Saviour, Jesus, and to preach the gospel anyway – even if in rather unusual circumstances! He has nothing to lose. He isn't interested in protecting himself. He is so single-minded that the only thing he wants to do is to tell others about the One who has transformed his life.

In this letter to the Philippians Paul wants to send reassurance to the church that, although from the outside things might look bad, from where he is sitting things are actually looking very good. The gospel is being preached and, because people are hearing about what is happening, others are also being encouraged to speak out more boldly for Jesus. How come? Well, word is getting out that Paul is not despondent about his imprisonment but is making the most of this opportunity to continue to serve God – and people can see that God is with him. His confidence is reminiscent of that of Joseph in Egypt, when he says to his brothers, 'You intended to harm me, but God intended it for good ...' (Gen. 50:20).

**For prayer and
reflection**

**Whatever is going
on in your life
right now, take
a moment to
acknowledge that
God is beside you
and wants to use
you – however
impossible that
might seem.**

No fear!

As a child, I was always frightened of dogs. My parents didn't really help me when they told me that dogs can tell when you are frightened! I learnt to stand my ground, though, and not to be intimidated, while inwardly chanting 'I am not afraid' in an attempt to calm my pounding heart. If I had run away, the dog would surely have chased me and my fear would have become a self-fulfilling prophecy. However I taught myself to send out signals that convinced the dog of my tremendous courage.

Fear can often lead to us feeling intimidated, which makes us feel and act as though we are powerless. Paul does not want this to be the case for the Philippians. He wants them to grasp that Jesus is Lord of the world at this very moment. He isn't waiting to be King but is ruling and reigning already in the heavenly places (Eph. 1:20–21); that means they have nothing to fear. The worst anyone can do is to kill them – which will simply send them to be with their Saviour and Friend, Jesus, a little sooner than anticipated.

You can often find stories on the internet which imply that there are many conspiracies in society trying to undermine Christianity. Some of these may be true and some most definitely are not. What they all do, however, is feed the belief in many Christians that the world is a hostile place and that everyone is plotting against them. Of course it is true, as Jesus says, that 'In this world you will have trouble' (John 16:33), but He also goes on to say, 'But take heart! I have overcome the world'. If you know of areas of your life that are influenced by fear, come to God now and decide to put your trust in Him, your Saviour, your King and your Friend.

Philippians 1:19–30

'… without being frightened in any way by those who oppose you.' (v.28)

For prayer and reflection

I'm sorry, Lord, for those times when I let fear influence me and I lose sight of You. I give You my fear today and choose to trust You. Amen.

203

WEEKEND

Sustained by God

For reflection: Psalm 119:113–120
'Sustain me according to your promise, and I shall live ...' (v.116)

L ast year I was away from home in a stressful situation and I experienced the Lord sustaining me in a way I'd never known before. What I really wanted was deliverance from the problem, but I learnt far more by trusting God than by being delivered from my difficulties!

The hardest thing was that I wasn't sleeping, and yet was very busy during the day. I became fearful that I would feel physically too weak to do what I needed to do. To my amazement, my energy levels remained high and I didn't need any extra sleep during the day. God was upholding me physically in an amazing way! As a result I found that I could keep going for far longer than I had expected.

Are you feeling worn out or at the end of your tether in a particular situation? Lean on God. Let Him sustain and support you, so that you can receive His supernatural resources.

Optional further reading
Psalm 55:22; Isaiah 46:4; Hebrews 1:3; Isaiah 40:28–31

How to **be happy**

While suffering from a bout of postnatal depression some years ago, I read an incredibly helpful book called Happiness is a Choice, by two American Christian doctors, Frank Minirth and Paul Meier. I am still benefiting from their advice even today. One particularly useful piece of advice was as follows: one way to decrease anxiety and help overcome [much] depression is to choose to think of other people more and to spend a little less time in unhelpful introspection. In a list of basic guidelines for a happy and meaningful life they write: 'Do something nice for one special person each week.' The doctors then explain how helping someone else can make us realise how useful we can be and can distract us from becoming overwhelmed by self-pity.

I know that Paul isn't writing a self-help book on depression, yet I'm struck by what he says to the Philippians about looking out for the interests of others. He also writes about this principle to the Corinthians: 'Nobody should seek his own good, but the good of others' (1 Cor. 10:24) and tells the believers in Rome: 'Each of us should please his neighbour for his good ... For even Christ did not please himself ...' (Rom. 15:2–3). Paul knows that a community of believers united in purpose and committed to loving one another will be a powerful witness to the non-believers around them. This is what Paul longs for. In prison and deprived of so much, nonetheless he states that what would bring him most joy is not a warm bed or a decent meal but that the believers were united in love and service to one another and to God.

Putting others' interests before our own is both a biblical command and a recipe for our own emotional and spiritual wellbeing. Let's get on with it then!

Philippians 2:1–4

'Each of you should look not only to your own interests, but also to the interests of others.' (v.4)

For prayer and reflection

Lord, when I am having a low day and feel nobody cares about me, please help me to step out and do something for someone else. Amen.

True **divinity**

**Philippians
2:5–11**

'Who, being in very nature God, did not consider equality with God something to be grasped …' (v.6)

For prayer and reflection

Thank You, Lord, that You gave up so much for me. My mind can't really take it in, but my heart responds today in worship and thanksgiving. Amen.

Try to imagine for a moment that you are Jesus before He came to earth! Equal with God, you have all His power at your disposal. Wouldn't you want to make the most of it? Wouldn't you be tempted to take advantage of your status to get your own way?

In Genesis 1 we read that Adam was lured by the thought of being like God and seized what he thought was the perfect opportunity to become just that. Christ, on the other hand, refused to exploit His position and did the opposite. As Adam tried to be like God, so God in Christ became a man.

This concept was profoundly shocking to the Philippians. The gods they once worshipped were portrayed as beings who seized power to use it to their own advantage. Earthly rulers, too, craved power, doing everything possible to amass ever more – wanting to be seen as great heroes, world conquerors. Caesar and Alexander even proclaimed themselves to have divine status because of their accomplishments.

Jesus didn't try to convince people of His divinity by taking advantage of His status. Instead He showed what true divinity was. He emptied Himself of selfish ambition and self-importance. In both life and death, He demonstrated the power, not of amassed wealth and armies, but of self-giving love. When Jesus came to earth as a man and died a death reserved for the lowest of the low He didn't stop being divine. His divinity wasn't diminished by the type of death He died. Instead He was showing us how revolutionary God's ways are and that they are not like the ways of man at all. After all, '"… my thoughts are not your thoughts, neither are your ways my ways," declares the Lord' (Isa. 55:8).

We can **work it out**

I t must be very encouraging for Paul to be writing to a congregation who are at least getting some things right! In verse 12 he says that the Philippians have always obeyed the teachings of Christ and now he tells them to continue to work out their salvation, implying that it is something they have already begun to do. He wants to encourage and exhort them to continue to live lives marked out by obedience, so that although living in a 'crooked and depraved generation' they can 'shine like stars in the universe' (v.15).

For me, the great encouragement in these verses is that I haven't got to work all this out on my own, but God is working with me and in me. Hurray! Working out my salvation with God's help is very different from working out my salvation independently. Salvation is His gift to us and not something we can earn by being nice. I like the picture of salvation – not as a destination to be reached by working incredibly hard, but as a precious possession to be unpacked and explored, enjoyed and understood. This unpacking entails working out what God has called me to do with my life, what gifts He has given me and where He wants me to use them. Working out my salvation means fulfilling my potential as the person God created me to be.

We have been given an awesome task which is not to be undertaken lightly but 'with fear and trembling', because we take God's work in our lives very seriously. It's an amazing thing to work in partnership with God to see His purposes fulfilled. We must remember, though, that God working with us doesn't mean that He does it for us but that He empowers us with His resources. In this way, just as the Beatles sang, we can work it out.

Philippians 2:12–13

'... continue to work out your salvation with fear and trembling, for it is God who works in you ...' (vv.12–13)

For prayer and reflection

Thank You, Lord, that You don't leave me on my own, but want to work with me and in me to make me the person You created me to be. Amen.

Holding on **and holding out**

**Philippians
2:14–18**

'… as you hold out
the word of life …'
(v.16)

**For prayer and
reflection**

**Think of those
with whom you
might come into
contact today.
Is there any way
in which you can
'hold out the word
of life' to them by
your words or by
your actions?**

ommentators are divided over the emphasis of this verse. Some feel that Paul is underlining the point that the Philippians need to hold on to the precious teaching he has given them about Jesus, while others feel he is writing with evangelism in mind, as the believers reach out to 'a crooked and depraved generation' (2:15). To me, the two concepts are not contradictory, but fit very well together. After all, if we truly grasp the good news of Jesus' love and hold it in our hearts, we will surely want to share it with the spiritually needy people around us.

It is true, to an extent, that when we are rooted in Christ's teaching and living it out, our lives will naturally bear witness to God's transforming power, the Word of life within us. Yet we also have a responsibility to be intentional about holding out the message to those around us. Our lives and our lips, surrendered to God, should be offering the gift of salvation to all we meet. Paul's isn't the only 'crooked and depraved generation': he is echoing Deuteronomy 32:5, where the phrase refers to the people of Moses' generation – and wouldn't we say the same applies today?

In the midst of a society that is full of fear, violence and corruption, we Christians have something priceless to offer those who are hungry for a different way to live. We mustn't keep this precious and amazing gift to ourselves but are required to hold it out to those around us. We are to be both containers *and* messengers of the gift God wants to give to a hurting world.

Look **out!**

What does it actually mean for you and me today to look out for the interests of Jesus Christ? From these verses we can see that it doesn't just mean singing worship songs or attending the church prayer meeting.

Looking out for the interests of Jesus Christ means both telling non-believers the good news of the gospel and encouraging people who already know Him to grow in intimacy with Him. It also includes reaching out to people with the love and care Jesus has shown to us by getting involved with the poor and needy in our own communities and speaking out for justice in our society – in this way putting other people's wellbeing before our own. Paul uses Timothy as an example of someone who has shown a genuine concern for the welfare of others in his care for the Philippians (v.20). Every time we care for someone in a way that shows them God's love we are looking out for the interests of Jesus Christ. Every time we put someone else's needs before our own we are acting in a Christlike way.

I wonder whether you have ever known the support of someone who has taken a genuine interest in your welfare? It can be a very powerful thing. While my husband was at theological college his fiancée broke off their engagement three days before the wedding, which was pretty devastating. One of his friends offered to come and pray with him once a week at 6am on his way to work and followed through on that commitment for many weeks. The friend put aside his own interests in order to help someone who was hurting. It was a powerful example of caring and concern at a very difficult time and was a real blessing to my husband.

Philippians 2:19–30

'For everyone looks out for his own interests, not those of Jesus Christ.' (v.21)

For prayer and reflection

I'm sorry, Lord, that so often I am too concerned with whether people are caring for me rather than eager to care for others.

WEEKEND

Where's your zeal?

For reflection: Acts 18:24–28
'… and he spoke with great fervour and taught about Jesus accurately …' (v.25)

The dictionary defines zeal as 'strong feeling, passionate ardour, intense enthusiasm'. In Romans 12:11 Paul writes, 'Never be lacking in zeal, but keep your spiritual fervour, serving the Lord'. So how do we get zeal? I know that one way to stir it up in me is to read about what God is doing in and through great men and women of God, often in other parts of the world. Reading biographies helps to inspire me, when I see what ordinary people can achieve with God's help.

Having passionate ardour may sound like something from a Jane Austen novel but it's what we need if we are going to make a difference to the people around us. It doesn't mean we become so heavenly minded that we're of no earthly good, but that we are fully alive with the energy God gives. Isn't that what you want?

Let's pray this weekend that we will understand what it means for us to be zealous for the Lord.

Optional further reading

Read Acts 2:1–3:26 to catch a glimpse of how zealous the early believers were for the Lord.
Simon Guillebaud, *For What It's Worth* (Oxford: Monarch, 2006)
Elisabeth Elliot, *A Chance to Die* (The Life and Legacy of Amy Carmichael) (Old Tappan: Revell, 1987)

Here we go **again!**

'It is no trouble for me to write the same things to you again, and it is a safeguard for you.' (v.1)

I once heard of a three-point guide to preaching that went like this: 'Tell them what you are going to say; say it; and then tell them what you have said.' We seem to need things to be repeated so that we can fully understand them and take the lessons on board. It's often only when 'the penny has finally dropped' that we can start to respond and change our lives accordingly. Even when something is for our own benefit, we may still need to hear the piece of advice more than once before we choose to act on it.

I see this happening in simple everyday situations – as with my daughter and her fight against adolescent acne. Telling her only once that washing her face is a good idea and will help reduce the embarrassing spots won't make a lot of difference. The advice needs to be repeated frequently, in different ways and at different times, in order for it to have any lasting impact (and without it sounding like nagging – which is quite an art!).

Paul understood this principle: he knew that the Philippians would need to hear some points repeated before they would really understand and respond to his teaching. He didn't get frustrated by having to repeat himself. Paul knew that the effort was worth it, as the result would be that these young Christians would be stronger and less likely to be led astray by false teachers.

My husband, a vicar, sometimes worries that he is repeating something he has already preached in a previous sermon. I don't think Paul would have had any such qualms! The fact is that God sometimes wants us to hear something we've heard before in our Christian lives because He wants to challenge us as to whether we are living out the truth of what we already know.

For prayer and reflection

Please show me, Lord, if there is something You have been trying to teach me that I am being slow to learn.

The right **qualifications?**

**Philippians
3:4–9**

'But whatever was
to my profit I now
consider loss for
the sake of Christ.'
(v.7)

I t's very hard for us today in the twenty-first century to understand how amazingly radical Paul's comments are in this passage. He is speaking to people who are incredibly proud of their ancestry in a society where being seen to keep all the rules means everything. Paul has been a paragon of rule-keeping and, if there were an exam giving people a place in the religious elite, he would surely get top marks! Coming from a family who can trace their Hebrew ancestry back to the ancient tribe of Benjamin, he was circumcised on the eighth day. Trained as an expert in Jewish law, Paul can hold himself up as an example of one who followed it to the letter. But a dramatic encounter with Jesus on the road to Damascus (Acts 9) has turned his life, and the rules by which he lived, upside down.

Paul now recognises that being born into the right family and following the laws of the Torah aren't actually what put you 'in Christ'. All these things he considers as rubbish, *skubala*, (a Greek word which actually means either food waste or human excrement!). This was radical teaching for the Philippians and is still hard for many to accept today. To Paul, circumcision without faith in Christ is purely a mutilation of the flesh. He despises the teachers who are insisting that Gentile believers undergo this ritual before they can be acceptable to God.

**For prayer and
reflection**

**Help me, Lord, not
to put my faith in
rituals or religion
but to know
the joy of being
acceptable to You
just as I am.**

Paul has learnt that the only righteousness that counts is the gift of a right relationship with God. And that comes through faith in Christ and not through being a good person. Following the rules laid down by the local church will never put us 'in Christ'. Putting our faith in Him and letting Him give us His righteousness are the only things that will do that.

Knowing Christ

Philippians 3:10–11

'I want to know Christ …' (v.10)

In my early twenties I went to work at Lee Abbey, a beautiful Christian conference centre on the North Devon coast. Part of the appeal of working there was that I hoped to do some serious study and gain a deeper understanding of my faith. I imagined that a lot of this learning would take place in the library, where I planned to read commentaries and other books that would help me understand this Man, Jesus, whom I had come to love. When I came to leave, after three happy years, the Lord reminded me of those early intentions, and I remember saying to someone, 'I came here to learn about Jesus through the books I read, but instead I have met Jesus in the people I've got to know.' I don't mean to imply that reading and study aren't important: of course they are. But my experience highlighted the difference between knowing *about* Christ and actually *knowing* Him and meeting Him in my everyday life.

The Greek word, *gnonai*, used here in verse 10, means more than intellectual knowledge, it includes personal knowledge too. Paul's focus in life, and his longing, is to know Christ personally and to enjoy an intimate and transforming relationship with Him. He wants to experience the power of Christ's resurrection – not just as an event in history but as a dynamic power which makes a difference in his life day by day (Rom. 8:11; Eph. 1:19–20). Knowing Christ isn't just about victory and power, though. It also involves sharing in the fellowship of His sufferings. As a follower of Jesus, suffering is inevitable (John 15:18–21; James 1:2–4). It isn't to be seen as a penalty or punishment but as a privilege, because we are sharing a tiny part of what Jesus chose to go through for us.

For prayer and reflection

Read verse 10 again and turn it into your own personal prayer that you will know Christ in a deeper way.

Don't look back!

Philippians 3:12–16

'But one thing I do: Forgetting what is behind and straining towards what is ahead, I press on …' (vv.13–14)

Looking back is a tricky thing. Sometimes it can be helpful, particularly if we are remembering what God has done for us and thanking Him for His faithfulness. Isaiah 46:9 exhorts us to: 'Remember the former things, those of long ago'; and Psalm 105 is dedicated to remembering the tremendous faithfulness of God. Sometimes, though, looking back can be negative and unhelpful. Elsewhere, in Isaiah, we are advised: 'Forget the former things; do not dwell on the past. See, I am doing a new thing!' (Isa. 43:18–19).

So what are we supposed to do? Remember or forget? I suppose it all depends on how looking back makes us feel, and whether it moves us towards greater intimacy with God or distances us from Him. Paul is eager that nothing should get in the way of the believers' wholehearted commitment to living their lives for God. He knows that if they are constantly riddled with guilt or disappointment about past failures, their progress will be slow and without much joy. Even looking back at great achievements might make them complacent about their need of God so that they take their eyes off Jesus.

For prayer and reflection

Help me, Lord, to look back with gratitude and to look to the future with excitement for all that You have in store. Amen.

We, too, need to get the balance right and live life in the light of the future, with our minds set on things above (Col. 3:1–4), rather than in the shadow of the negative things in our past. It's true that looking back with our hearts full of gratitude can spur us on, but looking back in regret or dissatisfaction will only hinder us. This is why Jesus said that no one who puts his hand to the plough but then looks back is fit for service in the kingdom of God (Luke 9:62). Paul himself knew the value of leaving behind the past and pressing on towards his future goal. In which direction are you facing?

Where is **your mind fixed?**

As I read Paul's words in these verses, I can hear his pain and heartache as he sees new believers being lured away from the truth by 'enemies of the cross'. These are people who have taken their eyes off Jesus and are letting their bodily appetites control the way they live.

In our society, we too can be tempted away from fixing our eyes on Jesus and sidetracked by our desire for 'earthly things'. Some people get out of the habit of going to church because they can't do without their weekly lie-in. I myself know the pull of sending emails or socialising on the internet while my Bible lies unopened by my bed. It's so easy to have our eyes fixed on the world and to allow God to get squeezed out from being the most important focus of our lives. I know that there have been evenings when I have slumped in front of 'rubbish' on the television – and have ended the day feeling cross with myself, when an hour spent with God would have meant going to bed in a completely different frame of mind.

So often we go through the week glancing at Jesus from time to time, as we pray or attend church, and at other times He slips out of our line of vision completely. We need to learn to live with our focus on the kingdom of God, which is what being a citizen of heaven is all about. Paul isn't just talking about where we go when we die. Philippi was a Roman colony and the task of a Roman citizen living there was to bring Roman culture, influence and rule to that place. This is our task too. We, as the body of Christ, a colony of heaven on earth, have the responsibility of bringing the life and the rule of the kingdom of heaven to the local communities and churches in which God has placed us.

Philippians 3:17–4:1

'Their mind is on earthly things. But our citizenship is in heaven.' (3:19–20)

For prayer and reflection

Help me, Lord, to keep my mind fixed on You at all times and not to be distracted by worldly things which divert me from Your will. Amen.

WEEKEND

What influences you?

For reflection: Deuteronomy 30:11–20
'… I have set before you life and death, blessings and curses. Now choose life …' (v.19)

know that I can be very easily influenced by the people around me. Even at the age of 49 I can still sometimes feel the tremendous power of peer pressure in certain situations. As a new Christian at college I was torn between two lifestyles. Sometimes I got drunk with friends from my course and at other times I went to prayer meetings with friends from the Christian Union. It wasn't a very satisfactory situation – often leaving me feeling guilty and confused as to whether I was really a Christian at all!

Many things can influence us, but we always have a choice over our words and actions. My desire is that as my heart is influenced more and more by God, so the pull of the 'sinful nature' (Gal. 5:16) will become less and less strong. I don't want to be drawn into things like gossip or lying; rather I want to stand up for what is right and be a witness for the God who has saved me.

Let's say with Joshua today, '… as for me and my household, we will serve the Lord' (Josh. 24:15).

Optional further reading
1 Kings 18:20–21; Matthew 5:13–16; Galatians 5:16–26

We need one another

Here is a situation which is clearly of great concern to Paul. Biblical scholars speculate over the identities of these two women, Euodia and Syntyche, and then speculate again about what they might have done. It's a bit frustrating not knowing exactly what was going on, but I think we can still take away important lessons from these verses.

Firstly, we see that Paul cared about these ladies, even though they may not have been very caring towards one other. The very fact that their names are mentioned shows that they had real status as Paul's friends. If they had been his enemies he would have been much more likely to keep them anonymous, which would have been considered a slur on their characters. Secondly, Paul's overriding desire isn't that Euodia and Syntyche are criticised or even punished for what they have done, but rather that they are helped and supported. These two people, who have fallen out with each other, need trustworthy friends to help them make up – and then to 'stand firm in the Lord'.

When we see people within the church family who have fallen out it's easy to ignore the situation, feeling that it is none of our business. Or else we can become critical or judgmental towards the people involved, and even make things worse by joining in and taking sides. From today's verses, Paul's teaching to the Ephesian church (Eph. 4:3) and Jesus' words to His disciples (Matt. 5:9), we can see that we are all called to be peacemakers and reconcilers within our congregations. We should offer help and support where it is needed, not criticism or judgment, so that broken relationships can be restored and healed – and the Body of Christ can function as it should.

Philippians 4:2–3

'… help these women who have contended at my side in the cause of the gospel …' (v.3)

For prayer and reflection

If you are feeling judgmental or critical towards anyone today, spend some time praying for them and asking God to be with them.

Liberated from worry

**Philippians
4:4–7**

'The Lord is near.
Do not be anxious
about anything …'
(vv.5–6)

I have to confess that I am a bit of a worrier and my anxiety levels are sometimes higher than I would like them to be. This passage has often made me feel guilty, as I've imagined God getting exasperated, and saying crossly, 'Stop being so anxious, Heather!'

I once shared a house with someone who told me off when I said that I was worrying about something. She informed me that it was a sin to worry, and told me how many times it says in the Bible, 'Do not fear'. I felt such a failure that I never dared admit any weaknesses to her again!

Recently, however, I read something that has started to transform my outlook on this passage – and my habit of worrying. In his commentary on Philippians, Marcus Bockmuehl says: 'Because the Lord is near, Christians are liberated from worry in any and all circumstances.' Wow! Can that really be true? As I read these words several times, in an effort to make them sink into my habit-hardened brain, I liked them more and more.

I love the picture of being liberated from something, rather than trying very hard to break free by myself and never quite succeeding! As is often the case where sin is concerned, it boils down to the choices I make in my heart over what Jesus has done for me. I can choose to trust Him, and replace my anxiety with faith in His goodness, or I can continue in bondage to my feelings and stay paralysed by worry about everything. Jesus has liberated me from the need to worry about anything! He has also placed me into His body so that I can share my burdens with my fellow Christians and benefit from their prayers, wisdom and guidance when I'm facing difficulties and am tempted to worry.

**For prayer and
reflection**

**Thank You, Lord,
that trusting You
liberates me from
my need to worry.
Help me to walk
in that freedom
today, by the
power of Your
Holy Spirit. Amen.**

Copy me!

I wonder if you would be happy to say to a new Christian, 'Whatever I do or say, just copy me and you will learn how to stay close to God'? I would find it a pretty big challenge, and would need to start asking for God's immediate help in some areas of my life! Paul is not ashamed to put himself forward as an example to the Christians in Philippi. His confidence is a huge challenge to me.

It's good for us to have role models, and I know that I have been encouraged and inspired by the lives of Christian women, both past and present. A couple of years ago, I read several books about the missionary Amy Carmichael for an article I was writing. Her life challenged me in ways that are still having an impact on areas of my life today. Christian friends can also be an example to us and can challenge us. For instance, we may be inspired to copy their generosity or their perseverance in prayer. Just as we look to others to see how they are living out their faith, so it is good to be reminded that people are watching you and me each day. Our friends, neighbours or work colleagues are looking to see whether how we live matches up to what we say we believe.

If we want to encourage and disciple new Christians then we need to be able to show them the way. We need to be able to say, 'Pray like me; give like me; love like me.' This doesn't mean that we have to be perfect (which is impossible anyway), but we can be an inspiration as we strive to be all that God would like us to be. God wants to use each one of us as an example to this world 'in which we shine like stars in the universe' – not because we are so fantastic but because *God's power* at work in us is truly life-transforming!

Philippians 4:8–9

'Whatever you have learned or received or heard from me, or seen in me – put it into practice.' (v.9)

For prayer and reflection

Take a few moments to think about what people could copy from your life which would deepen their relationship with God.

Contentment **whatever happens**

**Philippians
4:10–13**

'I have learned
the secret of being
content in any and
every situation …'
(v.12)

Having exhorted the Philippians to rejoice and not be anxious, Paul now shows them how these principles have been worked out in his own life. He has entrusted his life to God, and doesn't care whether that means being rich or poor. So often in our society we feel that the secret to contentment is having everything we want. An American millionaire was asked how much money a person needed to be happy. He answered: 'Just a little bit more than he has.' So, money can actually bring discontentment.

We may think that having too little prevents us from being happy, but having plenty can be just as difficult. I know people who are very well off, but can't enjoy their wealth because they feel guilty about the abundant life they have! Note that Paul isn't saying that it's bad to have plenty of food or possessions, but that these material things should not be the source of our contentment. He doesn't waste time feeling guilty when living in abundance but is grateful and enjoys it! It's also a privilege and blessing to be able to be generous to those poorer than ourselves when we have plenty. If we believe that God is our provider then we should praise Him when we have more than enough (Deut. 8:10–20) and when things are difficult (Hab. 3:17–19).

I recently heard a moving story of an elderly man living in a displacement camp in Burundi, who had seen his wife and children hacked to death and had lost absolutely everything. He was able to say with great humility: 'I never realised Jesus was all I needed until Jesus was all I had.'

May we learn what it is to be content with Jesus, so that material provision, whether plentiful or sparse, will not distract us from our relationship with Him.

**For prayer and
reflection**

**Are you content
with what God
has provided for
you materially?
Would you
like more?
Do you feel you
have too much?
Talk to Him about
how you are
feeling.**

A God **who meets needs**

As Paul comes to the end of this wonderful letter to his dear friends in Philippi, he wants them to know how grateful he is to them for their friendship and financial support. He wants to tell them that their generosity to him will reap a reward. As they give to him, so God will also be generous to them and meet their needs. Paul has learnt that giving is about investing. It's like planting a seed, watching it grow, and then seeing fruit appear.

Some years ago, I was staying with good friends on my birthday. I'd been given some money as a gift so that I could treat myself to something special. As I was going round the supermarket with my friends, I felt God nudge me to use my birthday money to pay for the shopping. I struggled and felt rather hard done by but, when I took out my purse and paid, I knew I'd done the right thing. On returning home the next day, I found an envelope, sent anonymously, waiting for me. It contained exactly the amount I'd been given – and which I'd then given away. God had fully met my needs, as I had been obedient to Him. We cannot outgive God!

Paul knows that he is in no position to put his hand in his pocket and meet the financial needs of the Philippian church. He is confident though, that as they rely on God and are generous with what they have been given, God will give back to them. And God's provision isn't just financial; it is also the joy and peace of God being poured into our hearts. We need to learn that just as the peace of God is beyond our understanding (4:7), so the riches of God are never-ending because He has the resources to supply every need we could ever have.

Philippians 4:14–19

'And my God will meet all your needs according to his glorious riches in Christ Jesus.' (v.19)

For prayer and reflection

Help me to be generous, Lord, with what You have given me; help me not to be unwilling to be a blessing to others.

WEEKEND

Enjoy **your** gifts!

For reflection: 1 Corinthians 12:1–30
'Now you are the body of Christ, and each one of you is
a part of it.' (v.27)

I wonder if you ever wish you were someone else or had
someone else's gifts? It's an easy trap to fall into but
one we must resist if we want to live our lives to the
full. Envying others will hold us back from living the life
God wants us to live.

Some people fear that if they surrender their lives to
God completely He will ask them to do something they
would hate. In actual fact, it is God who has put within each
of us a desire for, or enjoyment of, certain activities – and
serving Him can be a joy as we use the gifts He has given us.

I find evangelism hard and prefer talking to people who
are already Christians and encouraging them in their faith.
However I know people who find talking to Christians boring
and thrive on sharing their faith with non-believers. While
we do need to develop skills which don't come naturally,
we are all different and the Body of Christ will only work
effectively when I am being me and you are being you!

Optional further reading
Ephesians 4:7–16; Romans 12:1–8

The final word: **grace**

Paul's letter to the Philippians begins and ends with grace. In chapter 1 he wishes them, 'Grace and peace ... from God our Father and the Lord Jesus Christ', and now, as he concludes his letter, he wants them to continue to experience the grace of God which transforms lives. Grace sounds such a 'nice' word, and its meaning is often lost as we think of 'saying grace' before a meal or ending a prayer meeting by 'saying the grace'. It can so easily become just another word in our dictionary of Christian jargon – and its real meaning obscured.

I love the word 'grace'. It is one of my favourites, so I'm pleased that Paul thinks it is worth repeating. It's a 'big' word which can have a life-changing impact, but it can also cause offence. I remember hearing a speaker some years ago say that if you haven't been offended by God's grace then you haven't properly understood it – and I know what he means. Grace isn't fair; it isn't logical; it can't be understood by our puny, finite minds. This is because it comes from the very heart of God. Part of me wants to believe that if I work hard at being a nice person, I will be good enough to earn God's love by my good behaviour: but I can't do that and will never be able to. God's grace is experienced in the all-encompassing, supremely generous love of God being poured over you and me: not as a reward for our good behaviour but simply because God our Father loves us.

As we finish looking at Paul's letter to the Philippians and seek to put his teaching into practice in our lives, let us be encouraged that, even when we struggle to obey, the Lord says: 'My grace is sufficient for you, for my power is made perfect in weakness' (2 Cor. 12:9).

Philippians 4:20–23

'The grace of the Lord Jesus Christ be with your spirit.' (v.23)

For prayer and reflection

Take a few minutes to thank God for His grace and to bask in His love for you today.

2 Chronicles – lessons for life

Priscilla Reid

Priscilla Reid is on the leadership team of both the Lifelink team, (a group of churches in Ireland committed to planting and resourcing churches) and Christian Fellowship Church, Belfast along with her husband Paul. Priscilla is a frequent conference speaker around the world. Her current involvements include developing today's leaders for tomorrow's church, united prayer for Ireland and working to see women released into their full calling in God.

2 Chronicles – **lessons for life**

2 Chronicles
1:7–13

'Ask for whatever
you want me to
give you'. (v.7)

For prayer and reflection

**Father, thank
You for Your
generosity
towards me.
As You ask me
this question
today give me
wisdom to know
what to ask.
Amen.**

Some of my fondest memories are when my children were tucked up beside me as we read fairy stories together. A recurring theme in many of them is the offer of having a wish fulfilled. How often have you speculated with friends: 'If you could wish for anything, what would it be?' When God says to Solomon, at the beginning of his reign, 'Ask for whatever you want me to give you', it has that fairy tale ring to it.

It is not that God seeks to reinforce the twenty-first century view of Him as the manager of that great McDonald's in the sky, coming up with instant answers to all our problems. In asking us the question God is revealing two things: the nature of the amazing God we serve and the intent of our own heart. He wants us to understand His desire to bless us and that: 'Every good and perfect gift is from above ...' (James 1:17). Our heavenly Father is interested in our heart's desire.

Solomon asked for wisdom and God commended him. The Lord recognised that Solomon could have asked for anything, but his request revealed a heart that wanted to honour God and to do the job he had been given to the very best of his ability. In order to do that Solomon recognised that his own wisdom would fall far short – and he needed God's help.

Our desires are often very mixed. God wants to refine them, and that happens as we delight ourselves in the Lord. Then His promise is that 'he will give you the desires of your heart' (Psa. 37:4). Our God is not a harsh taskmaster. His loving question may come to you today because He wants to meet your needs. Don't be afraid to give Him an answer.

Giving **our best**

R ecently my husband and I visited Lincoln Cathedral. When you enter, the sheer size of the building makes you feel small; the beauty of the architecture and the stained glass takes your breath away. The original vision behind building cathedrals was to lift people's eyes to God and to stir their hearts to worship Him.

Solomon has the same vision when he embarks on building the Temple: he wants to erect a magnificent structure to reflect the greatness of God. However, he understands that while wanting to honour God in the eyes of men, God cannot be contained within a building – no matter how great. 'But who is able to build a temple for him, since the heavens, even the highest heavens, cannot contain him?' (v.6). Nonetheless the preparations are immense: they include employing thousands of people to do the work and strengthening his alliances with other kings in order that their resources will also be available. He orders the best materials, appoints people of great skill, craftsmanship and artistry. There is a spirit of excellence in everything that is being done.

In the twenty-first century Church we need to display the same spirit in all we do for God. The 'anything will do' attitude, when it comes to church, is just not good enough. Of course we want to avoid being slick or so image conscious that people feel excluded because they are not clever, talented or good-looking enough. Many of us have limited resources, but it is amazing what you can do when you want to produce something that will honour God. The world doesn't expect much from us – let's surprise them. We want to reflect the fact that as God's people we are in relationship with a great God who deserves our very best.

2 Chronicles 2:1–18

'The temple I am going to build will be great, because our God is greater than all other gods.' (v.5)

For prayer and reflection

Lord, in everything I do help me to give You my very best. Let it be part of my worship to You, to reflect Your glory to others. Amen.

The beauty of birdsong

2 Chronicles 3:1–17

'He adorned the temple with precious stones.' (v.6)

Lord Jesus, thank You for the beauty of birdsong, the inspiration in a painting and the hope in a rainbow. Stir up the creativity You have placed in me as Your child – may I reflect Your beauty to those around me.

In her book *Wild Swans* chronicling the story of three generations of women in China, Jung Chang describes a time during the Cultural Revolution when Mao ordered the destruction of all birds in the cities. Anything of beauty was discouraged – even the sound of birdsong. The effect was devastating on people's spirits; depression and hopelessness were the order of the day. As they sought to proclaim that God was dead so beauty had to die as well.

The God we worship is a God of beauty. You only have to stand on a mountain top or sit by the edge of a wave-crashing ocean to understand the importance of beauty to God and also to us, the ones He created in His image. Beauty feeds something deep inside us.

Solomon had an understanding of this as he built and furnished the Temple. It must have been magnificent, with its gold walls studded with precious stones, ornate carvings, delicate embroideries and unique furnishings. Some might have objected to the excess: surely something more functional would serve? However, I believe Solomon not only wanted to reflect to the worshippers a sense of the glory of God, but he also wanted to feed their spirits with the beauty of their surroundings. It is time to recapture this truth. For too long the world has believed that the God we worship is grey. I believe God by His Spirit is at work among us to stir up the creative gifts within us. We need to value and encourage creativity, inspired by the Holy Spirit. The Church should be the place where the best artists, poets, musicians, dancers and so much more are found. Our God wants to 'paint the town red' and surprise people with this beauty and grace and He wants to do it through us.

A divine **interruption**

I like to think of myself as being spontaneous but, if I'm being honest, I don't like my routine to be disrupted. We can pay lip service to one thing but live another. Sometimes we can fool ourselves that all we want is to experience God's presence among us, but we are not prepared for how that might impact our lives. Yet it is this that differentiates us as the people of God.

The ark of the covenant represented the presence of God to Israel. They carried it with them throughout their wanderings in the desert. After a false start, David brought it to Jerusalem and now Solomon had provided a magnificent building for it. As they installed the ark in the Temple, four things accompanied the event: sacrifice (v.6), unity (v.3), consecration (v.11) and worship (v.13). This resulted in the presence of God being so strong among them that they were unable to continue their routine services (v.14).

The presence of God can seem an illusory concept and yet we all recognise its absence. We long for more of God's presence among us, but have we any part to play in fulfilling that desire?

As we come together as God's people in unity, sacrificially giving our time, gifts and money, consecrating ourselves to the One who is Lord of our lives and worshipping together, we prepare the way for more of God's presence to be evident among us. We do what He has called us to. Should He then come and disrupt our routines, let's embrace Him and not fret – because the focus of our lives is God alone and not the service we bring Him. Then when others who haven't yet encountered the living God are among us, they will experience the reality of what we are trying to communicate to them in words.

2 Chronicles 5:2–14

'… the priests could not perform their service because of the cloud, for the glory of the LORD filled the temple of God.' (v.14)

For prayer and reflection

Father, we are hungry for more of Your presence. Help us to pay the price; to be whole-hearted in our devotion to You and, in unity, to worship You, the Lord of our lives.

WEEKEND

History lessons

For reflection: 2 Timothy 3:10–17
'All Scripture is God-breathed and is useful for teaching, rebuking, correcting and training in righteousness ...' (v.16)

On a visit to the Bayeux Tapestry I was basking in the glow of being a great mother. I had gone round, hand in hand with my seven-year-old, explaining in a simple but entertaining way the history behind the great work of art. My pride was deflated on overhearing her say to her sister: 'Well that was a really boring morning.'

When it comes to the history books in the Bible sometimes we can find it just as hard to engage. What relevance do these stories of kings, who lived so long ago, have to our lives in the twenty-first century? Paul instructs Timothy that 'All Scripture is God-breathed ...' and can teach and equip us for our daily lives.

We can find ourselves disapproving of the actions and attitudes of the characters to whom we are introduced but, with the Holy Spirit's guidance and revelation, we realise that our behaviour can be remarkably similar – only in a different context. Let's be open to the Holy Spirit challenging and changing us as we respond to God's Word.

Optional further reading
2 Chronicles 1:1–36: 23
Michael Tunnicliffe, *The People's Bible Commentary: Chronicles to Nehemiah* (Abingdon: BRF, 1999)

Delivery **guaranteed**

Too often, in my enthusiasm, I promise more than I am capable of delivering. I overestimate my abilities or the time available and it's frustrating for friends and family when I fail to do what I have promised. I am so glad that God is not like that.

Solomon is blessing the people and praising God on the day of the dedication of the Temple. The first thing he acknowledges is that none of it would have been possible apart from God, who not only had given them promises but now had made them a reality. God's actions are always consistent with what He has said and when He speaks He always follows through. We worship a God who is completely dependable, true and faithful. He is able to perform everything He has promised.

Satan will always tempt us not only to doubt God's Word but also, in a crisis, he will try to make God seem small and ineffectual. Isaiah reassures us that it is impossible for God's Word to return to Him empty. As the Lord declares, it '... will accomplish what I desire and achieve the purpose for which I sent it' (Isa. 55:11).

This is foundational to our spiritual lives. We can often be shaken, but we are called to return to this rock of truth over and over again. Perhaps you have received a promise about a prodigal child or a husband who doesn't know the Lord; today they appear to be further away than ever. Refuse to listen to the lies of the enemy. Don't be afraid to remind yourself of God's promise to you because He has it in hand and will not let you down. When circumstances seem to challenge this truth, choose to believe what God's Word says and let fresh hope spring up within you.

2 Chronicles 6:3–11

'Praise be to the LORD, the God of Israel, who with his hands has fulfilled what he promised with his mouth ...' (v.4)

For prayer and reflection

Today, begin to praise God for His promises and His ability to do what He has said.

Captivity **or freedom**

**2 Chronicles
6:36–39**

'… if they have a
change of heart
in the land where
they are held
captive …' (v.37)

**For prayer and
reflection**

**Are you struggling
with unconfessed
sin in your life?
Right now come
to your heavenly
Father and admit
what you have
done; you have
nothing to fear –
He is waiting to
forgive.**

Guilt is a very unpopular subject in today's world and is viewed as an old-fashioned concept which hinders our enjoyment of life. Even among Christians we are wary about bringing up the subject, afraid lest the person should feel condemned or rejected. We live in a blame-orientated society, but most of us find it increasingly difficult to admit to being at fault. Yet the whole premise of our faith is that Jesus died in order that we could know the freedom of forgiveness.

Solomon is not afraid to say it like it is: 'When they sin against you – for there is no-one who doesn't sin …' (v.36). A large part of Solomon's prayer is concerned with asking God to forgive His people when they get it wrong. In a literal sense, the result of Israel's sin is being taken into captivity, but when they have 'a change of heart' and repent God comes to their rescue.

Unrepented sin brings us into spiritual captivity. It affects our relationship with God and one another, and we become frustrated and joyless. John agrees with Solomon: 'If we claim to be without sin, we deceive ourselves …' (1 John 1:8), but the incredible truth is: 'If we confess our sins, he is faithful and just and will forgive us our sins and purify us from all unrighteousness' (1 John 1:9).

This is true freedom. Don't let the enemy lock you up in a prison of unconfessed sin. Be prepared to admit that you were wrong and receive the forgiveness God promises you. Satan tries to convince us that guilt is a destructive emotion, but to feel guilty when you have done something wrong is healthy. Confessing our guilt opens the door to renewed relationship with the One who paid such an incredible price in order to offer us forgiveness in the first place.

Healing communities

I n the 30 years of civil strife in Northern Ireland, when the Church came together to pray, verse 14 of 2 Chronicles 7 was probably the verse quoted most often. We were under no illusions that our society was broken, and so God's promise to '... hear from heaven and ... forgive [our] sin and ... heal [our] land' got our attention. As with many of the promises in Scripture there were conditions attached. They included humility, seeking God's face and repentance. We longed to see an end to violence and a change of heart in our divided community, but this verse made us realise that the starting point had to be with us, God's people.

The Church is called to be salt and light in our society; to be a prophetic voice representing the heart of God. However, if we interpret this as standing on the outside, pointing the finger at the wrongs which are all too evident, we miss the point. When things were going wrong in Israel, the prophets did not focus on external forces but called God's people to put their own house in order. In God's response to Solomon's dedication of the Temple we see the same principle at work: it is when '[His] people, who are called by [His] name ... humble themselves and pray'.

God has responded to the cries of our hearts in this part of the world. Of course we recognise there is still much to be done, but it began with the Church recognising that we were part of the problem. As we are confronted with the problems in our communities, we should feel neither helpless nor detached. If we take responsibility and allow the Holy Spirit to shine His light on us, seeking God in prayer and repentance, we can expect to see God move in renewing and redeeming whole communities.

2 Chronicles 7:11–22

'... if my people ... will humble themselves and pray ... and turn from their wicked ways, then will I hear ...' (v.14)

For prayer and reflection

Father, I long to see my broken community experience Your healing power. Help me play my part in humbly seeking You in prayer and repentance. Amen.

Wise up

**2 Chronicles
9:1–12**

'… not even half
the greatness of
your wisdom was
told me; you have
far exceeded the
report I heard.'
(v.6)

The Queen of Sheba's visit to Solomon is the stuff of blockbuster movies. An exotic monarch arrives with great pomp to check out the man with the 'X-Factor'. She came, she conversed, she observed and she concluded that everything she had heard '… about [his] achievements and [his] wisdom is true' (v.5). It's striking that it draws from her heart a declaration of praise, not of Solomon but of God: 'Praise be to the Lord your God, who has delighted in you and placed you on his throne …' (v.8).

We too are called to live as people of wisdom. Perhaps you think it's unrealistic for us to compare ourselves with the great Solomon, but who was the source of his wisdom? It was God – and that same source is available to you and me. James makes it very clear that if we need wisdom all we have to do is ask God 'and it will be given' to us (James 1:5).

God's ways haven't changed. He wants us, as His people, to influence the world around us. If ever the wisdom of God were needed, in families, the workplace, economics and government, it's today. When people observe our lives does it produce in them the same response as that of the Queen of Sheba? The apostle Peter puts it like this: 'Live such good lives … that … they may see your good deeds and glorify God …' (1 Pet. 2:12).

The Queen of Sheba's insight is remarkable. Not only does she see that God is behind Solomon's success, but she remarks that it shows God's delight in His servant and His desire to bless the nation through Solomon.

God delights in you and has given you as a gift to those around you. Be the woman of wisdom He has called you to be and it will result in pointing others to the God you serve.

**For prayer and
reflection**

**Father, I ask for
Your wisdom in
my relationships
and the situations
I am facing right
now, so that those
around me will
understand what
an amazing God
I serve. Amen.**

Commonplace **riches**

We often value things because of their scarcity. Summer strawberries taste sweeter than those out of season. I don't feel as good in clothes from a cheaper chain store as I do in the outfit bought for my daughter's wedding from a more exclusive shop – even if it was in a sale!

This chapter describes Solomon's incredible wealth. Gold flooded into his kingdom so fast that even everyday objects in the palace were made of gold, 'Nothing was made of silver, because silver was considered of little value in Solomon's day' (v.20). God fulfilled His promise to Solomon that he would be the richest king who'd ever lived, because he had asked God for wisdom, not wealth.

God's people have a different value system to the world around us. Like Solomon, we understand where true wealth is found. In the Sermon on the Mount, Jesus presents the manifesto of the kingdom of God that runs counter-cultural to our world. We are children of the King, with untold spiritual riches available to us. Our Father 'has blessed us in the heavenly realms with every spiritual blessing in Christ' (Eph. 1:3) and has lavished on us 'the riches of God's grace' (Eph. 1:7–8).

Like Solomon we can make precious and normally scarce commodities become commonplace. Ask yourself: 'What is lacking in my community or workplace that I'd like to see become commonplace?' Hope, generosity, love for those outside 'my clan', healing, righteousness, concern for the less fortunate, forgiveness, grace? We're called to live in such a way as to make these riches of God's kingdom available to those among whom we live; and to pray that God moves in our communities to make these godly qualities as commonplace 'as stones'.

2 Chronicles 9:13–27

'The king made silver as common in Jerusalem as stones …' (v.27)

For prayer and reflection

Father, thank You for the spiritual riches I have in You. Help me make them available to others through my life and my prayers. Amen.

WEEKEND

Women of wisdom

For reflection: Proverbs 3:15
'She is more precious than rubies; nothing you desire can compare with her.'

Proverbs makes it clear that it is not diamonds that are a girl's best friend, but wisdom. Many women struggle with a low opinion of themselves. As we embrace God's wisdom we can be confident and fulfilled, with treasure to share. In Proverbs, Solomon, Israel's wisest king, outlines the benefits of wisdom:

Wisdom protects (4:6)
Wisdom guides (4:11–12)
Wisdom teaches the fear of the Lord (2:5)
Wisdom brings health to our bodies (3:8)
The wise will be discerning (14:33)
The wise will not be easily offended (12:16)
The wise will be patient (19:11)
The wise honour God (3:9–10)
The humble will be wise (11:2)
The one who wins souls is wise (11:30)

Take time this weekend to discover other blessings.

'By wisdom a house is built, and through understanding it is established; through knowledge its rooms are filled with rare and beautiful treasures' (Prov. 24:3–4).

Optional further reading
Read through the books of: Proverbs and James
Kate Hayes, *The Journey to Wisdom* (Milton Keynes: Scripture Union, 2007)

Good and bad **advice**

Have you ever followed someone's advice and it turned out to be a disaster? Shortly after being crowned, Rehoboam is faced with making an important decision. Israel has become wealthy and influential under the leadership of his father, Solomon, but it has come at a price. The high taxes and forced labour have become a heavy burden on the people: now they appeal to the young king to 'lighten the harsh labour and the heavy yoke' (v.4) under which they are suffering.

At first the king's response shows wisdom. He doesn't make a hasty decision but consults the elders who have served his father. Unfortunately, he doesn't listen to their advice and turns to his peers, young men who seem to have let their new-found status go to their heads. As a result, he responds to the people harshly. Because of this Israel becomes a divided kingdom, leading to years of conflict.

The moral of this story is: be careful to whom you listen. Sometimes we run around consulting people about a problem, but we are just looking for someone to agree with us. Rehoboam 'rejected the advice the elders gave him' (v.8). He obviously didn't like what he heard; perhaps he felt he had something to prove following in the footsteps of a famous father.

If you have a decision to make at present and have been seeking advice, perhaps you need to listen to that person who is older and wiser rather than to your friend who is merely confirming what you have already decided. The problem is: if you are not open to another viewpoint from people you respect, you can end up making decisions with far-reaching consequences – not just for yourself but also for others.

**2 Chronicles
10:1–19**

'He asked them,
"What is your
advice?"' (v.9)

**For prayer and
reflection**

**Father, please
bring wise
counsellors into
my life. Give me
humility to listen
to their advice and
discernment to
know what to act
upon. Amen.**

Going **for gold**

2 Chronicles
12:1–12

'... so they
may learn the
difference between
serving me and
serving the kings
of other lands.'
(v.8)

**For prayer and
reflection**

**If you or someone
you know is
contemplating
walking away
from God, stop
and think about
the consequences;
then pray for a
fresh revelation of
His goodness and
faithfulness.**

The Israelites never seemed to get the concept 'You've never had it so good'. The grass always seemed greener on the other side and their history is littered with stories of their turning their backs on God. Once again, the king and the people 'abandoned the law of the Lord' (v.1) because they were well established and had become strong.

I am always amazed at their stupidity: did they not get it? The reason for the Israelites' success was that they were living for God and according to His principles. However, the Holy Spirit often stops me in my tracks and asks me: 'Are you really so different?' He teaches us things that, if put into practice, make us strong in our faith and equip us for everyday living. Yet we so easily abandon them and, like the Israelites, we have to live with the consequences. God handed them over to their enemies so that they could experience the difference between serving Him and serving them. The Egyptian king, Shishak, carried off all their treasures and they had to replace the gold shields with ones made of bronze.

We also have an enemy who wants to rob us of God's best for us. I remember one of my daughters struggling with her faith, thinking that her friends were having a much better life than she was. She said to me: 'It's just too hard to be a Christian.' I replied, 'There will be times in your life when it's too hard not to be one.' Let's not be tempted into thinking that if we stop trying to live for God life will be so much easier. God wants to give us gold – let's not settle for bronze. As Paul says: 'Run in such a way as to get the prize' (1 Cor. 9:24).

Ambushed **but rescued**

Perhaps that's how you are feeling today: you don't know which way to turn because you are under attack on all sides. Judah was in a literal battle, hemmed in at the front, and with an ambush set by their enemy behind them. Paul explains in Ephesians 6:12: '... our struggle is not against flesh and blood, but against the rulers, against the authorities, against the powers of this dark world and against the spiritual forces of evil in the heavenly realms.' Just because our battles are spiritual doesn't make them any less real. Satan still uses this tactic of a frontal attack but then ambushes us from behind.

We have battled in our lives as we worked to plant and build a church in our home city of Belfast. Satan threw the usual tactics at us: disappointments, setbacks, disrupted plans, but the most painful thing was the ambush he set to take out our children. It's then you feel like giving up; there's no way forward and no way back.

This was not the first time God's people had been in this position: it had happened at the Red Sea when they were fleeing from the Egyptians. The key in both cases was that 'they cried out to the Lord' – and God came to their rescue.

God has already defeated our enemy at the cross of Christ. He has '... disarmed the powers and authorities, he made a public spectacle of them, triumphing over them by the cross' (Col. 2:15). Remind yourself of this victory and His ability to give you a strategy to overcome. Allow a battle cry (2 Chron. 13:15) to rise up within you and refuse to be intimidated. When the people cried to the Lord, the sea parted and the enemy was routed and fled. Your God can make a way for you where there is no way.

---

2 Chronicles 13:1–18

'Judah turned and saw that they were being attacked at both front and rear. Then they cried out to the LORD.' (v.14)

For prayer and reflection

Father, I don't know which way to turn but I know You are my deliverer. Help me not to give up but to know You have heard my cry and are coming to my rescue. Amen.

Courage **to continue**

**2 Chronicles
15:1–19**

'But as for you,
be strong and do
not give up, for
your work will be
rewarded.' (v.7)

A t whatever stage you find yourself, life circumstances can arise that make you feel like giving up. Perhaps you have been faithfully serving God, persevering, and yet nothing seems to be happening. We can get battle weary. In fact, King Asa hears these words as he returns from a battle in which the enemy was defeated. We think we are at risk when things are going wrong, but sometimes our most vulnerable times are when we have experienced success.

For many years I have been involved in the Transformations prayer movement. It was a continual battle to get people together to pray; small numbers attended the events we planned. Then, on the Global Day of Prayer in both 2005 and 2006, we saw thousands of Christians come together at our local parliament building to pray for our nation at a crucial time in the peacemaking process. We experienced a miracle of financial provision as well – and political breakthrough followed.

For prayer and reflection

**Lord, thank
You for Your
timely promise.
Strengthen me
and help me to
keep going as
I know You are
faithful and the
outcome will be
rewarding. Amen.**

In all the years of hard work I was never tempted to give up, but 'success' made me fearful. How could we top what had happened? Perhaps you are on the brink of quitting and God's word comes to you today, as it did to Asa, so that you can take courage (v.8). Asa went on to remove the idols from the land, to repair the Lord's altar and to encourage the people to seek the Lord. The result was that '... the Lord gave them rest on every side' (v.15). If you are tired, feeling fruitless, dispirited, or even a bit fearful because of having to live up to success, God's promise is reiterated in Galatians 6:9: 'Let us not become weary in doing good, for at the proper time we will reap a harvest if we do not give up.'

Guard **your heart**

**2 Chronicles
16:1–14**

I n the early part of his reign Asa was committed to seeking the Lord with all his heart. Now, as he neared the end of his life, something changed. His first reaction wasn't to seek the Lord but to opt for a practical solution which worked! God sent a prophet to him to challenge him because it was an affair of the heart. Unfortunately, Asa reacted badly and imprisoned the prophet and began to oppress the people. There were far-reaching consequences which even affected his health: 'Though his disease was severe, even in his illness he did not seek help from the Lord, but only from the physicians' (v.12).

> 'For the eyes of the LORD range throughout the earth to strengthen those whose hearts are fully committed to him.'
> (v.9)

Proverbs 4:23 encourages us to: 'Above all else, guard your heart, for it is the wellspring of life.' God is on the lookout for people who remain single-minded in their devotion to Him so that He can pour strength into them. This is the solution to finishing well, so that we can say with Paul: 'I have fought the good fight, I have finished the race, I have kept the faith' (2 Tim. 4:7).

We are easily tempted to depend on pragmatic solutions rather than on the Lord. When problems arise we need to remind ourselves of God's faithfulness to us in the past and trust Him in the present. Also, if we get it wrong, we need to handle God's rebuke with humility and repentance, not resorting to abusing the messenger. Perhaps these challenges become even greater in the latter part of our lives. God was as committed to Asa in this part of his reign as He was at the beginning. God hadn't changed; Asa had. God's heart is always for us – so let's make sure we finish well by guarding our hearts towards Him.

For prayer and reflection

Let the Holy Spirit search your heart. Has anything come into your life which has seduced you away from the Lord? Repent of it and recommit yourself to Him.

WEEKEND

Stands and delivers

For reflection: Jeremiah 51:19
'He who is the Portion of Jacob is not like these ...'

The books of Chronicles tell the story of how the worship of idols promises much but fails to deliver. Only when God's people worshipped and served the Lord were their lives fulfilled and blessed.

Many things today call for our allegiance, but the God who is our portion 'is not like these'.

Promising security but failing to deliver
– He is not like these
  Offering relationship but leaving you broken-hearted
– He is not like these
  Promoting rewards but you pay the price
– He is not like these
  Proclaiming freedom but enslaving you
– He is not like these
  Promising fulfilment but leaving you with frustration
– He is not like these
  Showing the pinnacle but not being there when needed
– He is not like these
  Offering love but with conditions attached
– He is not like these
  The Lord who is my portion is the maker of all things,
The Lord Almighty is His name.

Optional further reading
Psalms 9,16,18,19,23

Ears **to hear**

I paraded the new dress I'd just bought in front of my husband and then asked the fateful question: 'Well, do you like it?' The truth was I only wanted one answer and when he expressed his doubts I was none too pleased. We often find ourselves in situations where we only want to hear our own opinions confirmed – and this can also be true in our relationship with God.

King Jehoshaphat had a high regard for God's Word. He had sent his officials into the towns of Judah to teach the people from the Book of the Law. He respected God's written Word and the prophetic word. It was he who advised King Ahab to 'seek the counsel of the Lord' (18:4) when they were planning to go into battle together. Ahab produced 400 prophets who, to a man, told him what he wanted to hear. However, Jehoshaphat was unimpressed by them and asked: 'Is there not a prophet of the Lord here whom we can enquire of?' Micaiah, knowing King Ahab's heart, agreed with what had been said, but the king insisted that he tell him 'nothing but the truth'. Nevertheless the king ignored what God said to him and ended up being killed on the battlefield.

We are in relationship with a God who speaks to His children, but it is imperative we not only have an ear to hear but a heart to obey. Jehoshaphat wanted to hear what God thought but he still made the wrong decision and went to war. God doesn't always say what we want to hear. Even if it's unpalatable and conflicts with what others are saying to us we need to respond in humility and obedience because God has our best interests at heart.

---

2 Chronicles 17:7–9; 18:1–17

'First seek the counsel of the LORD.' (18:4)

For prayer and reflection

Lord, Your word is a lamp to my feet and a light to my path. Give me a discerning heart to hear Your word and to act on it – even if it isn't what I want to hear. Amen.

Look who's **on my side**

**2 Chronicles
20:5–26**

'Do not be afraid
or discouraged
because of this
vast army. For the
battle is not yours,
but God's.' (v.15)

Facing a vast army, the people of Judah felt completely overwhelmed. King Jehoshaphat, however, did not panic: he brought the people together to 'seek help from the Lord' (v.4).

Whatever the situation you are currently facing that has left you feeling powerless and overwhelmed, instead of panicking, remember who's on your side. Jehoshaphat reminded himself and the people of who their God was. He remembered what God had done for them in the past and the promises God had made to them. He declared that while they had no idea what to do, they were looking to God for help.

The enemy wants to keep us cowering in a corner, but God's word to us is: 'Do not be afraid; do not be discouraged. Go out to face them tomorrow, and the Lord will be with you' (v.17).

Many times in my life the threats of the enemy, Satan, have either immobilised me or have made me want to turn and run. In Ephesians 6, we are instructed to: 'Put on the full armour of God so that you can take your stand against the devil's schemes' (v.11) and 'to stand your ground, and after you have done everything, to stand' (v.13).

The king realised that the people needed to get their eyes off 'the vast army' and on to God. He appointed worshippers to go ahead of his army and they sang 'Give thanks to the Lord, for his love endures for ever' (v.21). Satan knows he has won the day if we begin to doubt God's faithfulness.

Step out of that corner in which you are huddling. Refuse to believe Satan's lies. You don't have to come up with a solution: God is going to ambush the enemy for you and the valley of your greatest battle will become the valley of victory.

**For prayer and
reflection**

**Lord, I feel
powerless and
don't know what
to do, but my
eyes are on You.
I worship You
because You are
my faithful God
who promises to
be with me and to
fight for me. My
hope is in You.
Amen.**

Creating an epitaph

The story of Jehoram does not make for happy reading and it finishes with the saddest comment: 'He passed away, to no-one's regret ...' He destroyed his family, made enemies at every turn and led the whole nation astray.

Some people might feel that to live our lives with an eye on our passing is morbid, but we won't live forever. God's plan and purpose for us is that our lives would make a difference. Library shelves are full of the life stories of men and women who made an impact on the world in which they lived. However, the names of many will never be known: people who lived their lives loving God, being led by His Spirit and positively touching the lives of others.

Just think of the number of people who would raise their voices in praise and appreciation of the woman described in Proverbs 31. At the head would be her husband, then her children, employees, fellow business people and the poor. Her epitaph is very different to Jehoram's: 'Give her the reward she has earned, and let her works bring her praise at the city gate' (Prov. 31:31).

Women in the twenty-first century are put under pressure to try to hold back time; to succumb to the culture of youth where death is a taboo subject. The result: self-obsession and superficiality. Let's not allow the world 'to squeeze [us] into its own mould' (Rom. 12:2, Phillips). God wants to raise up beautiful women who make a difference in their families, workplaces and communities because of their strength, wisdom and grace.

Life is a wonderful gift from God. We can let it slip away or embrace each day as an opportunity to affect the lives of others for the good. What would you like your epitaph to be?

2 Chronicles 21:4–20

'Jehoram ... reigned in Jerusalem for eight years. He passed away, to no-one's regret ...' (v.20)

For prayer and reflection

Do I enrich the lives of others? It's in our hands to create and shape our epitaph – ask God to give you a vision of what it should be.

Lives **to influence**

2 Chronicles 22:2–3; 23:16–24:2

'Joash did what was right in the eyes of the LORD all the years of Jehoiada the priest.' (24:2)

For prayer and reflection

Father, lead me to one person to whom I can be a spiritual mother. I feel inadequate, but I know you can strengthen me for the task. Amen.

As the story continues to unfold in chapters 22 to 24 of 2 Chronicles, two characters stand out. Athaliah, the queen mother, was power hungry, ruthless and manipulative; actively encouraging her son to do wrong (22:3). Jehoiada, the priest, was a man of integrity and wisdom who served God. His counsel resulted in the young king leading the nation of Judah back to serving God and restoring the Temple.

As I look back over my own life I'm so grateful for God-given mentors, including my parents, who guided, instructed and challenged me. Today, there is a great need in the Church for spiritual mothers and fathers who, through their love, support and wisdom, can encourage those younger in their relationship with God.

In the New Testament older Christians are often exhorted to instruct and help younger ones. The heart of the Great Commission is discipleship – not just introducing people to the good news but, as Jesus said, 'teaching them to obey everything I have commanded you' (Matt. 28:20).

Many of us feel inadequate for such a task. Our thoughts immediately go to a need to be trained in how to do it. Or perhaps you think, 'I need a mentor'. My experience, of both receiving and giving in this area, leads me to believe it works best through informal, relational interaction. Women are uniquely suited to what I call 'kitchen sink' discipling. Don't underestimate what God has taught you over the years. If you're willing to pass it on to others it will enrich their lives, perhaps even protecting someone from losing their way. Whatever our age, we all have the capacity to pass on what we've learned to others and, like Jehoiada, to encourage them to do what is 'right in the eyes of the Lord'.

My Lord and my God

Being the mother of four daughters, I have no greater desire than that they all have a relationship with God which is real and are not carried on the back of their parents' faith. Unless they encounter God for themselves, eventually they will flounder. Our faith will not be sufficient to carry them through.

That's why a little phrase in the middle of the story of Joash is so significant. Under the guidance of Jehoiada, the king is making wise decisions, including collecting money from the people to restore the Temple and leading them away from idol worship again. However, as he gives instructions to the priests, he reveals something in his heart by referring to 'your God' (v.5). He doesn't say 'my God' or even 'our God'.

It becomes evident from Joash's actions after Jehoiada dies that something is missing. The people of Judah return to idolatry and when God challenges them, through Zechariah, Jehoiada's son, 'they plotted against him, and by order of the king they stoned him to death ...' (v.21). You can play the game for so long, but what is in your heart eventually becomes evident. Joash had obviously never moved on to seeing God as his God.

Perhaps you're reading this today and, from the outside, your life looks OK. Brought up in a Christian home, you appear to say and do the right things, yet in your heart you know that you haven't encountered God in a meaningful way for yourself. The elder brother in the story of the prodigal son did the right thing, stayed at home and served his father, but he needed to encounter the father's love every bit as much as his prodigal brother. It's not too late. Be honest with yourself and God – He is waiting to turn 'your God' into 'my God'.

---

2 Chronicles 24:4–5,17–22

'... collect the money due annually from all Israel, to repair the temple of your God.' (v.5)

For prayer and reflection

Lord, I want You to be my God. I give myself to You and choose to encounter You for myself – not through the faith of my parents or friends. Please reveal Yourself to me. Amen.

WEEKEND

The Father's embrace

For reflection: Luke 15:20
'… he ran to his son, threw his arms around him and kissed him.'

How reassuring it is to be in relationship with the God of the second chance. If the history of Israel teaches us anything, it is that God never gives up on us. In fact, His mercy extends even beyond a second chance. The books of Chronicles relate some very ugly episodes in Israel's story but God comes to the people again and again to give them an opportunity to be restored.

This history book also makes it abundantly clear that when we take control of our own lives and ignore God there are dire consequences to be faced. However, when our lives are submitted to a loving Father who wants the best for us we can live fulfilled lives.

Both lessons are echoed in the parable of the prodigal son. There are times in our lives when we feel restricted and want to escape from the Father's house, only to discover that what the world promotes as freedom is actually bondage in disguise. Every day we live we are writing our own history. May it be one of remaining in the protective embrace of the Father's love.

Optional further reading
Luke 15:11–32
Francine Rivers, *A Lineage of Grace* (Illinois: Tyndale House, 2003)

All or nothing

I n our world today, many people see good and evil as a balancing act. We may not do the right thing all the time, but we can make an effort to see that the good outweighs the bad. Unfortunately, wrong attitudes and actions can have devastating consequences. Amaziah made some good decisions, but because he was not wholehearted in his devotion to God he began to live in a way that endangered himself and others.

In our relationship with God there is no room for half measures. Jesus was unapologetic when He explained to people the cost of following Him: '... anyone who does not take his cross and follow me is not worthy of me' (Matt. 10:38). God has held nothing back in His pursuit of us, giving His own Son to face punishment and death in order for us to be reconciled to Him. God requires His people to fulfil the greatest commandment: 'Love the Lord your God with all your heart and with all your soul and with all your mind' (Matt. 22:37–38).

Amaziah was sidetracked and started to worship other gods, even though they'd proved themselves powerless (v.15). As a result he stopped listening to God and went his own way, suffering defeat and disgrace at the hand of his enemies. The wall of Jerusalem was broken down and the enemy carried off their most treasured possessions.

When we hold back and don't give all of our heart to the Lord there is a problem: we can then give it away to something else. We make a few good decisions and, as a result, our lives are blessed; then we turn around and begin to give our devotion to things that are both false and futile.

Our God is worthy of wholehearted devotion: we dare not offer Him anything less.

2 Chronicles 25:1–2,14–16

'He did what was right in the eyes of the LORD, but not wholeheartedly.' (v.2)

For prayer and reflection

Lord, You are worthy of my wholehearted devotion. I give myself to You afresh, holding nothing back. Amen.

Believing **your own publicity**

2 Chronicles 26:3–21

'But after Uzziah became powerful, his pride led to his downfall'. (v.16)

Famous or influential people sometimes begin to believe their own publicity. We read of their ridiculous demands to be treated differently to lesser mortals. The saying: 'Pride comes before a fall' echoes verse 16 in this chapter.

Uzziah was very successful. He defeated Judah's enemies, developed the country economically and established a well-trained, modern army. His fame spread throughout the surrounding nations. Unfortunately, the power went to his head and he thought that he could do anything – including burning incense in the Temple. God had assigned this task to the consecrated priests. By his actions, the king was communicating that he didn't have to live by God's commands.

He had forgotten who was responsible for his success story. Several times we read: 'God gave him success' or 'God helped him'. As a result of his unfaithfulness to God, he was afflicted with leprosy and had to live in isolation until he died.

God is incredibly generous. He shapes us, gives us gifts and opportunities to use them and then empowers us by His Spirit to do the job. We then receive all the comments of 'Well done!' and, if we are not careful, we begin to believe that it was down to us – while paying lip service to God's part in it all. It's a bit like giving my children pocket money which they use to buy me a present – and then they want to be congratulated for being so generous!

It is perfectly acceptable to feel a sense of fulfilment when you have done something well. We don't need to resort to false humility, but we must never forget that all that we will ever accomplish is because of God. Let's determine to always give Him the glory.

For prayer and reflection

Father, forgive me for the times I have allowed pride to make me forget that I can do nothing of value without You. Amen.

On the **move**

I am a self-confessed queue dodger. The affliction is a determination to believe that every other checkout queue is moving faster than the one you are in and that your checkout operator is the newest and most incompetent employee of the company. Waiting does not come easily to me and Scripture seems to be full of instructions about waiting. When I read verses like: 'Be still, and know that I am God' (Psa. 46:10), I feel like the child fidgeting and squirming on the naughty chair in nursery. Therefore when I read a verse that tells me about God acting quickly, my ears prick up.

Hezekiah has the unenviable task of undoing 16 years of unbelievable wickedness during the reign of Ahaz. The horror of those years rings out when you read: 'They also shut the doors of the portico and put out the lamps' (v.7). However, the king was undaunted by the magnitude of the task. He set about it with energy and commitment and, as you read chapter 29, you feel you are running to catch up.

Don't get me wrong: I am under no illusions that you can bypass waiting on God. However, when God begins to move I am often amazed at the speed with which He acts – especially in issues of restoration and redemption.

Be encouraged – that person for whom you have been praying for so long can be turned around more quickly than you could ever imagine. That ongoing problem you have been struggling with can be solved overnight when God begins to move. If you've been away from God for a long time, the road back may seem too long even to contemplate. But when you repent and turn around, the Father's embrace is only a short step away. The door opens and the lights come on to welcome you home.

2 Chronicles 29:1–17,35–36

'... the people rejoiced at what God had brought about for his people, because it was done so quickly.' (v.36)

For prayer and reflection

Meditate on the fact that when God moves things can happen very quickly. Let this fact encourage you to persevere in prayer.

The beauty of worship

Gill Beard

Gill Beard currently leads two outreach initiatives in Reading – Prayer Cafe and Prayer Stop. She trained as a cellist at the Royal College of Music, and played with the Royal Ballet Company. She was a singer, song writer and worship leader for 25 years. Married to Nick for 43 years, she has two sons and three gorgeous and hilarious grandchildren. Her passion is to see Prayer Cafe or Prayer Stop in every town, village or community.

The beauty of worship

'Worship the LORD in the splendour of his holiness.' (v.9)

For prayer and reflection

Lord God, I know that You are worthy of all honour and praise. May I renew my passion to worship You in all of my life and discover new joys of surrender. Amen.

Worship. Where shall we start? One dictionary definition states: 'to show profound religious devotion and respect to; to adore or venerate (God *or any person or thing considered divine*).' Well, I think chocolate is divine – there are even brands called 'Divine' and 'Heaven' – but that can't be right, can it? The word comes from the old English, *woerthscipe*, which means affirming the inestimable worth of God. The Greek word for worship, *proskuneo*, meaning 'to kiss the hand', suggests a humble, reverent intimacy.

Archbishop William Temple says this: 'Worship is the most important thing in life and conduct is the test. If it's not there then your worship is not real. It is the submission of *all* our nature to God. It is the quickening of conscience by His holiness; the nourishment of the mind by His truth; the purifying of imagination by His beauty; the opening of the heart to His love, the surrender of will to His purpose and all this gathered up in adoration ... the most selfless emotion of which our nature is capable.'

How awesome! So much for chocolate then!

Richard Foster, a Christian theologian, writes: 'To worship is to experience reality, to touch life. It is to know, to feel, to experience the resurrected Christ in the midst of the gathered community. It is a breaking into the shekinah (the radiance/glory) of God, or better yet, being invaded by the shekinah of God.'*

I'm sure that we each have our own ideas about what constitutes worship and I hope that we'll explore some of them this month. As we do, may we allow our thinking to be expanded and our lives taken afresh into the presence of the divine, the One and only true God.

* Richard Foster, *Celebration of Discipline* (London: Hodder and Stoughton, 1984)

Worship ... **offering my all**

Today I want to unpack the William Temple quote from yesterday's notes.

'*Worship is ... submission*' We must put aside our self-centredness. To submit means to surrender oneself completely to God. We have to choose to come to Him. He will never force us, but isn't it a relief when we make that choice?

'*Worship is ... quickening of conscience*' When in the presence of God, we become aware of our own wretchedness; the Holy Spirit prompts us about wrong things in our lives. This leads us into confession.

'*Worship is ... nourishment*' The truth is God's Word in the Bible. It is the source of our information on Christ. The more we learn about Jesus, the stronger our desire to worship and adore Him.

'*Worship is ... the purifying of imagination*' 1 Corinthians 2:16 tells us that 'we have the mind of Christ'. I wonder what our minds are like? If we centre our thoughts on the beauty of Jesus, we ourselves become lovelier, because we become more like Him.

'*Worship is ... the opening of the heart*' God loves us so much that He wants to cleanse us of our sins, so that we may get closer to Him.

'*Worship is ... surrender of will*' We need to be willing to go in God's direction, not our own. The only way to achieve this is to allow Him into every part of our lives, holding nothing back.

'*Worship is ... adoration*' So, let's focus our hearts, minds and spirits on God, just sitting in His presence, loving Him and giving generously of ourselves.

You can only truly worship when you experience the deepest love imaginable. The very heart of worship is falling in love with Jesus.

Psalm 103

'Praise the LORD, O my soul; all my inmost being, praise his holy name.' (v.1)

For prayer and reflection

'When I fall in love, it will be forever ...' – if I fall in love with Jesus.

WEEKEND

'Show Me'

For reflection:
Ask God how you can play your part in changing the situation for a child you know.

The song below was written as a response to the awful murder of James Bulger in 1993. It started in me a train of thought about the desperate world in which we live. More than twenty years later things are even worse. Knife crime and murdered teenagers are constantly in the news. How must Jesus' heart ache with sorrow for the little children. He didn't say, 'Let the little children suffer.' He said, 'Suffer [Let] little children … to come unto me' (Matt. 19:14, AV).

Show me a world without Jesus,
And I'll show you a world full of hate,
A world in which children kill children,
And the innocent suffer abuse.
Show me a world full of Jesus,
And I'll show you a world full of grace,
A world in which children are cherished,
And the innocent look upon His face.

'Show Me' (1st verse) © Gill Beard 1993

Optional further reading
John 17:20–26; Ephesians 3:14–19; Mark 10:13–16

Whom do we worship?

Matthew 4:1–11

The Bible is pretty clear about whom we should worship and is equally clear about whom or what we should *not* worship. Jesus reminds Satan, as he tries to tempt Jesus by offering Him the whole world, that in Deuteronomy 6:13–14 we are commanded to: 'Fear [worship] the Lord your God, serve him only ... Do not follow other gods, the gods of the peoples around you ...'

Jesus has no doubts whatsoever that His Father in heaven is the only God and the One we are designed to worship. Our spiritual DNA (figuratively speaking) has, at the very core of our being, the inbuilt need and desire to honour the Creator of all things. We recognise His majesty, authority and power.

One of the simplest songs I learnt as a new Christian put it beautifully in just three lines. The writer, Terrye Coelho, talks of our love and adoration of the Father, which leads us to lay our lives before Him. If we are able to truthfully sing and genuinely live out those words, then we are the kind of worshippers God seeks (see John 4:23–24).

As we lay down our lives in worship, we abandon self, selfishness and self-centredness. We give ourselves completely to Father God, seeking to bless and adore Him, submitting our hearts, souls, minds and bodies as an overflow of the love that He first gave to us. Let's offer that love back to Him with the passion He deserves.

Why not spend a few quiet moments now remembering the God who loved us so much that He was willing to see His only Son die a criminal's death, so that we might live with Him forever.

Lift your voice and let your heart worship in words that the Holy Spirit provides.

'Jesus said … "Away from me, Satan! For it is written: 'Worship the Lord your God, and serve him only.'"' (v.10)

For prayer and reflection

'Come, now is the time to worship. Come, now is the time to give your heart. Come, just as you are to worship. Come, just as you are before your God. Come ... come.'*

* 'Come Now Is The Time' by Brian Doerkson © 1998 Vineyard Songs UK/Eire. Used by permission.

257

Worship ... **is also praise**

**Psalm 27:4;
Psalm 145**

'I will praise your name for ever and ever.' (Psa 145:1)

I never differentiate between worship and praise, as I believe our whole life can become an act of worship. It doesn't make it *not worship* if we are singing joyfully along with the drums and guitars. Equally, it doesn't make it *not praise* if we are quietly humming a spiritual song around the supermarket. Worship with music comes from hearts yearning to bless God.

Take King David, who introduced music into the tabernacle and Temple services. Can you imagine the massive volume of sound, coming from the numerous instruments, choirs and worship leaders? I bet they didn't hassle the PA operator to ... 'Turn it down!' And yet David's greatest desire was to: '... gaze upon the beauty of the Lord ...' (Psa. 27:4). This speaks of tender moments, of intimacy, of a deep relationship. David totally appreciated the awesome magnificence of God. He loved those quiet moments in the house of the Lord, seeking His face.

Have you ever found yourself guilty of complaining or criticising the worship team as they do their very best to encourage you in worship? My hand is high in the air ... speck and plank come to mind (Matt. 7:5)!

In this consumer society, with so much choice, do we really want a 'pick and mix' service? I love classical music, whilst my youngest son prefers jazz. But we both love God and want to bless and serve Him to the best of our ability.

So, let's agree to honour God wherever we worship corporately, knowing that He knows our thoughts, hears our hearts and receives what's deep in our minds – not what comes out of our mouths (Isa. 29:13).

Is 'My Way' your song today – or are you singing 'I will offer up my life ...'?

For prayer and reflection

Lord, please forgive me when I am too 'picky' and teach me to honour You as I worship in Your house. Amen.

Worship ... **give thanks**

When we receive a gift with which we're *really* pleased, our response is a genuinely enthusiastic 'Thank you'. Let's take a moment to read the whole of Psalm 136. The psalmist here remembers many facets and actions of God for which to thank and praise Him.

As Christians, how often do we thank God for all Jesus gave for us on the cross and for the complete work of salvation He bought for us there? He set us free from sin and provides, through His resurrection, an eternal home in heaven. We might remember to give thanks, occasionally, as we sing the anointed worship songs centred on the cross.

This was the most momentous act of selflessness that could ever affect the soul of mankind. This sentence has caused me to stop writing as the impact of its truth has brought me to tears. *JESUS DIED for ME.* Say with me ... *JESUS* died for me, Jesus *DIED* for me, Jesus died for *ME.* What *can* we say but, 'Thank You! Thank You! Thank You!'

As our act of worship today, let us give thanks to God for *all* the good things He gives us. Family, friends, college, work, food, peace, patience, life itself ... As we do so, we will discover the glorious impact in our hearts as we recognise just how much we have to thank God for. Such love endures for ever.

We could write our own personal psalm today. Here's the start of mine:

Give thanks to the Lord for He is true
His love endures for ever
Give thanks to the Lord for He is mine
His love endures for ever
Give thanks to the Lord for He is risen!
His love endures for ever

Psalm 136:1–3

'Give thanks to the LORD, for he is good.' (Psa. 136:1)

For prayer and reflection

Thank You for saving me ... this *is* what I can say. Amen!

Worship ... **be holy**

. . . .

1 Peter 1:15–16

. . . .

'Be holy, because
I am holy.' (v.16)

hat does this mean for us? What *is* holiness and how do we attain it?

In our reading, it says: 'But just as he who called you is holy, so be holy in all you do; for it is written: "Be holy, because I am holy."' This isn't an optional extra for Christians; it is a command: Be holy.

As followers of Christ, we are sanctified (made holy) when we are set apart for sacred use, offering Him devoted lives of worship. As we bow before His awesome purity, we tremble at His majesty; we prostrate ourselves in the light of His holiness and we surrender our lives to Him (see Isa. 6:1–4).

The more we submit ourselves to God in worship, the greater our desire to honour and adore Him, and to glorify His name. The more we read and understand the life and character of Jesus, the greater our awareness of our own *un*godliness.

God's nature is always to have mercy. As we recognise our sinfulness in direct comparison with His holiness, our response must be to fall at His feet, repent of our sin and ask for His forgiveness. This He freely gives because Jesus has already paid the price by dying on the cross and releasing us from the debt of sin past, present and future. Hallelujah, what a Saviour!

We *can* be holy, because God sees the beauty of Jesus in us and loves us deeply, even though we are but a pale reflection of His Son, who was without sin.

Have we ever polluted our eyes, minds and thoughts by watching inappropriate TV or reading pulp fiction? Do we gossip about each other rather than talking about Jesus (see Phil. 4:8)? Shall we bring such things into the presence of Father God and pray this prayer?

. . . .
**For prayer and
reflection**
. . . .

**Lord, I am often
weak and foolish
and so easily fall
into sinful ways.
Please show
me what is true,
noble, right, pure,
lovely, excellent
and praiseworthy
for, from today, I
choose to be holy.**

Worship ... **bowing down**

There are many physical positions we can adopt when coming before the Lord Jesus in worship. The Magi fell down in the presence of this divine baby, recognising, even in this humble human form, the Saviour of the world.

Matthew 2:1–12

'... and they bowed down and worshipped him.' (Matt. 2:11)

How do you express yourself physically when worshipping? The psalms speak of raising hands, dancing, clapping, shouting, kneeling ... Have you tried any of these? Did you know that you can even get keep-fit videos set to praise songs? Why not offer your whole body to the Lord in worship and, if you are able, find a new way to physically express your praise. You will find a freedom that will bless your socks off!

My husband, Nick, recently took to lying flat on his face whilst seeking to bless God and come into close communion with Him. As he lay down one day, he had a picture. He saw himself on a beach closely examining a grain of sand, then rising a few feet in the air, watching the grain becoming smaller and smaller. Next, he was transported into space, 170 kilometres above earth's surface. (Men just know these things!) He asked God: 'How is it that You are concerned about me, when I am such a tiny part in Your whole creation?' He heard God reply: 'Because we are joined at the heart.' Nick then had a picture of those who do not yet know God, joined to God by a spiritual umbilical cord that was clamped – stopping the flow of God's love to them – and he asked God how it felt. On understanding that God felt physical pain, Nick was led to pray more passionately for those outside God's kingdom.

As we seek to explore new expressions of worship in our times alone with God, we too can expect to meet with God in deeper, more intimate, ways.

For prayer and reflection

Heavenly Father, as we surrender ourselves to You today, may we hear Your voice and be joined to Your heart of love.

WEEKEND

'Show Me'

For reflection:
Read the story of the Samaritan woman at the well (John 4:1–26).
Bring into Jesus' presence the first person who comes to mind.
Pray that this person will come to know and love Him.

When you think of your 'not yet Christian' friends and family, do the words below strike a chord? The teenager needing to know God, but finding drugs instead. The grandparent, lonely and isolated; the restless husband; the best friend who is suffering from mental illness. All these people not only need to meet their Saviour, they need you to show them the way. Keep loving, keep praying. Jesus is near. He who is faithful will answer.

Show me a life without Jesus,
And I'll show you a heart full of pain,
A life that is drifting and hopeless,
Where the darkness can drive you insane.
Show me a life full of Jesus,
And I'll show you a heart full of love.
A life that is anchored and fearless,
With the light of His Spirit within.

'Show Me' (2nd verse) © Gill Beard 1993

Optional further reading
Philippians 2:1–11; Luke 19:1–10

Worship ... **God's voice**

What an amazing thought! God rejoices over you and me with singing. When? we might ask. Zephaniah suggests this happens when we faithfully follow Him and obey His commands. It seems like a wonderful reward, considering all He has *already* done for us.

What sort of voice do you imagine God to have? Basso profundo ... deep and resonant? A boy soprano's, clear and pure? Could He sing like a babbling brook or a nightingale in full song? I imagine that God can sing in any key, style or expression He chooses. He can even sing in three-part harmony! He might croon lullabies when we're desperate for sleep or hum a melancholy tune as He watches us stray into sin. He may belt out wonderful melodies as He rejoices over our restored relationships.

I wonder if He whistles a piercing call, like the Shepherd bringing His sheep back home or prompting the prodigal's return to his Father. Would He gently quieten us with a melodic whisper, when we are fearful and downcast? Or, maybe He sings *the* love song that brings us, through His Son, into His kingdom forever.

During a period of deep depression, as two friends prayed for me, I 'heard' God singing over me words from the *Student Prince* musical: 'Drink, drink, drink, true lover.' Those words helped me to realise how dry and thirsty I had become, and how much God wanted to refresh me with His Spirit and remind me of our intimate relationship. As I listened and drew closer to Him, I started to see the light at the end of my tunnel.

Let's take a moment to imagine God's voice for each one of us as we listen for the love songs He sings over us. *What do you hear?*

Zephaniah 3:17

'... he will rejoice over you with singing.' (v.17)

For prayer and reflection

Thank You, Father, that your song of love is written on my heart for eternity.

Worship ... **taming the tongue**

James 3:9–10

'With the tongue we praise our Lord and Father ...' (v.9)

Yes, we do – praise our Lord! But ... read on in verse 9: '... and with it we curse men, who have been made in God's likeness.' I was suddenly horribly aware, when I read these verses 9–10, how easy it is, when gathered in congregational worship, to end up cursing man, rather than praising God. If you don't know what I'm talking about, then I truly praise God for you. You are a rare treasure in His kingdom.

As we open our mouths in worship, our tongues enable us to declare aloud great truths and to express deep emotions of love and gratitude to our awesome God. Equally, we recite creeds and utter our deepest confession. But, what may our tongues be saying as we leave our worship services? 'I didn't think much of the worship today, did you?' 'That sermon was so boring.' 'Weren't the prayers long?'... what have we just done?

We have possibly cursed those who, with honest hearts and good intentions, have sought to bring us into the throne room of our Father in worship. We have heaped curses and condemnation upon the speaker, trying his or her best to train and teach us in the ways of God. The tongue has 'done it again'!

Who do we think we are? Is what we are saying really coming from the overflow of our hearts? How have we blessed God by what has come out of our mouths? What offering have we brought Him today?

Perhaps it would be a good time to bring to mind anything of this nature we have said that makes us feel ashamed of ourselves ... *God knows.*

'My [sisters], this should not be' (v.10). If we confess our sins, God is faithful and just and will forgive us our sins.

For prayer and reflection

'Take my tongue and let it be, pure and beautiful for Thee' and for (insert the name of anyone we may have 'cursed') ... and let me remember this before I speak in future.

Worship ... **in nature**

My mother-in-law lives on a farm. Each morning she opens her curtains and looks out upon a magnificent spruce tree. It forks in the middle and its two main branches seem to her like arms raised as an offering of worship.

One day, she realised that the 'arms' of her tree were drooping. Investigating further, she discovered that her beloved tree was being choked by ivy. My father-in-law's saw soon released the tree to 'praise' again.

How many times have we found ourselves choking and unable to freely praise our wonderful God? We can all too easily find ourselves bound and bowed down, not in awe and wonder, but by the pressures of life, finances, fear, family, frustration ...

How do we get ourselves untangled from the 'ivy' in our lives in order to find such freedom in worship? Maybe this freedom is something we have always longed for, but have never known how to express.

Let's take heart, sit down, tune in and simply 'be'. Instead of striving and struggling, let's endeavour to rest as we invite Jesus to come and sit with us for a while. In the stillness, we open our hands to receive Him. Lift *your* arms high and bless Him in return. We don't need to speak. Just: 'Be still, and know that I am God' (Psa. 46:10).

Allow the Holy Spirit to bring to mind the things that make you feel choked when you try to worship. In your heart, and perhaps in words, release them into God's safe keeping. Let them go, let yourself go ... into His arms of love.

Like the tree, His arms are strong and secure, inviting us to rest with Him; a place of deep serenity. They are there for you now: '... my peace I give you' (John 14:27).

Psalm 96:10–13

'Then all the trees of the forest will sing for joy ...' (v.12)

For prayer and reflection

I bless You, Father, for Your everlasting arms. Receive my heart of worship. 'You lift me up, when I fall down.' Amen.

Worship ... **the Creator God**

Genesis 1:11–13

'Then God said, "Let the land produce vegetation: seed-bearing plants and trees …"' (v.11)

As I looked out of my bedroom window this morning, I was overwhelmed by the vision of beauty before my eyes: bounteous hues and glistening tones, from subtlest greens through flame reds to deepest purples. An artist's palette could never be wide enough to paint this scene. A photographer with the greatest expertise could never capture such a view. Only God, the Creator of all things in heaven and on earth, could produce every aspect of gorgeousness set out before me.

Why is God *so* extravagantly generous in creation? Because He is! It must have given Him such joy to make all that *was* made, knowing what pleasure He would bring to His 'very good' creation of man and woman. He also gave us *every* seed-bearing plant on the face of the whole earth and *every* tree that has fruit with seed in it, for our food (Gen. 1:29). Wouldn't it be amazing to walk with God in the Garden of Eden, chatting about the plants and flowers, discovering how He designed them to grow and the best way to look after them? What worship there would be!

Being in a garden always brings me pleasure. I marvel at the tiniest shoot that between spring and summer becomes a blossoming shrub of intricate beauty. Or seeing an oak tree, stark and bare in winter, burgeoning to abundant life again in the spring. God then seems to be extraordinarily ordered and precise, but He always allows creation its freedom, as everything bursts forth into glorious life in its season.

Take a moment today to use the creativity God has placed in *you* to offer Him your worship: by writing a poem, drawing or painting something He created for your pleasure; or by just recalling a beautiful walk where you felt His presence.

For prayer and reflection

Please open my eyes today, Lord, to appreciate *all* You have created for me. Amen.

Worship ... the King

Looking out of my bedroom window before writing these notes on *this* morning, I couldn't believe my eyes. The overwhelming vision of beauty from yesterday had been exceeded today! Overnight, God had clothed the grass in a garment of purest white snow and capped the trees with headdresses fit for a bride. The sun made everything glitter and sparkle under the clear blue sky. Suddenly, it felt like Christmas was just around the corner and I was transported, in my mind, back to the time when the Magi came to worship Jesus.

The wise men had travelled a very great distance, possibly thousands of miles, to find the Messiah who was to save all mankind. God provided the guiding light of a star to bring them unerringly to Bethlehem, as prophesied in Micah 5:2, hundreds of years before Jesus was born. Jesus would have been a very young child when they visited Him. The moment they saw Him, however, they knew without doubt that He was the One they had been looking for. Their instinctive response was to bow down and worship. They also brought with them expensive gifts, fit for a King.

This is true worship: recognising and honouring Christ for who He is, giving Him our lives and following His example of how to live and love.

It may be that you haven't yet met the Son of God, whom the Father sent to save you. It is so simple to find Him. Get to know Jesus by reading about Him in the Gospels of Matthew, Mark, Luke and John. Ask Him into your life today, say sorry for the things you know you have done wrong in the past, and receive the most valuable gift of all time ... total forgiveness, freedom and eternal life.

Matthew 2:1–12

'On coming to the house, they saw the child ... and they bowed down and worshipped him.' (v.11)

For prayer and reflection

Lord Jesus, I admit that I'm a sinner and I confess my sins to You. I believe You died on the cross to take away my sins. I come to You now and welcome You into my life.

WEEKEND

'Show Me'

For reflection:
Spend a moment remembering when you gave your life to Jesus.

You may have had the privilege of being born and brought up in a loving Christian home. Many, like me, did not. Having suffered a nervous breakdown in my early thirties, I gave my life to Jesus, after reading *You Must Be Joking* by Michael Green.

Christ showed me what true love is when He humbled Himself for *me* by dying on the cross for *me*, taking upon Himself *my* sin, *all my sin* … gone, finished. He was humbled. He died. He took all our sin. How could I not love Him?

Show me the one without Jesus,
And I looked in the mirror to see,
The one with the saddest reflection,
The one in the mirror was ME.
Show me the One who is Jesus,
Who died and was raised and is real,
The man full of love and compassion,
The King with the power to heal …

'Show Me' (3rd verse) © Gill Beard 1993

Optional further reading
Luke 7:1–10; Luke 15:11—32

Worship ... **Jesus**

This story in the Gospel of Luke gives us an intimate picture of a woman worshipping Jesus. She was well known by the townsfolk as a 'bad' woman, possibly a prostitute. However, she knew in her heart that Jesus was in very essence God and, with fear and trembling, she entered a house where she was not welcome and worshipped her Lord with utter abandon.

Setting aside her fear of man, the woman washed Jesus' feet with her tears and dried them with her hair. This would have horrified Simon the Pharisee, but she was oblivious to him because she was motivated solely by her love for Jesus and her deep gratitude for receiving forgiveness for her sins.

In stark contrast, Simon showed no reverence or respect for such a prominent guest. Even acts of common courtesy were absent. His thoughts were judgmental and his attitude begrudging and self-serving.

Which are we? Extravagant and abandoned in our worship? Do we offer our whole selves to the King of kings and the Lord of lords, careless of man's niceties and traditions? Or are we miserly in our expressions of love and worship, looking around to see what others are doing and thinking? Luke 12:48 reminds us: 'From everyone who has been given much, much will be demanded ...' What has Jesus given you?

Jesus saved me from the pit of despair and brought me into His kingdom because He loves me more than words can express. He loves you just as much. This sinful woman knew that love too. Jesus is worth everything I can offer Him through my feeble acts of worship. This life is simply a rehearsal for the glorious worship we will experience when we meet Him in heaven!

Luke 7:36–50

'... she wet my feet with her tears and wiped them with her hair.' (v.44)

For prayer and reflection

Let's start practising now. Taking a simple phrase, such as, 'I adore You, Jesus', or even just the word, 'Jesus', open your mouth and sing ... No one is looking – let yourself go.

Worship ... **a lifestyle**

**Hebrews 13:15;
Psalm 34:1**

'I will extol the
LORD at all
times ...'
(Psa. 34:1)

Worship is an act of will. We can choose whether or not we worship. However we are feeling, God is still worth our worship. Indeed, the whole of our lives can become an act of worship.

God sees what goes on inside us. If we are using our mouths to say or sing words of worship, but are inwardly disconnected, complaining or pretending, then that is what God will receive from us. Daunting? Read on. Hebrews 13:15 says: 'Through Jesus, therefore, let us continually offer to God a sacrifice of praise – the fruit of lips that confess his name.' 'Hang on a minute,' some might say, 'surely worship is something that happens in church on Sundays?' Oh no! We can make every moment an act of worship.

Shall we start as we mean to go on? On waking, take time to listen to the sounds around you. Hear those birds? God made every one of them. Can you hear the wind? A reminder of God's breath breathed into Adam to give life to you and me. Now, look at your body – go on, it really is rather wonderful. It may be imperfect in your eyes, but you and I are the pinnacle of God's creation, each of us unique, beautiful and filled with God Himself by His Spirit. Maybe you can smell toast and coffee being prepared downstairs. How blessed are you! So, as we rise, let's thank God for all these things, and so many more, at the start of our day.

I wonder how many of us pick up the post before we pick up the Bible. Is the junk mail more important than the living Word of God? The more we read about God and come into relationship with Him, the more we want to honour Him in worship.

For prayer and reflection

Heavenly Father, I delight today to worship You with every part of my being, because I am fearfully and wonderfully made. Thank You for designing me to live in close relationship with You. Amen.

Worship ... **is relationship**

Do you belong to a home group, cell group or a prayer triplet? Are you perhaps a 'Robinson Crusoe' Christian, preferring to be on your own? If the latter, you may be excluding yourself from your place in the body of Christ.

In our reading in Matthew Jesus tells us that *He* is with us *whenever two or three are gathered together* ... What an amazing truth! What huge impact it has! *Whenever* we come together with another Christian, Jesus is also there.

'How?' we ask. He is with us through the Holy Spirit indwelling us. So, if two or three people agree about anything that falls within God's purpose, they have more power in their agreement than thousands who do not have such a majestic companion.

Jesus adores being in this close relationship with us. Do we ache to be in such depth of relationship with Him? How can we get closer to this 'eternal triangle'?

Get to know Him in the same way you would anyone whom you truly love. Spend time with Him, listen to Him, sing love songs for Him and receive the songs He sends you. Read about His life in the Gospels. He's infinitely more interesting to read about than any passing celebrity of the moment! Talk about Him, laugh with Him as you share your joys, and cry with Him when you are in despair. Build your relationship daily. Why? Because He is the lover of your soul, the partner who'll never let you down and the brother who gave up His life to save yours.

The more you get to know Jesus, the more you'll want to become like Him. Becoming like Him gives us the capacity to love the *un*lovely. John 17 tells us how Jesus wants us to be. Such unity and love is beyond comparison; perfect and complete.

Matthew 18:20; John 17:20–26

'For where two or three come together in my name …' (Matt. 18:20)

For prayer and reflection

Jesus, I love You. I want to know You more.

Worship ... a delight?

'I delight greatly in the LORD; my soul rejoices in my God.' (Isa. 61:10)

So many verses in the Bible, especially in the Psalms, speak of rejoicing, boasting, praising, singing, giving thanks to God. In James 5:13 we read: 'Is anyone happy? Let him sing songs of praise.' In Ephesians 5:19 Paul writes, 'Speak to one another with psalms, hymns and spiritual songs. Sing and make music in your heart to the Lord ...' In Philippians 4:4, he says: 'Rejoice in the Lord always. I will say it again: Rejoice!' OK, Paul – we get the point!

Does this sound like you on a daily basis? No? Me neither. I would *love* it to be, but I freely admit that 'life' gets in the way. Or does it? Perhaps I should say that I allow life to get in the way. If I awake and start thanking God, I am more likely to make space for worship, study and prayer. If I rush into the day, I never recover that lost moment of joy. Fifteen minutes more sleep never compensates for being with my Father.

In the Anglican Communion liturgy we say: 'It is our duty and our joy at all times and in all places to give thanks and praise, Holy Father, heavenly King ...' The word 'duty' sounds heavy and difficult, but if it is accompanied by joy, it *can* become delightful. Even if we aren't happy, let us choose to worship today.

For prayer and reflection

Oh Daddy, we are so silly letting life get in the way, when You gave us our life. You gave us Jesus, You filled us full of joy, and always will, as we worship You each day.

Start with reading a psalm of praise out loud (eg Pss. 113,117,134,145,148). No, even *louder* than that. Why not shout and declare Psalm 150? Wow! Now I want to rejoice some more – do you?

All heaven holds its breath to see what we will do next. Put on a praise CD and sing along as you wash up last night's dishes or hoover the cat! You get the picture. How is your soul doing? Has your duty become more joyful? Let's praise God!

Worship ... **producing fruit**

Keats's poem, 'To Autumn' perfectly describes the scene from my window on some mornings! It speaks of a 'Season of mists and mellow fruitfulness', which I often see before my eyes. The thick mist of the morning seems to enclose me in a shroud, reminding me that we died with Christ and our lives are now hidden in Him (Col. 3:3). My thoughts return to that empty tomb where Jesus was released from the grip of death by His loving Father, setting you and me free to live with them for ever.

A life surrendered to Jesus longs to grow and become like Jesus. What better way to express our love for Him than by surrendering all that corrupts our lives? All those hidden sins like gossip, anger, lust, envy, greed, covetousness, pride, jealousy ... need I go on?

That season is now gone from our lives. God's Holy Spirit shines His light into all those dark, hidden places and, burning away the mist, reveals, with perfect clarity, the life of Jesus growing within us.

The good qualities we read about in Galatians 5:22 aren't automatic when we come to faith. We may be kind and gentle by nature, but lacking in self-control. (Why am I now thinking about chocolate?)

In my life, nearly 30 years of being a Christian have been punctuated by moments of revelation when God has been pruning and feeding me, enabling me to grow. Being disciplined may feel uncomfortable at the time, but the love with which God's discipline is ministered has always led to spiritual growth, often accompanied by physical health too.

Even when we fall far short of Jesus' perfect example, it is never too late to turn back to God and ask for His help as we try again.

Galatians 5:16–25

'But the fruit of the Spirit is love, joy ...' (v.22)

For prayer and reflection

Lord God, I thank You for the fruitfulness You *have* produced in my life. Holy Spirit, I long for even more. Keep me close, as You nourish me with Your Word and shower me with Your love.

WEEKEND

Fruit of the Spirit

For reflection:
Let's read again Galatians 5:22–23. How can we better grow in the fruit of the Spirit? Perhaps you could memorise these words and ask the God of the impossible to water them in your heart.

Lord, I want to be like You in everything,
Lord, I want to worship You in every song that I sing,
Father, I need to be, Spirit, help me to be,
Jesus, I long to be more like You.

Fill me with *joy* when my spirit touches Yours, Lord.
Clothe me in *peace* when my heart beats close to Yours.
Let me be *kind* to the ones who've hurt us both, Lord.
Help me to wait for *Your timing*, not my own.

Chorus: *But teach me how to love, to love like You.*

Show me by grace how Your *goodness* makes me holy,
Give me a *faith* that won't deny You even once.
Soften my touch; make me *gentle* in Your strength, Lord.
Firm my resolve to *restrain* my human desires. (Chorus)

'Fruit of the Spirit' © Gill Beard 1996

Optional further reading
James 3:17–18; John 15:1–17

Worship ... **but I can't sing!**

love to sing in worship ... always have, always will. From the age of eight I have sung with a voice, so I'm told, that stands out from the crowd. Have you ever been in church, standing in front of someone singing their own harmonies that blend seamlessly into the overall sound, making you want to weep because it is *so* beautiful?

Are you disappointed when your vocal cords don't live up to your expectations? Don't be! What *really* matters to God, when you open your mouth to worship Him, is whether or not it comes from a heart of love. Also, God gave us our voices, and every other wonderful part of our bodies, for His glory not ours. We are simply grateful recipients.

Did you know that God's heart aches if we don't sing to Him? It's like an orchestra minus a flute or a piano without middle C. You are an important part of the heavenly choir. He needs to hear *you* to complete the harmony. When we sing to God with our whole heart, He listens to each tender whisper of love and receives the depth of passion we daren't express vocally. We are here to bless Almighty God, not the other way round.

Have you ever said, 'I'm tone deaf'? There is no such thing as far as God is concerned. Open your heart up to Him and He will receive your symphony. He can hear the concerto inside, where you are the soloist with an audience of One.

Today, let's banish negative thoughts that say: 'I can't sing.' Who are we trying to impress? Instead, let our hearts pour out to God the sweetest love song ever written. Maybe, as in the words of the well-known carol, we can say: 'What can I give Him, poor as I am? ... Give my *heart*.'

Psalm 9:1–2; Psalm 30:11–12

'... that my heart may sing to you and not be silent.' (Psa. 30:12)

For prayer and reflection

Beloved Lord God, I thank You that You don't need me to 'perform' for You. Please accept my widow's mite and turn it into purest gold for Your pleasure and glory. Amen.

Worship ... **through psalms**

'The LORD will
keep you from all
harm – he will
watch over your
life ...' (Psa. 121:7)

How many psalms do you know from memory? Most of us will probably think of Psalm 23, as it is the most often quoted. Reading and memorising psalms is, in itself, an act of worship. The breadth and depth of the Psalms cover so many aspects of our daily walk with God. They speak of God's generosity and goodness. They remind us of our daily need to repent and seek forgiveness, Psalm 51 being a well-known example. The Psalms comfort us when we are troubled or distressed; strengthen and help us to grow in confidence, faith and trust. We can be free to be who we really are, warts and all! We have no need to hide from a God who hears our cries – whether of despair or ecstasy.

We can use praise psalms as examples for us to follow as we rejoice in all that God has done for us. We can certainly identify with King David when he shouts in anger and frustration, but he always comes back to a place of confidence in his God. God respects our honesty when we genuinely communicate our need for Him – in the bad times as well as the good.

This wonderful book is a collection of songs and prayers in a unique expression of worship. They express words of honest relationship with our Father God; He *loves* to hear from us too in this way. We also bring Him blessing when we pour out amazingly joyful praise! (See Psa. 145–150.) Which is your favourite psalm? Mine is Psalm 121 – and I mustn't forget Psalm 92 also. Mind you, I couldn't do without Psalms 51,133,131 and ...!

Choose one psalm, if you can, and memorise it. Through it worship the God who cares for you *so* deeply that He wants to be with you every moment of your life ... *every* moment.

....
**For prayer and
reflection**
....

**Lord, I long to
know You more
deeply each day,
and to love You
as You love me.
Amen.**

Worship ... **not today**

Psalm 38

'I am bowed down and brought very low; all day long I go about mourning.' (v.6)

Do you ever have days when you feel that you just can't worship? Oh no! I forgot, we're Christians! Does that prevent bad days, moods or situations that, like David in this psalm, bring us to the depths of misery? I think not.

David is aware of his sinfulness and cries out for God not to punish him whilst He is angry. He is suffering spiritually, mentally and physically, separated from God because of his actions. He is depressed.

I have suffered on and off from depression, triggered by undiagnosed postnatal depression 32 years ago. Recently, I decided to try and come off my pills, having felt well for years. It took six months to come off the antidepressants and six months before I needed to go back on them, triggered by two very painful nerve conditions. I tried *so* hard to stay off the pills. Secretly, I felt ashamed that, having been a Christian for years, I couldn't cope without medical intervention.

Having been a worship leader for 25 years you would have thought that I could have praised God. I just couldn't, try as I might. I read the Psalms out loud and called and called on God for healing. I listened to worship CDs, becoming more and more miserable as I couldn't join in. I examined my heart, soul and spirit before God for every possible sin, stronghold or area of attack from the enemy, wearing myself out in the process.

It seemed like I couldn't worship anymore.

Now that the chemical imbalance in my brain has been rectified, I can see that in reality, like David, I was calling out to my 'Abba' (Daddy). Nothing *seemed* to change my situation, but I wanted Daddy to hold me and make it better. No one else would do! Perhaps that *was* worship?

For prayer and reflection

Abba, I know that as I cry out to You, You receive the worship of a broken heart, mind or spirit. I love You because You first loved me. Amen.

Worship … **love in action**

....

1 John 4:7–21

....

'And [God]
has given us
this command:
Whoever loves
God must also love
his brother.' (v.21)

God *is* love. This is the very nature of God. His greatest act of love was sending Jesus into the world who, through His sacrifice on the cross, gained for us forgiveness of sin and life with God forever. What is His command to us? To love one another that much too. When we show love to our family, friends and neighbours, it becomes an act of worship as we reflect our Father's love. This too may involve sacrifice from us.

I am privileged to co-lead a venture at my church called Prayer Café. For two hours every month we invite perfect strangers in for refreshment of every kind. Those suffering physically, mentally or spiritually are offered healing prayer. The lonely and needy find a listening ear, comfort and support. Those seeking after truth are introduced to their Saviour.

Worshipping in this way is an awesome experience of the almighty love of the Father flowing into us and then out to our neighbours. As we trust God to provide each month, His love always exceeds our expectations.

It is humbling as we see unity growing among the team members and their willingness to serve in any way needed. It's exciting to know that, each month, up to 80 people have been brought to the Lord in prayer. This is a small example of love in action.

God is love and He lives in us. *We* are love, because He is in each of us. God loves every human being on this earth and wants them to know that they're loved. *We* are His hands, His feet and, most of all, His heart. What an honour to represent Jesus here on earth today! 'Dear friends, let us love one another …' (v.7).

We all have a part to play. Why not ask God how He wants you or your church to worship Him in *your* community.

....

**For prayer and
reflection**

....

**Father of love,
please show me
today what I can
do to worship
You in the wider
community in
which You have
put me. Amen.**

Worship ... **a glimpse of heaven**

Worship will be absolutely central to our role in heaven. This becomes clearer as we look at this chapter in the last (and often most difficult to understand) book of the Bible. Can we even begin to visualise the scene?

John has been invited into heaven by Jesus, whose voice sounds like the high-pitched sound of a trumpet. He then sees an awesome figure, seated on a throne, who is almost impossible to describe in human language. The throne is surrounded by 24 elders wearing crowns of gold, dressed in white. Stop and imagine how you might *feel* at this point. *I* feel as if I have stopped breathing and am shivering all over, partly with excitement but mostly in awe.

Some commentators believe that the 24 elders represent the 12 tribes of Israel, God's very own people. The other 12 represent the 12 apostles, Jesus' very own friends. Together they seem to represent all those whom Jesus came to redeem.

We are in the throne room of God Himself. What is everyone doing? The only possible activity that is appropriate ... worshipping, in words that are peculiarly familiar to us. These words seem so natural here, so obvious, so ... *right*. Now, *we* are singing with God's highest order of angels and yet, somehow, there is a harmony that the finest composer could never have written. Love, so deep, enfolds us in its ocean of joy. Freedom, never experienced like this before, breaks out in heart-bursting adoration.

In this temple, in heaven, we too will have crowns to lay down, reverently offering homage to the Lord God Almighty, the King in His kingdom, before shouting aloud glory and honour and power to *the Creator* of all things.

Revelation 4:1–11

'... the twenty-four elders fall down before him ... and worship ...' (v.10)

For prayer and reflection

Take some time today to try and imagine the scene described. Now shut your eyes and see if you can picture yourself worshipping there. Glory to God in the highest!

WEEKEND

I wonder ... thoughts of heaven

For reflection:
Read John 14:1–6. Do you find the idea of going to heaven scary or exciting?

No one wants to face dying, but I wonder what joy awaits us there? Why not allow yourself to wonder too? Do you ever wonder what it might be like in heaven? These were my thoughts as a young Christian 24 years ago. They haven't changed!

Sometimes as I sit alone, I wonder ... what will I see,
How will He be in heaven?
Sometimes as I sit alone, I wonder, that Jesus loves me.
Yes, Lord, oh yes, Lord, I want to see Your face,
To look into those loving eyes, and to know such grace.

Sometimes as I walk along, I wonder ... what will I see,
How will it be in heaven?
Sometimes as I walk along, I wonder, that He died for me.
You, Lord, my true Lord, I want to feel Your hands,
To touch and see those sacred scars, and to understand,
Just understand.

'I Wonder ... Thoughts of Heaven' © Gill Beard 1985

Optional further reading
Selwyn Hughes, *Heaven Bound* (Farnham: CWR, 2003)
Christina Baxter, *The Wounds of Jesus* (Grand Rapids: Zondervan, 2005)

The wonder of the Word

Helena Wilkinson

Helena Wilkinson trained in counselling at CWR and subsequently joined the staff as a tutor, counsellor and editor of *The Christian Counsellor*. She is the author of nine books including the bestseller *Puppet on a String*, her personal account of overcoming anorexia. Helena is now based at the Swansea City Mission's retreat centre, Nicholaston House, on the Gower Peninsula where she runs courses. For further information visit www.helenawilkinson.co.uk

Lamp to my feet

Psalm 119:
105–120

'Your word is a
lamp to my feet
and a light for my
path.' (v.105)

We live in an age where reading has been largely replaced by what appear to be more tantalising means of communication: multichannel TVs, portable DVDs, iPods, the Internet, Twitter, Facebook and Skype, to name but a few of the attractions. I certainly read far less now than I did 15 years ago. How about you? For most of us life is lived in the fast lane and 'busyness' is an enemy of not only reading for pleasure, but also reading the Bible. Finding that we have less time to read the Bible is one means by which our faith and our sense of authority in Christ is weakened. We can easily forget that actually we require God's Word for spiritual nourishment and strength. Reading it needs to be a discipline we exercise as well as a desire at work within us.

I recall when I gave my life to Jesus as a teenager, 25 years ago, how I was 'magnetically' drawn to the Bible. I just wanted to open its pages all the time and, on each occasion I did, what I read seemed incredibly relevant to me. As a new Christian the Word was, as the psalmist states, 'a lamp to my feet' as I endeavoured to walk in new ways, and 'a light for my path' as I sought guidance and direction for my life. I have always loved the Bible and I never tire of delving deeper into it in an attempt to understand a little of the original language and context in which it was written. However, there was something electrically exciting in those early days when I used to open its pages and feel the words were written just for me!

The way I see it, *the Bible is God's gift to us*. Let's spend time with His gift and enjoy what He has given us.

For prayer and reflection

Father, please place in me a deep longing for Your Word that nothing else can satisfy. I am so sorry that I have allowed it to have less priority in my life than it deserves. Amen.

More than words

The word 'Bible' comes from the Greek word *biblios* which means 'roll' or 'book'. It is divided, as we all know, into the Old Testament and the New Testament; the word *testament* meaning *covenant*. The *whole* Bible records the Old and the New Covenant. The Old Testament is the foundation for the New Testament as it sets the scene for man's need for a Saviour and foretells the coming of the Messiah. Hence, we can only fully appreciate the New in the light of the Old.

The original text would have been written on a 'roll' or 'scroll'. We see an example of this where Jesus is teaching in the synagogue. 'The scroll of the prophet Isaiah was handed to him. Unrolling it, he found the place where it is written: "The Spirit of the Lord is on me, because he has anointed me ..."' (Luke 4:17–18). Jesus is reading a prophecy about Himself written by a prophet who lived some 700 years before Him. Awesome! Not only does the Bible contain incredible accounts of history and the fulfilment of many prophecies but: '... the word of God is living and active. Sharper than any double-edged sword, it penetrates even to dividing soul and spirit, joints and marrow; it judges the thoughts and attitudes of the heart' (Heb. 4:12). It is not merely words on a page – but brings life to us spiritually and emotionally. In its original language and context the word 'living' means 'being alive' and 'causing to live'.

So, God's Word, written by the people He chose, *brings* life to us and also *sustains* that life. As you read the Bible, whichever version you prefer, do you expect it to speak to you and change your life?

Hebrews 4:12–5:10

'For the word of God is living and active.' (v.12)

For prayer and reflection

Have you ever considered that our spirit without the Word of God is like our lungs without fresh air?

What do *you* believe?

....

2 Timothy 3:1–17

....

'All Scripture is
God-breathed ...'
(v.16)

....

....

**Lord God, open
my eyes to see
the incredible
detail in Scripture
which reveals that
every word was
breathed by You.
Help me to share
these revelations
with others.
Amen.**

Do you ever ask yourself questions like: 'Is the Bible really accurate, really from God?' It's good to ask difficult questions and seek out answers rather than just believe what we are told. Jesus encouraged people to think for themselves, 'Who do *you* say I am?' (Luke 9:20, italics mine). When I first began to read the Bible I didn't think too deeply about how the knowledge was gained, but as I have grown in my relationship with God I have often stopped in the middle of a reading and asked myself, 'How could the writer possibly have known that God had been the One to reveal it to him?' To me, the Bible is an amazing book, like *no other* book, and I have to say that *I do* believe that its writers (although fallible men) were inspired by God and that it is God's way of revealing His nature, plans and purposes. How about you, what do *you* believe and why?

There are lots of reasons why I believe it is the inspired Word of God. For starters, so many of the different writers, most of whom didn't know each other, *claim divine inspiration*, and I guess they can't all be wrong! The apostle Paul sums it up this way: 'All Scripture is God-breathed ...' (2 Tim. 3:16).

Other reasons are that there are so many biblical prophecies which have apparently been fulfilled; and archaeological confirmations of biblical accounts have been recorded outside the Bible. Take, for instance, a number of Babylonian documents* which describe the same worldwide flood as written about in Genesis 6–9.

When the enemy sows seeds of doubt about aspects of the Bible, can you hold on to the fact that other historical documents verify the truth of God's Word?

*eg *The Antediluvian Patriarchs and the Sumerian King List* by Raul Lopez (*CEN Technical Journal 12* (3) 1998).

Wonder of the Word

t's so easy to take the Bible for granted. Most of us have more than one copy and aren't restricted as to when, where and how much we read it. Yet it's incredible we have the Bible at all. After all, how many other books in our homes were written over 2,000 years ago, with around 1,500 years between the writing of the first and last chapters?

Consider too that there were 40 plus authors from all walks of life: kings, peasants, philosophers, fishermen, poets and scholars, using three different languages: Hebrew, Aramaic and Greek. The places in which it was written varied enormously too: in the wilderness, a dungeon, a palace, a prison, as well as whilst in exile and during a military campaign. Finally, add to this the complexity of its content which covers hundreds of controversial subjects. Despite all this, there is harmony and continuity, with one major theme from beginning to end: God's relationship with and deliverance of man.

There have been numerous attempts to destroy God's Word, only highlighting its significance. The Roman emperor, Diocletian, conducted the empire's largest and bloodiest attempt to systematically destroy the Scriptures and persecute Christians from AD 303–311. Yet after AD 324, Christianity became the preferred religion under the empire's first Christian emperor, Constantine. In 1776 the French philosopher, Voltaire (1694–1778) is said to have declared: 'One hundred years from my day there will not be a Bible in the earth except one that is looked upon by an antiquarian curiosity seeker.' Ironically, 233 years later, we are still reflecting on those comments in the light of the 'Living Word'.

1 Peter 1:23–2:10

'... but the word of the Lord stands for ever.' (v.25)

For prayer and reflection

Father, You have the victory! Your Word is the most widely read, most influential and best-selling book ever written. It changes lives. Amen.

The **Word** became flesh

....

John 1:1–18

....

'In the beginning
was the Word,
and the Word was
with God, and the
Word was God.'
(v.1)

think what is so incredible about the Bible is that it isn't merely a book of words on paper. The Bible actually talks about two types of 'word'. The Greek language, in which part of the Bible was written, uses both *logos* and *rhema* for 'word' which gives far greater insight into the nature of the Bible than the English language does.

Logos essentially refers to the *written* Word, which tells us what God says about Himself, His relationship with His creation and His Church. It is interpreted both as the Bible (God's written Word) and in the Person of Jesus (God's Word in the flesh, as in our verse today).

Rhema means 'an utterance'; a personally spoken word of revelation, prophecy or knowledge, from God to us. It can be a passage of Scripture that 'speaks to' or 'leaps out at' us.

The work of the Holy Spirit brings alive the truths of Scripture and changes our lives as a result of our reading the Bible; the words on a page (*logos*) become *rhema*, bringing us supernatural comfort, reassurance, guidance and direction. Is it not true that the same Spirit who inspired the Old and New Testament writers is still with us today?

For prayer and reflection

Thank You, Father, for sending Your Holy Spirit who speaks Your very words of comfort and direction to me. Amen.

The *logos* and *rhema* Word together make the Bible stand out from any other book, because we have operating in our lives the *written* and the *active* Word of God. The Holy Spirit enlightens us when reading Scripture, imparting wisdom, knowledge and understanding to impact our lives. Jesus put it another way: 'It is written: "Man does not live on bread alone, but on every word [*rhema*] that comes from the mouth of God"' (Matt. 4:4). 'The words [*rhema*] I have spoken to you are spirit and they are life' (John 6:63).

WEEKEND

The wonder of the Word

For reflection: Psalm 119:97–104

Reading the Bible has consequences! We are going to look at some of those consequences, along with the uniqueness of the Bible and its relevance to us. We'll reflect on verses from Psalm 119 which reveal the difference the Bible makes to our lives, and we'll weave our way around the Bible looking at God's incredible revelations about Himself and His covenants with mankind.

One outcome of reading the Bible which the psalmist highlights for us in Psalm 119 is that it *makes us wise*. The psalmist speaks of how God's words and precepts* give birth to wisdom, insight and understanding; making him far wiser than his enemies. Many say wisdom comes with age but, in reality, it is more to do with where we invest our time and energy. James reminds us that if we lack wisdom we should ask God, who gives generously (James 1:5).

Would it be helpful for you to invest time this weekend asking God for wisdom concerning anything?

Optional further reading
Matthew 7:24–25; Joshua 1:8; John 1:18.

*A precept is a decree which directs a specific individual or group to do (or not to do) something, especially to urge observance of the law, eg 'You have laid down precepts that are to be fully obeyed. Oh, that my ways were steadfast in obeying your decrees!' (Psa. 119:4–5).

God reveals **Himself**

1 John 4:7–21

'We love because he first loved us.' (v.19)

Have you ever been apart from someone you really love? The person is on your mind all the time and when they make contact you find yourself hanging on their every word. As you absorb what they have written you feel close; what they say and how they say it tells you something of their character and what is important to them; you long for the next 'instalment'. It is not dissimilar in our relationship with God. He loves us with an everlasting love but we are separated from Him – we cannot see Him face-to-face. 'No-one has seen the Father except the one who is from God ...' (John 6:46) so the Bible is God's communication to us. It is God's love letter through which He reveals Himself.

I find that the more I read my Bible the more I get to know God, but also the more my love for Him grows. It works the other way too; the more I love God and express my love for Him, the more I desire to read His Word. If you ever feel 'dry' in your relationship with God, try asking Him to show you how much He loves you and how to increase your own passion for Him. He delights to reveal Himself to us and He won't disappoint you, but you must seek Him with *all* your heart.

When we spend time basking in God's love and really embracing the truth that He loves us, not only do we find peace but we are changed in our reactions to other people. John reminds us that 'perfect love drives out fear' (1 John 4:18) – we can know security through the love of God. John also reminds us that 'Whoever loves God must also love his brother' (1 John 4:21) – when we allow ourselves to be enveloped in the love of God, our love for others is enriched.

For prayer and reflection

Father, thank You that You love me with an everlasting love. As I understand more fully the extent to which You love me, I pray that my love for You will increase beyond measure. Amen.

Revelation means what?

The whole of the Bible is a 'revelation'; God revealing Himself and His plan to us. The word 'revelation' comes from the Greek word meaning 'the unveiling'. I like that concept, don't you? When you think of the bride in the marriage service whose face is covered and whose veil is gradually lifted to reveal her full beauty there is an air of anticipation and excitement. The same is true of the Scriptures which bring with them an unveiling of the Almighty God, Creator of heaven and earth. Had God not chosen to unveil Himself in this way, we would know so little about Him. The fact that He *has* unveiled aspects of Himself in the written Word creates in me a desire to go on seeking Him and to find out even more about Him.

God unveiling Himself through His Word also answers so many questions that nearly every person asks at some stage in life: 'How did mankind come into being? What is the point of our existence? How should we live? Will the world go on forever? Is there life after death? Does it matter how we act on earth?'

What would our lives be like if we didn't have the Bible in which to find out more about God and His love for us? I think I would find that hard. I want to get to know the God with whom I'm going to spend eternity, don't you? How do you think your identity, worth, value, security and sense of hope would be affected if there were very limited revelation? I think I would feel insecure and would question my value; I know my motivation and sense of destiny would be lessened too.

What aspect of God's character would you like Him most to reveal to you?

Isaiah 40:1–8, 18–31

'And the glory of the LORD will be revealed …' (v.5)

For prayer and reflection

Father, thank You that You have chosen to reveal Your very nature through Your Word. I ask that this week You will open my eyes to see more of what You are like and Your love for me.

It's truly **inspired**

2 Peter 1:12–21

'We did not follow cleverly invented stories when we told you about the power and coming of our Lord Jesus Christ …' (v.16)

Do you ever doubt that the Bible is God's Word and not man's ideas? I love the fact that when Thomas doubted the resurrection Jesus didn't scold him, but lovingly held out His hands and encouraged him to see for himself (John 20:24–29).

Is the Bible truly inspired? The Bible itself is clear on the matter. 'Above all, you must understand that no prophecy of Scripture came about by the prophet's own interpretation. For prophecy never had its origin in the will of man, but men spoke from God as they were carried along by the Holy Spirit' (2 Pet. 1:20–21).

Biblical prophecies are then confirmed by their fulfilment. Psalm 22, for example, prophesies the crucifixion of Jesus, detailing every aspect of Christ's suffering, yet it was written about 1,000 years before Jesus' birth. In fact a huge number of Old Testament prophecies relate to the coming of the Messiah and the statistical chances of any man fulfilling a fraction of these are slim. But Jesus fulfilled virtually all of them and those which remain are concerning the future.

Another reason why we say that the Bible is God's Word is because many Old and New Testament writers use phrases such as: 'the Lord said'. These words aren't said once or twice but, according to Arnold Fruchtenbaum,* 3,808 times in the Old Testament alone! Jesus Himself constantly made reference to the Old Testament and declared that He had come to fulfil the Law and the Prophets (Matt. 5:17; Luke 24:44).

God planned the coming of the Messiah from before the beginning of time. In the same way, He chose you before the creation of the world to be adopted as His child (Eph. 1:3–6). Quite incredible, don't you think?

For prayer and reflection

Yes, Lord, You commanded every word in the Bible and not one of Your words is without relevance and meaning to me, as Your child! Thank You. Amen.

* *The Understanding Series Vol. 1. The Word of God* (Tustin, CA: Ariel Ministries, 1983) p.35.

There's **no mistake**

All my life I've been a deep thinker, fascinated by facts. Whilst I trust the Bible and most certainly believe in its accuracy, I still feel excited when I discover new things which confirm what is written in Scripture.

I remember when I first discovered that there are ancient writings about Jesus other than in the New Testament, Flavius Josephus (AD 37–c.100) being one of the best-known writers. My reaction was 'Wow! Jesus is mentioned elsewhere!' Then I found out how accounts in the Bible have been scientifically verified* to be accurate on many points and that was awesome! Did you know, for instance, that the Bible told us that the Earth is round (Isa. 40:22) 300 years before Aristotle suggested it might be, and it was almost another 2,000 years before Columbus sailed around the world to prove it? Then there's the hydrologic water cycle which was only fully understood in about 30 BC by the Roman engineer Marcus Vitruvius; yet every aspect of the water cycle was revealed in 1600 BC and the Bible's description is in harmony with modern science (Eccl. 1:6–7; 11:3; Job 26:8; Amos 9:6).

Our text for today speaks of the Law of the Lord being perfect. The Hebrew adjective for 'perfect' refers to something that is sound and free from blemish. I think that's a pretty good description of the Bible, don't you? Yes, there are altered meanings in the translation process but the original writings are free from blemish. For this reason, I like to look at key words in their original language to consider the context and background and hence attain a fuller picture which I love to share with others.

* Lee Strobel, *The Case for a Creator* (Grand Rapids: Zondervan, 2005)

Psalm 19:7–14

'The law of the LORD is perfect, reviving the soul …' (v.7)

For prayer and reflection

Father, Your Word is truth and life to me; truly reviving my soul. I want to praise You for such a wonderful book! Amen.

There's **a plan**

Isaiah 46:1–13

'I make known
the end from the
beginning …' (v.10)

▌n Isaiah 46 and in other places in Scripture, God makes two points very clear: 1. There is *no one* to whom God can be compared (v.5); 2. God's purpose *will* stand or, in other words, *will* be accomplished (v.10).

Throughout Scripture God has a plan and purpose – or rather plans and purposes. The Bible has distinct sections (sometimes relating to time periods) and within them are overlapping and interwoven plans and purposes. Key figures are appointed by God to whom revelation is given with responsibility. We then read of the successes and failings of these key men and women, and God's response of judgment and grace.

We will focus on these different sections during next week and see how God's purposes are woven throughout the various books. The more I study God's plans and purposes in Scripture the more it inspires me to trace what He has worked in my life. It fascinates me to see how He has used my many different experiences over a long time period and woven them together to fulfil His calling in my life today.

Can you trace the ways in which God has been working in your life? It's so easy to take things for granted and miss the often subtle ways in which He leads and guides. Life may not have worked out as we had anticipated but I believe that if we turn to God and put our trust in Him, He will fulfil His plans – even if we may divert them for a while. Think of the Israelites who were told that they would enter the land 'flowing with milk and honey' which had been promised by God (Exod. 3:17). It wasn't far away – and yet their unbelief and fears resulted in them taking 40 years to reach it. But God said they would enter the land – and they did!

For prayer and reflection

Father thank You that nothing is wasted in Your economy. Sometimes I feel my life hasn't quite worked out as I'd have liked – help me to surrender it to You and watch You work.

WEEKEND

The Bible offers us comfort

For reflection: Psalm 119:73–80

Last weekend we saw how one outcome of reading God's Word is that it makes us wise. Another outcome is that it *offers us comfort*. Unlike Job's three comforters, Eliphaz, Bildad and Zophar, who endeavoured to offer Job consolation when he had lost everything but in fact made him feel worse, the psalmist speaks of how God's unfailing love brings comfort (v.76) and His compassion brings life (v.77). Even those who have no faith have been known to find comfort when picking up a Gideon Bible next to their bed in hospital or in a hotel.

In Psalm 30, David speaks of how in his despair he cried out to God for mercy. He reflects back to God: 'You turned my wailing into dancing; you removed my sackcloth and clothed me with joy …' (v.11). Unlike Job's comforters who frustrated him, David's comforter, the Lord, not only brought comfort but transformed his sorrow. As we put our trust in God and allow Him to comfort us through His Word, He will make sense of our worst moments.

Optional further reading
Philip Yancey, *The Bible Jesus Read* (Grand Rapids: Zondervan, 2002); Isaiah 40:6–8; Romans 8:3–11

Covenant-keeping God

**1 Chronicles
16:8–27**

'He remembers
his covenant for
ever …' (v.15)

The concept of a covenant between God and His people is one of the central themes of the Bible. A *covenant* is an agreement between two people, but biblically it implies much more than a contract between two potentially fickle parties; it involves promises by God who is faithful to what He says. My experience is that we, as fallible people, can easily let each other down; in contrast, God keeps His promises forever. We talked about the Old and New Testaments meaning the Old and New Covenants, but in fact the Bible has more than two covenants – there are said to be eight in total.

Even though the covenants were written many thousands of years ago (some specifically for the nation of Israel), each time I read an aspect of them, I learn something more about God and about myself too! Doesn't that just show how the Bible, which is living and active, is also outside time? I find it exciting that biblical prophecies, for instance, were given for a person or a group of people at a given moment and yet, on occasion, have been the means by which God has spoken very powerfully into my own life. This is what is meant by the term: 'Living Word'.

Of the eight covenants we are going to look at, two are conditional: 'If you do this then I will fulfil my promise …'; and six are unconditional: 'I will fulfil my promise and there is nothing *you* can do about it …' Have you ever noticed that God operates in a similar pattern in your own life: 1. God calls you to do something and blesses you in response; and 2. God speaks into your life and brings it to pass, irrespective of what happens around you or your own failings?

**For prayer and
reflection**

**Lord, it is so good
to know that You
are faithful to
Your promises.
Please help me to
be responsive to
Your words and
to honour You.
Amen.**

The Lord **is Almighty**

The first covenant is known as the 'Edenic' Covenant, between God and Adam (and his race, appearing in Gen. 1–3). It was a *conditional* covenant and was based on all points being fulfilled. God's instructions to Adam were:

1. To fill the earth with the influence and order of mankind; 2. To subdue the earth; 3. To have dominion over the animal creation; 4. To eat vegetables, herbs and fruits; 5. To tend the garden; and 6. To refrain from eating of the tree of the knowledge of good and evil, on penalty of death. Beyond these instructions Adam and Eve enjoyed complete liberty, along with the ability to commune directly with God.

However, Adam and Eve *did* reject God's rule and authority – resulting in their (and all mankind's) spiritual death. If you had been given a perfect environment in which to live, in the full knowledge of being loved, would you have done the one thing God told you not to do at the risk of dire consequences? Would curiosity have got the better of you?

We are very easily tempted. Jesus Himself was tempted, but never sinned (Matt. 4:1–11). Led by the Spirit into the desert, the devil tried all sorts of tactics to cause Him to sin but, using the Word, Jesus stood against temptation and refuted the devil's lies and innuendos. Satan still seeks to tempt and deceive us in all sorts of ways and it's good to remind ourselves that Jesus is able to help us in our weakness and time of need (Heb. 2:18; 4:14–16).

Despite Adam and Eve's rebellion (and no doubt we would have rebelled had we been in their position) God, in His mercy, sent a 'second' Adam (1 Cor. 15:45–47) through whom there would be the offer of a way back to Him. Thank You, Lord!

Genesis 1:27–30; 2:15–3:8

'… but you must not eat from the tree of the knowledge of good and evil …' (2:17)

For prayer and reflection

Father, the voice of the enemy tempting surrounds me. Help me to remember that You have *made* a way for me to withstand and that I don't need to fight this on my own. Amen.

God **of grace**

'So the LORD God said … "Because you have done this …"' (v.14)

The second covenant is known as the 'Adamic' Covenant (Gen. 3:14–19) which replaced the first covenant. It was also established between God and Adam and Eve, representing the human race. Unconditional, it is still in effect today and describes the consequences of Adam's and Eve's choice not to obey the rule and authority of God.

Spiritual death was already in operation as a result of breaking the first covenant and to it physical death was added. As well as death, the result of man's rejection of God's authority was: 1. Enmity between Satan and Eve (and her descendants); 2. Pain in childbirth; 3. Marital disunity; 4. The soil cursed (with thorns and thistles); and 5. Hard toil; a struggle to survive. Can you see how these go on affecting our everyday lives?

As you reflect upon this covenant I wonder how you view God. Do you see Him as punitive for pronouncing curses upon mankind or faithful to what He says He will do? Can you see the bigger picture of the necessity of consequences and of our dependence upon a Saviour? The consequences of man's disobedience may seem harsh but God, in His grace, makes known a plan thousands of years before it happens. In Genesis 3:15 God declares the battle against Satan. The battle *will* be won and the curse of death *will* be broken – through Christ the Redeemer who is born of the 'seed' (or children) of Eve (Heb. 2:14). Through Christ's death the curse of sin has been broken – so although the *presence* of sin is still in the world, we are freed from the *power* and the *penalty* of sin. Can you do as Paul suggests: '… count yourselves dead to sin but alive to God in Christ Jesus' (Rom. 6:11)?

....
For prayer and reflection
....

In raising children we understand the importance of conditions, and consequences for breaking them, so why do we struggle with the concept of a God who works within the same principles?

New beginnings

The third covenant is the 'Noahic' Covenant (Gen. 9:1–17) a covenant between God and Noah (and the generations to come). Mankind had greatly increased in number but had become so wicked that God, in an act of judgment, wiped the earth clean with a flood, leaving only Noah and his family (plus pairs of animals and birds) as representatives once again to populate the earth. God knew that sin had already entered mankind and so this time, although He pronounced His blessing, He didn't declare mankind 'good' (Gen. 8:21).

Do you ever wonder why, if mankind had sinned and alienated themselves from God, God didn't just start again? Instead, He left a remnant alive in which sin was already operating (because of the legacy from Adam and Eve). Wasn't it obvious that, in time, life would be back at square one? Perhaps God wanted us to see that the natural inclination of the human heart is sinful – hence our need of a Saviour.

God's choice was to preserve the world until His redemptive purposes are complete. None of us knows when that will be. We only know that God's heart is patient: '… not wanting anyone to perish, but everyone to come to repentance' (2 Pet. 3:9). In His grace He has given this time for people to turn to Jesus. Is there anyone who comes to mind, perhaps someone dear to you, whom you long might find Christ? Why not take a few minutes now to pray for them?

Although we don't know when the end will come, we do know that it will happen in a flash (see Matt. 24). So, as in the days of Noah, we need to be aware of those around us, to stay spiritually alert and prayerful and to make the most of every opportunity to share our faith.

Genesis 9:1–17

'Be fruitful and increase in number and fill the earth.'
(v.1)

For prayer and reflection

God left us with a reminder that He would never destroy mankind again by a flood – the rainbow (Gen. 9:13). It is also an awesome reminder of how privileged we are to be saved.

Promises **and blessings**

Genesis 12:1–7;
13:14–17

'… all peoples
on earth will be
blessed through
you.' (12:3)

The fourth covenant, the 'Abrahamic' Covenant, makes me tingle with excitement! God promises Abram (later renamed Abraham), a childless 75-year-old man married to a barren old woman, Sarai (later Sarah), that he will have many descendants and that through him will be the 'seed' (Jesus) through whom there will be redemption (delivery from sin) for the world. It's an unconditional covenant: God makes promises to Abraham which *only* God can bring about. Abraham himself can do nothing to make it happen or to stop it happening (although he tries to bring it into being prematurely, by having a child with his wife's servant, Hagar).

The covenant includes the promises of: 1. Land (Gen. 12:1); 2. Descendants (Gen. 12:2); 3. Blessing and redemption (Gen. 12:3), each of which is built upon in further covenants. Scripture is like an incredible art piece; each individual brush stroke of the artist is art in itself and together they make up the complete picture. Likewise, each covenant stands alone but is also part of God's overall plan.

I love the 'Abrahamic' Covenant for two reasons: 1. When we accept Christ *we receive the inheritance promised to Abraham*; and 2. This covenant so clearly *forms a bridge between the Old and New Testaments.* Abraham is told he will be the bearer of the 'seed' and yet Christ does not appear in person until the New Testament. The fact that Christ is to come again, speaks to me of how God is *God of the past, the present and the future.* Being inheritors of the Abrahamic Covenant, we have been blessed by God. How can we be channels of blessing to the world around us and live in such a way that 'all peoples on earth will be blessed' through us?

For prayer and reflection

Can you allow the Eternal God to give you hope and comfort when you struggle with issues from the past, with present anxieties or with concerns regarding the future?

WEEKEND

The Bible gives us peace

For reflection: Psalm 119:165–168

Another outcome of reading the Bible is that it *gives us peace* in our everyday lives. The psalmist links peace with not 'stumbling'; in other words giving us a sense of stability and security. In that place of peace God sets our feet upon a rock and gives us a firm place to stand (Psa. 40:2).

The peace we need in our lives is a peace that only God can bring about. Such peace transcends (rises above) all understanding. It is beyond human logic and it carries the hallmark of guarding our hearts and minds in Christ Jesus (Phil. 4:7). It is a peace we find in knowing God and in living within the bounds of His will for our lives. We can endeavour to create peace as we attempt to build security but, just as the man who built the house upon the sand discovered, it does not withstand the storms of life. Only the house built upon the rock, or the life built upon obedience and trust in Christ, withstands the storm (Matt. 7:24–27) and experiences peace within. What's your house built on?

Optional further reading

Psalms 40; 45:6; Isaiah 40:8–17

Look at: www.pleaseconvinceme.com and www.christiananswers.net

Sacrifice for sin

Leviticus 17:1–15

'... it is the blood
that makes
atonement for
one's life.' (v.11)

T he fifth covenant is the 'Mosaic' Covenant which is between God and Israel (Moses being Israel's representative). We are probably familiar with the Ten Commandments. It may come as some surprise that the covenant is *full* of commandments, *613 in total*, involving blessings for obedience and curses for disobedience. If you thought ten was hard enough, can you imagine endeavouring to live by all these laws, covering food, sacrifice, clothing, sexual relations, circumcision and much more?

We may interpret the Mosaic Law as 'hard work', but it is a vital part of the overall picture of God's redemptive plan. An essential part of the Mosaic Law is the blood sacrifice (Lev. 17:11) – the atonement for sin. Sin separates man from God (Isa. 59:2). Sin cannot exist in the presence of God (being pure holiness) and therefore our sin must be 'covered' if we are to be in His presence. The Hebrew word for 'atonement' means just that – 'covering'. Within the Mosaic Law, the blood sacrifices (the killing and shedding of blood of a specific animal without defect) covered the sins of those concerned. When Jesus died, His blood was shed on the cross and became, for all who trust in Him, the ultimate and final blood sacrifice. His blood did not only 'cover' our sin but *removed* it. It is only the blood of Jesus that has the power to do that.

The Mosaic Covenant was fulfilled with the death of Christ (Matt. 5:17–18; Rom. 10:4) and it still has lessons to teach us today. What might God be saying to you? Is there anything you want to confess to God now? 'If we confess our sins, he is faithful and just and will forgive us our sins and purify us from all unrighteousness' (1 John 1:9).

For prayer and reflection

Oh Jesus, may I never take the blood You shed for granted, but instead increasingly realise what You have saved me from. Amen.

Relationship **of love**

The intention of the Mosaic Law was to expose sin and drive the Israelites to God's grace – as God had provided for them a means of forgiveness through the sacrificial system. However, the Israelites failed in their keeping of the Law of Moses, hence another covenant came into being. With each covenant we see a similar pattern: God establishes something with mankind (be it an individual, a nation or ongoing generations); mankind often fails to keep their part of the bargain; God reveals His displeasure at disobedience but also reveals an aspect of His grace. The sixth covenant, the 'Palestinian' Covenant (Deut. 29:1–30:20) between God and Israel, is no exception to the pattern.

In order to demonstrate the extent of God's love for Israel (and for us as believers) the book of Hosea portrays the imagery of God choosing Israel (or, in Ezek. 16:8–14, the city of Jerusalem) as a wife. God is expressing love, intimacy and trust. However, Israel's response is to play the harlot (see Hosea 1:1–3:5; Ezek. 16:15–34) putting idols in place of the one true God. God is no longer first; He is no longer Israel's only love. I wonder if we act similarly with God ourselves, displacing Him from the central position in our lives by putting other people, money and possessions before Him?

In Revelation Jesus accuses the church in Ephesus of having forsaken its first love (Rev. 2:4). How easy it is for us to do likewise. Let's remind ourselves that we, the Church, are the bride of Christ. Our hearts should be beating with excitement and longing for intimacy with our bridegroom – Jesus. He is everything to us and, as our one true love, all else pales into insignificance compared to Him.

Deuteronomy 30:1–20

'See, I set before you today life and prosperity, death and destruction.'
(v.15)

For prayer and reflection

Father help me to love with more of the passion and sincerity of Your Son, Jesus. Amen.

Eternal throne

....

1 Chronicles 17:11–15

....

'… his throne will be established forever.' (v.14)

For prayer and reflection

....

Father, I thank You that however insecure my life is now, my future is completely secure with You and that one day Your Son will rule and reign. Amen.

The seventh covenant, the 'Davidic' Covenant, is between God and David (2 Sam. 7:1–29; 1 Chron. 17:11–14; 2 Chron. 6:16). God promises David (and Israel) through the prophet Nathan that the Messiah (Jesus Christ) would come from the lineage of David and the tribe of Judah and would establish a kingdom that would endure forever.

The Davidic Covenant is an unconditional covenant; God does not place any conditions of obedience upon its fulfilment – it is completely dependent upon God's faithfulness, not on David's or anyone else's obedience. An event is foretold and, although the one to whom it is told may not see the fruit (David was not around to see the Messiah and to know that He really did descend from his lineage), future generations can confirm it to be so.

We are in the same position in regard to the remaining promises and prophecies of the Bible which are yet to be fulfilled – not least the 'second coming' of Christ. We have to live by faith that *He will return.* But we're privileged to be able to read the biblical prophecies that have already come to fruition, which encourage us to trust God for what is yet to come – even if we don't fully understand all we read.

Are there areas of your life in which you are trusting God to fulfil His personal word or promise to you? Be encouraged that what God has clearly spoken (and personal prophecy needs always to be weighed and tested against biblical truth) He will perform – in His way and His timing. Our God is a faithful God.

New covenant

magine being given a mission by God to bring prophetic words for more than 40 years. Now imagine not wanting to do the job, not being listened to and feeling depressed because of the opposition. This was the position in which the prophet Jeremiah found himself. He had been called to the prophetic ministry as a young man and served the Lord faithfully, putting God before his own desires and circumstances. He had to constantly confront people with the joyless message that they had put other gods before the Almighty God and that their disobedience would bring destruction.

Amidst all the heaviness, what a wonderful moment it must have been when God spoke to Jeremiah of the restoration of the people to the land and of the new covenant to come. '"The time is coming," declares the Lord, "when I will make a new covenant ..."' (Jer. 31:31). I wonder if it was in conjunction with this message that Jeremiah wrote his words of hope in the book of Lamentations, the rest of which is pretty melancholic: 'Because of the Lord's great love we are not consumed, for his compassions never fail. They are new every morning; great is your faithfulness' (Lam. 3:22–23).

Jeremiah began prophesying around 627 BC. I find it quite incredible that God brought the revelation of a new covenant (Jer. 31:31–34) hundreds of years before it came into effect. Jeremiah's prophecy that each of us would know God and that our sins would be forgiven became possible through Jesus' sacrificial death on the cross. Through the life-giving Holy Spirit, who lives in all believers (Rom. 8:9–11), we can now share in the inheritance of Christ, enjoy relationship with God and receive the blessings spoken of throughout Scripture.

Hebrews 9:11–28;
Jeremiah
31:31–34

'For this reason Christ is the mediator of a new covenant, that those who are called may receive the promised eternal inheritance ...'
(Heb. 9:15)

For prayer and reflection

Lord, I am so blessed! What can I say? I praise Your holy name! Amen.

Feed on the Word

....

John 15:1–17

....

'If you remain in me and my words remain in you, ask whatever you wish, and it will be given you.' (v.7)

....

For prayer and reflection

....

Lord, I ask that Your Word would be living and active within me. May I be a true witness to You – not just in what I say but in how I relate to others. Amen.

I was sitting chatting with a friend over a drink one day when he suddenly said, 'I'm not sure the Bible is really all God's words ... How do you know?' Quite amazingly, this particular question came while I was writing these notes! I tried my hardest to offer him a taste of what I'd recently committed to paper: how I wished at the time I had my notes in front of me! It highlighted how important it is that we *feed on* the Word. When the Word becomes a part of us, it oozes out of our being and its treasures are on our very breath.

The psalmist wrote: 'I have hidden your word in my heart that I might not sin against you' (Psa. 119:11). He had taken what God said right into his being. In accordance with the new covenant, God puts His law in our minds and writes it onto our hearts (Jer. 31:33). In addition, God has sent the Holy Spirit to teach us all things and to remind us of Jesus' teaching (John 14:26). We cannot live the Christian life in our own strength; rather we need to rely on the Holy Spirit to guide us into all truth (John 16:13).

Daily submission to the Holy Spirit helps us to follow God and to walk in His ways. Our lives as believers do not consist of following a set of rules but, as Paul says, 'The commandments ... summed up in this one rule: "Love your neighbour as yourself"' (Rom. 13:9). Jesus Himself was clear in His message to us. 'My command is this: Love each other as I have loved you' (John 15:12). The Bible may be complex, but the message is simple: *Love.* As we share God's truths, our lives must reflect the love of Christ.

In what new ways can you show Christ's love to those around you today?

WEEKEND

The Bible brings light

For reflection: Psalm 119:129–136

Imagine being in a dark room day and night and how you might feel. Then imagine shafts of light pouring in and transforming the darkness. How different things would look and how differently you would feel. The psalmist declares: 'The unfolding of your words gives light …' (v.130). God's Word *brings light* into our dark places.

In the beginning, God spoke and light came into being (Gen. 1:3); the world was transformed. God speaks into our lives, light pours into our lives and we too are transformed.

The psalmist found that it was the *unfolding* of God's words that brought light. As you read the Bible and ask God to bring you understanding of the truths contained in it, have you tried praying that He would, at the same time, bring light into the dark places of your life? Perhaps there are aspects of your work, relationships, family life or patterns of behaviour which are problematic and you long to see a solution or change. Try praying that God will speak into these situations and bring change through His living Word.

Optional further reading
Galatians 4:4; 1 John 3:8; Psalm 18:28–29; John 8:12

Live **by the Word**

....

Colossians 3:1–17

....

'Let the word of Christ dwell in you richly …' (v.16)

As we move towards the end of our readings about the Word of God, Paul reminds us to let the word of Christ dwell in us richly (Col. 3:16) and James tells us: 'Do not merely listen to the word, and so deceive yourselves. Do what it says. Anyone who listens to the word but does not do what it says is like a man who looks at his face in a mirror and, after looking at himself, goes away and immediately forgets what he looks like. But the man who looks intently into the perfect law that gives freedom, and continues to do this, not forgetting what he has heard, but doing it – he will be blessed in what he does' (James 1:22–25).

Why do we study God's Word and buy Bible-reading notes such as *Inspiring Women Every Day*? It's not to score Brownie points with God or because the church tells us we *ought* to have a daily time with God. The reason we study the Bible is because *it is God's communication to us*, telling us about Himself, His relationship with us, the hope we have and the way in which we are called to live. The Bible is our manual for living, our compass, our road map, our source of nourishment, our protection and our means of defence against the enemy. Jesus Himself used the written Word in His warfare against Satan when tempted in the wilderness, in saying back to the enemy: 'It is written …' (Matt. 4:4,7,10). Don't you think it's incredible that we have available to us the same Scriptures to use for ourselves?

I hope and pray that your understanding of the Bible has developed during this month. I wonder what has had the greatest impact on you and if there are any changes you would now like to make to your daily life?

....

For prayer and reflection

....

'The decision to study God's Word in order to do His Word is a meaningful act of submission and reverence – in short, it is worship'
(Dr John D. Garr).

The Bible results in **freedom**

he psalmist rejoices by saying, 'I will walk about in freedom, for I have sought out your precepts' (v.45). An obvious result of meditating on and following God's truth is that we experience freedom. I love the concept of 'walking about' in freedom; it creates a sense of healthy, joyful pride in what God is doing in our lives. It proves to be something that impacts our everyday life and that others can clearly see.

What aspects of freedom are you seeking at the moment? Freedom from fear, isolation, emptiness, hopelessness, rejection, despair, resentment, guilt, jealousy, negative thoughts, self-condemnation, doubt? We live in a fallen world and we are affected every day by the world and its ways; but the good news is that we have a Deliverer: 'For he will deliver the needy who cry out ...' (Psa. 72:12). We are *all* needy in one way or another and we need our Deliverer as much as our bodies need oxygen to breathe!

Why not spend some time considering all that Jesus has delivered you from? If God has brought change in your life – and no doubt you have witnessed Him transform the lives of others too – remember, He also has other great things in store for you.

Psalm 119:41–48

'I will walk about in freedom for I have sought out your precepts.' (v.45)

For prayer and reflection

Father, thank You for Your changes in my life and for all that my future holds in You. Amen.

The power of
the tongue

Jeanette Henderson

Jeanette Henderson serves God itinerantly in the UK and East
Africa. She is also a freelance writer whose publications include
the first two books in a series of biblical studies called 'LLT' –
Life's Like That: Meeting God In the Everyday and *Life's Like
That: Meeting God in Life's Challenges*. An avid reader of murder
mysteries, Jeanette also contributes to UCB Inspirational radio's
'Godspot' slots. During term-time she is a part-time primary
school secretary and leader of its team of midday supervisors.

The power of the **tongue**

Matthew
12:22–37

'For out of the overflow of the heart the mouth speaks.' (v.34)

Our studies over the next few weeks will focus on one of the smallest yet most powerful parts of the human body – the tongue. A rather unusual theme, you might think? Certainly – if we were studying merely from a scientific point of view. (All I remember from school biology lessons, however, can be written on the back of a postage stamp!)

Our main reason for considering the human tongue is the fact that James and others thought it so significant that they just had to write about it (see James 3:1–12). And why did they reckon it so important?

Think back to times in your childhood years when you told your mother that you weren't feeling well. After touching your brow to check your temperature what did she usually do next? If she were anything like my mum, she would ask to see your tongue because, by some amazing maternal instinct, she could tell from its colour and condition the exact state of your physical health! Somehow she could work out what was going on physically inside you and then recommend a cure for whatever was wrong. (For me, this usually involved a massive dose of the dreaded castor oil!)

For prayer and reflection

In His clash with the Pharisees Jesus states (vv.33–35) that by examining a person's tongue and what it conveys, *He* can tell the exact condition of the person's *spiritual* health. Our tongue expresses what is going on inside us – in our heart and spirit (v.34). Someone who has a careless, offensive or critical tongue, says Jesus, is far from healthy in the spiritual sense (vv.36–37).

**'May the words of my mouth and the meditation of my heart [always] be pleasing in your sight, O Lord, my Rock and my Redeemer'
(Psa. 19:14).**

As we invite the Holy Spirit to examine the 'fruit' (v.33) of our mouth and heart, may we be honest and humble enough to accept *His* cure for any problems He might find.

Where did it **all go wrong?**

Recently I was invited to speak at a significant anniversary service in a local church. It had been planned and advertised as a very grand affair. The church was beautifully decorated, the musical instruments highly polished and the choir finely tuned. Everyone was dressed in their 'Sunday best' – with the result that I was very nervous!

Everything went well until it came to the pastor's choice of Bible reading. I would have chosen something else, as the version I had to read from contained an awful 'tongue twister' – the phrase 'the rich young ruler'.

For days beforehand, I had practised saying this until my tongue was almost numb, but standing there before an ornate lectern and even more daunting congregation ... you've guessed it ... my tongue let me down! Because of nerves, the words came out in a muddled 'heap' making me sound like a drunken Martian! Everyone laughed good-heartedly, but I was so embarrassed.

How James would have sympathised with me! 'We all stumble in many ways. If anyone is never at fault in what he says, he is a perfect man' (3:2) or, putting this another way, our tongue lets us down (and not just in tongue twisters!) because we are not 'perfect'. Mankind lost the perfection we were created with after Adam and Eve disobeyed God (Gen. 3) and sin distorted the human personality as a result.

The more spiritually depraved the human heart became, the more uncontrolled the tongue. Although intended for *good*, fallen men and women are now *mis*using the tongue for *evil* purposes (Rom. 1:29–30).

Outside of Christ, says James, the human tongue is a 'restless evil' that cannot be tamed (3:8). In Christ Jesus, however, it's a different story!

**James 3:1–12;
Romans 1:18–21,
28–31**

'They are gossips, slanderers, God-haters, insolent, arrogant and boastful ...'
(Rom. 1:29)

For prayer and reflection

Lord, please help my tongue to express only godly things today, for Your glory.

Picture this ...

James 3:3–8;
Proverbs
10:12–21

'The tongue of the
righteous is choice
silver ... [Their]
lips ... nourish
many ...'
(Prov. 10:20–21)

James' letter is one of the most practical and 'down to earth' in the New Testament. Although only five chapters long he assigns 15 out of the 108 verses (that's nearly 14 per cent) to the unusual subject of the human tongue.

In chapter 3, James gives us three pairs of pictures, each describing what the tongue is really like. The first pair, the 'bit' and 'rudder' (vv.3–4), tell us how God intended the tongue to be used when He first created it (ie to *guide* and *direct*). The second and third pairs, the pictures of 'fire and poison' (vv.5,8) and 'water and fruit trees' (vv.11–12), describe how the tongue has come to be *mis*used (to *destroy* and *deceive* instead) since the human personality became tainted and distorted by sin.

Over the next few days we will take a more detailed look at these pictures, beginning with the most negative (pairs nos. 2 and 3) and ending on a very positive note with pair no. 1.

Pair no. 2: In verses 5 and 8 James uses, as examples, the pictures of 'fire' and 'poison' to describe how the tongue is very often used for the negative purpose of *destruction*. Although these can certainly destroy, both were given originally for a very positive purpose. When used responsibly, they can actually achieve a great deal of good in society.

For prayer and reflection

Prayerfully consider: 'Is there any wickedness on *my* lips?' (Job 6:30, my emphasis).

In many countries, for example, naked fire is still used today for heating, lighting and cooking. In the field of medicine, certain poisons are often used in small doses (eg digitalis is used to treat chronic heart disease). Likewise, when used responsibly, the human tongue can achieve a great deal of positive good in people's lives. But, says James, should any of these ever be used carelessly (vv.5–6), watch out!

WEEKEND

Nothing but the truth

For reflection: Isaiah 9:1–7

To see how the tongue has been used to direct people (see James 3:3–4) towards God and His kingdom, look no further than the Old Testament prophets. Their prophecies would originally have been spoken or even shouted out – not just in temples but on street corners and in busy marketplaces. The prophecies both foretold and forth-told (ie 'proclaimed') the will of God concerning the advent of His Son and the setting up of His supernatural kingdom within the hearts of all who would believe and receive Him as Saviour and Lord.

God's prophetic words, now written down for us, are absolutely oozing with divine truth (like the Scriptures as a whole). In this passage from Isaiah a veritable feast of truth is set out for us declaring 'what *is*' and 'what *will be*' in Christ Jesus. For example, the names of Jesus (v.6) reveal just some of the benefits available to us in Christ, such as wise advice and guidance when we seek the 'Wonderful Counsellor' in faith-filled, trusting prayer.

So, if such positive truth (ie 'what *is*' in Christ Jesus) is available for Christians to feed on spiritually, why do we waste so much mental and emotional energy worrying about the 'what *ifs*?' of life that Satan sends to torment us?

Optional further reading

Romans 12; Philippians 4

What a **terrible waste!**

Proverbs 18:7–21; James 3:5–6

'The tongue has the power of life and death …'
(Prov. 18:21)

Fire can greatly benefit society. 'But', says James, 'when out of control it can cause untold damage.' He writes about a 'great forest' (v.5) but let us imagine something more familiar, like a field of crops.

Think of how *long* it would take to prepare the ground, especially if only the most basic equipment was used: how long to sow the seed, especially if done by hand. Think of the months it would take for the sun and rain to nurture the growing plants until finally they are ready for harvesting. Now think of how *short* a time it would take for one evil person with petrol and matches to set the field ablaze and destroy the whole crop. What a terrible waste! All that time and effort for nothing!

It doesn't matter what it is: the principle is the same. It may take months to produce but only a matter of hours to destroy. And it doesn't matter if the fire was started wilfully or by accident, the end result is exactly the same – total ruin!

James says that the tongue is like fire. It can be useful but can also cause needless damage – even in the kingdom of God! The following happened to a friend of mine. After sharing her faith for almost fifteen months, two young people became interested and began going to church. One day, however, a Christian at her church lost his temper and wrongly accused them of something, without bothering to check his facts or even to put his brain into gear before opening his mouth. The result: the youngsters stormed out and have never returned. They've even stopped asking about Jesus.

See what James is saying here? Months of faithful witness ruined in seconds because someone who should have known better could not control his tongue!

For prayer and reflection

'A gentle answer turns away wrath, but a harsh word stirs up anger'
(Prov. 15:1).

Deadly poison!

Today we see how James uses the example of 'poison' to show how the tongue is often *mis*used for the purpose of destruction (v.8). When used responsibly some poisons can actively benefit society by controlling weeds, vermin, bacteria etc. Poison, however, can also be used to kill *people* and that rarely happens by accident. Usually it is given deliberately, without the victim's knowledge.

Likewise, the tongue being 'full of deadly poison' can be just as destructive. People can use it maliciously to 'poison' the lives of others through gossip, lies and criticism and, sadly, even Christians can be guilty of this.

This is usually how it starts ... One person meets another and says, 'Have you heard what happened to So-and-so? It's awful! I shouldn't really say anything because I don't know *all* the facts, but I thought you should know so you can pray about it ...' That person then meets another and says, 'I've something for you to pray about. You won't believe it!' and so on ... Only this time a few more so-called 'facts' are added – usually the product of someone's fertile imagination. Over the weeks *more* people join in this game of 'Chinese whispers' (all with very 'spiritual' motives, of course!) and the 'deadly poison' spreads.

Or perhaps you have come across some of the people who do more damage by what they *don't* say – by what they deliberately leave out. They will share only part of the story and stop rather suddenly (hand over mouth) as if they really ought *not* to say more. Our imagination is then left to make up what we *think* happened next and this can often be far more harmful than if the whole truth had actually been told in the first place.

Proverbs 11:1–13; James 3:7–10

'With his mouth the godless destroys his neighbour ...' (Prov. 11:9)

For prayer and reflection

Has your own tongue ever been 'full of deadly poison'? Confess this, asking God to show you how you can put things right again.

There's **no taking it back!**

**James 1:19–27;
3:7–8**

'If anyone considers himself religious and yet does not keep a tight rein on his tongue, he deceives himself …' (1:26)

The human tongue can certainly cause terrible damage that cannot be *un*done, no matter how much we might like to do so.

When speaking publicly to children, I've been known to use this simple yet powerful visual aid. Those who volunteer (adults included!) take it in turns to empty a tube of very cheap toothpaste into a clear plastic bag. Sounds mindless, I know, but they love this. You should see their faces as they squeeze every last drop out of the tube and into the bag. (It's actually a great stress-reliever!) However, their faces are a picture when I say at the end, 'OK! Now put *all* of the toothpaste *back* into the tube again.' It cannot be done, of course, although several (adults included) have had a go! Once that toothpaste is out of the tube it cannot be put back inside again. The damage has already been done.

The same is true of every word the tongue produces. Once out of our mouths those words cannot be taken back again, whether or not we meant to say them. And if they have been negative and destructive, the damage has already been done. Trying to *un*do it is impossible.

We cannot go back to how things were before we said them. We *might* be able to put right the *content* of what we said, though I'm told it takes at least *fourteen* compliments to neutralise the effect of just *one* criticism. However, we can never fully repair the hurt and embarrassment that our damaging words caused in the first place.

An uncontrolled tongue can destroy someone's self-confidence and reputation. Even worse, it can ruin their testimony and effectiveness for God. And God's enemy, the devil, is delighted because we are doing his work for him!

For prayer and reflection

Lord, please help me to 'watch my ways and keep my tongue from sin' (Psa. 39:1). Show me how to 'put a muzzle' on my lips so that I may not use them for evil.

We all have **expectations**

We have seen how James uses his pictures of 'fire' (v.5) and 'poison' (v.8) to show how the tongue is often misused (even by Christians) to *destroy*. A 'restless evil' (v.8), it will not stay still. And long after the original words have been spoken, they can still go on doing their evil work. False rumours are started, more people join in along the way and the damage spreads. An 'untamed' (v.8) tongue can destroy someone's self-esteem and reputation. It can destroy their chance of success and prosperity and, even worse, it can ruin their fruitfulness for God. I am sure that the Lord is grieved when His people use their tongues for the purpose of destruction.

James now introduces his *third* pair of pictures to describe how the tongue is often misused to *deceive*.

Pair no. 3: Giving examples of 'water' and 'fruit trees' (vv.11–12) he makes the point that people always have expectations.

When I lived in Scotland and had more time for relaxation I used to enjoy hill walking around Edinburgh. I never used to worry about carrying bottled water with me to refresh me when I became hot and thirsty. Natural streams and springs bubbling up amongst the rocks were a familiar sight along the way. We could always rely on the water from these to be fresh enough to drink.

Weary and very thirsty after a long walk one day, we found a cool, clear and seemingly clean flow of water from which to sup. From its outward appearance, everything looked normal but, on tasting it, the water turned out to be bitter and undrinkable. Not at all what we'd expected!

Imagine how disappointed we were: the spring water had failed to meet both our need and our expectation.

Matthew
23:23–28;
James 3:9–12

'Can both fresh water and salt water flow from the same spring?'
(James 3:11)

For prayer and reflection

Lord, please make my mouth a 'fountain of life' (Prov. 10:11) that always refreshes others.

Figs from a fig tree!

**James 3:9–12;
Matthew 7:15–29**

'… by their fruit
you will recognise
them.' (Matt. 7:20)

Through his example of 'water' (vv.11–12), James makes the point that people have certain expectations of life in general. For example, we would never expect a fresh water spring to produce salt water – and vice versa. Citing 'fruit trees' (v.12) as a similar example, he says that people expect a fig tree to grow figs – not olives (or avocados) but figs! Likewise they expect a vine to produce grapes as its fruit – not figs (or bananas) but grapes!

In the same way, society (and God, Himself!) has certain expectations of His people. Those who profess to be Christians, with the Holy Spirit living inside, are *not* expected to produce 'bad' or unrighteous fruit (Matt. 7:18). They should *never* use their tongue to lie or deceive. Only truth should come out of their mouths. God desires it and people expect it!

The Lord certainly never expects the same tongue that offers up praise to Him (James 3:10) to be used to spread gossip, rumours or unhealthy criticism. People around us should be able to rely on everything we tell them because we are Christ's 'ambassadors' here on the earth (2 Cor. 5:20).

When we make a promise, we should make it a priority before God to keep it. Better still, if we cannot give an absolute guarantee with our promises, we should be less hasty in making them. Why? Well, if *we*, as God's representatives, let people down, they might be tempted to wrongly assume that *He* will too; and then they might struggle to believe and put their trust in Him.

Why not try a very different kind of 'fast' today? See how long you can go – not without food, but without using your tongue for ungodly purposes (eg gossip, lies, hurtful comments).

**For prayer and
reflection**

**Have you made
any promises
this week? How
determined are
you to keep them?**

WEEKEND

The Lord's servant

For reflection: Luke 1:26–38

I love writing short stories. I can place my characters in unusual situations and put my own words into their mouths. I can have them behave in any way I choose because they are fictional.

Were I to rewrite today's story as fictional, what words would I 'put' into Mary's mouth when she hears what God is asking of her (vv.31–35)? Considering the awful maelstrom of misunderstanding, change and criticism that would be loosed upon her life as soon as she agreed, I might be tempted to write a different reply for her, eg: 'It's such a huge decision, I'll need ages to consider it.' Or: 'Perhaps when I'm older and more experienced.' Or: 'Are you kidding me? Mess up my life and have everyone hate me? No way!' Or even: 'I'm not listening! Go and find somebody else.'

Of course, Mary's story is absolutely true. The choice she made and her words in reply (v.38) were truly her own: 'I am the Lord's servant. May it be to me as you have said.'

Were I to write your real-life story describing the very costly things God may have asked of you, which of the above replies would I mostly be recording?

Optional further reading
Joyce Meyer, *Me and My Big Mouth* (Nashville: FaithWords, 2002).

Live as **children of light**

Ephesians 5:1–20;
James 3:9–10

'… (for the fruit of
the light consists
in all goodness,
righteousness
and truth) …'
(Eph. 5:9)

I n today's reading James condemns what he sees as double standards in Christians. Many will use their tongues to worship, pray and express an outward show of 'spirituality' in church, but as soon as they are outside the church doors they will *mis*use them to deceive others. And, says James emphatically, '… this should *not* be!' (3:10, my emphasis). Why not? Many who live outside God's kingdom watch and listen carefully to all that is said and done by those claiming to be its members. In fact, very often the first impressions they will have of God's kingdom and of God Himself will come from what they hear and see in the lives of His people.

This is why Paul exhorts us to 'live as children of light' (Eph. 5:8) and as 'blameless and pure, children of God without fault … as [we] hold out the word of life …' (Phil. 2:15–16). The words 'blameless and pure' in the Greek carry with them a sense of being 'crystal clear and see-through'. In other words, there should be no inconsistency between how we live as Christians and what comes out of our mouths.

For prayer and reflection

Lord, may the pure light of *Your* Spirit shine within my own soul and spirit today, exposing and cleansing anything there that robs You of glory, for Your name's sake.

What people hear us say on the 'outside' should reflect how we really are on the 'inside', in our soul and spirit. And when they approach us they should expect to be blessed and helped in their need, as if they had gone directly to Jesus Himself (in the same way as we would expect a natural spring to refresh us when we are thirsty). What they do not expect, says James, is to be criticised, cursed or condemned instead (3:9–10). He goes on to say that whoever curses others is, in fact, also cursing God because we were created in His image. And cursing God is *serious* business!

No **double standards!**

The apostle James speaks out against double standards in the lives of Christians because deceit and dishonesty can ruin our effectiveness and spiritual fruitfulness for God (James 3:9–12).

One day I met a friend in a rather grand hotel popular with local businessmen. A group of young lawyers were lunching at the next table. They sported expensive designer clothes, highly polished footwear, expertly cut hairstyles and manicures. They looked extremely successful and professional – and I was impressed! Well, only until they opened their mouths, that is! I was absolutely disgusted by what I heard them say. They constantly made foul-mouthed comments about the waitresses, every other word was a swear word and they kept verbally harassing a young colleague who was with them.

And what a waste! Having spent all that time and effort creating the perfect, professional image, they then completely spoiled it by what came out of their mouths.

Similarly, people outside the Church, looking in, judge us not only by what they see us do but also by what they hear us say. This is why the Word of God reminds us that a Christian's words should always match the godly image that is set out for us in Scripture: 'Lord, who may dwell in your sanctuary? ... He whose walk is blameless ... who *does* what is righteous, who *speaks* the truth ... and has no slander on his tongue, who does his neighbour no wrong and casts no slur on his fellow-man ...' (Psa. 15:1–3, my emphases). How we speak should always be in harmony with how we live and how we behave should never contradict what we say. If it does, we will no doubt struggle to be effective and fruitful in our spiritual witness.

Matthew 15:1–20; Proverbs 17:27–28

'... it is not what goes into ... but ... what comes out of the mouth that defiles.' (Matt. 15:11, NRSV)

For prayer and reflection

'Lord, may my words *and* actions honour You always – for Your glory.

Choose the 'power of life'!

**James 3:3–4;
1 Peter 3:8–17**

'Be ready … to answer anyone who asks you to explain the hope you have …'
(1 Pet. 3:15, GNB)

We have seen how the tongue has been *mis*used to destroy and deceive. When God created it, however, He originally meant it to *direct* and *guide*. Here, at last, we have a healthy and positive purpose for the tongue! James uses his first pair of pictures to describe this.

Pair no. 1: the 'bit' (v.3) and 'rudder' (v.4). These have two things in common:

(i) size: The bridle 'bit' is the metal bar that goes into the horse's mouth to direct the horse and to keep the reins in place. Compared to the size of the horse itself (especially if a huge Clydesdale), the actual 'bit' is tiny. The same can be said of a ship's 'rudder' compared to the huge bulk of the ship itself (especially if as vast as an ocean liner!). Small they may be, but also vitally important. Just think what might happen if they weren't there or were faulty in some way!

(ii) potential: The second thing they have in common is what they can achieve despite their size. Although tiny, when properly controlled, they can actually guide the horse and steer the ship in whatever direction they need to be moving.

It's the same with the human tongue, says James. God intended it for the purpose of directing or 'steering' men and women towards Himself and His kingdom. Yet how many of us don't realise this? How many of us pay little attention to the actual words we allow our tongues to utter every day? Do you take more notice of the coins you dole out of your purse than the words you dispense from your lips? Are you tempted to think that words are so small and insignificant they just don't matter? Remember what the tiny bit and rudder can achieve when controlled and used correctly.

For prayer and reflection

**'The tongue has the power of life and death …'
(Prov. 18:21).
Choose the 'power of *life*' today!**

Words **are powerful**

When used correctly, words can be as powerful as the 'bit' and 'rudder' (James 3:3–4). Politicians and salespeople are actually trained in how to put words to their best use because they realise that the right words can have a positive influence in persuading people.

In the world of commerce, advertisers choose their words carefully because how they express themselves when introducing their product can mean either great success or financial ruin. Words are chosen that will stimulate our minds and stay forever in our memory. For example, if you live in the UK can you remember whose toothpaste claimed to give you a 'ring of confidence' and which petrol put a 'tiger in your tank'?

Our focus verse reminds us of how vitally important the right words are – especially a mother's words as she wisely instructs her children. And, of course, the same is true for all of us. Working in a primary school with almost 200 impressionable youngsters, I am always aware that my own words can either inspire them or crush their spirits; and can either help to mould their maturing characters or to 'mess them up' forever. The right words (eg of encouragement, acceptance, respect) offered in the right way for the right reasons can make a powerful difference for good in the future lives of these children.

Christians also need to realise the amazing potential in the various types of words we release from our lips every day: words that have the power to either 'bear much fruit' (John 15:5) for God's kingdom or cause it serious, and sometimes irreparable, damage. Ensuring that the words we utter daily will be of the spiritually fruitful kind will involve a challenge, a choice and perhaps, for some, a change of focus.

Proverbs 31:10–31

'She speaks with wisdom, and faithful instruction is on her tongue.' (v.26)

For prayer and reflection

Lord, help me to speak only faithful and fruitful words for You today.

Submit to God ...

James 4:1–12

'Submit yourselves, then, to God. Resist the devil, and he will flee from you.' (v.7)

How can we ensure that our words will bear spiritual fruit? The first step involves a personal *challenge*. We must always adopt a 'zero tolerance' attitude to sin in our lives. The apostle Paul writes, 'Therefore do not let sin reign in your mortal body so that you obey its evil desires. Do not offer the parts of your body to sin, as instruments of wickedness, but rather offer yourselves to God, as those who have been brought from death to life; and offer the parts of your body [tongue included!] to him as instruments of righteousness' (Rom. 6:12–13). A surrendered tongue has the potential, with God's help, to become a 'tamed' tongue.

The second step involves a powerful *choice*. Over the years in my walk with God, I have come to believe that whenever *we* supply the willingness and obedience to achieve something in Him that is in line with His Word and His specific will for our lives *He*, in turn, will supply the supernatural power to help it become a reality. So if you sincerely want only godly and gracious words to come from your mouth then declare in faith with David, 'I *will* watch my ways and keep my tongue from sin; I *will* put a muzzle on my mouth as long as the wicked are in my presence'; and with Job, '... as long as I have life within me ... my lips *will not* speak wickedness, and my tongue will utter *no* deceit ...' (Psa. 39:1; Job 27:3–4, my emphases).

When we allow God to search our hearts and He sees there a sincere desire to use our tongue, lips, mouth and voice as an effective means of steering others towards Jesus and His amazing kingdom, He is then able to take that willingness, to crown it with His abundant power and to help us to speak faithfully and fruitfully for Him.

For prayer and reflection

Lord, I surrender every part of me into Your loving hands and ask that You will turn my willingness into spiritual fruitfulness for the sake of Jesus.

WEEKEND

Praise not petulance

For reflection: Luke 1:39–56

A group of my friends and I recently discussed teenagers. Somebody said that her daughter is so grumpy that she stomps off whenever she doesn't get her own way! Someone else shared that whenever her son is in a huff he slams the doors so hard it almost starts an earthquake! Another commented, 'Our Joe grumbles so much, he could make a career out of it!'

What a brilliant contrast we have in teenager Mary's attitude. No, I haven't got it wrong! Mary would have been no more than a teenager when God called her to become the earthly parent of His Son, Jesus. Her pregnancy would have created problems for her. Joseph, her fiancé (they married young in that culture), could have rejected her, leaving her to the merciless scorn (and endless gossip!) of others. And, if accused of adultery, she'd have faced the real possibility of death by stoning (Deut. 22:23–26). If any teenager had the right to complain or storm off in a huff, Mary surely did! But does she?

Instead she lifts her heart and voice to God and composes one of the most moving songs ever. She counted her blessings and then turned any worry and stress she might be feeling into thanksgiving and praise (vv.46–56). Do you?

Optional further reading

Merlin Carothers, *Prison to Praise* (Sevenoaks: Hodder Christian Paperbacks, 1977)

Blessed are **the merciful**

Matthew
5:1–10,13–16;
Proverbs 31:8–9

'Speak up for those
who cannot speak
for themselves …'
(Prov. 31:8–9)

The *final* step in ensuring that we speak spiritually fruitful words, involves a radical *change of focus*. Jesus states that the source of the tongue's problems lies in the human heart (Matt. 12:34) because the tongue mainly expresses what the heart is fixated upon: for example, football fanatics tend to spend most of their waking hours talking about football!

A mouth that constantly offers negative, hurtful or critical comments tends to reveal a heart that has itself been the victim of long-term hurt and criticism and has yet to have the effects of these fully dealt with in God. The more we fix our eyes upon Jesus, however, holding out our damaged souls for Him to heal, the more our focus becomes centred on Him; the more we become securely and contentedly settled in His loving presence, the more we find ourselves wanting to speak only words that will please Him and bless others in His name.

Our final weekday studies will show exactly how we can do this – how we can actively choose (with God's help) to release positive words into people's lives that will encourage and bless; words that the Holy Spirit can use to direct them towards Jesus and His kingdom.

Before speaking to others on behalf of God, however, we must always remember to speak firstly to *God* on *their* behalf. Sadly, too many times, we rush into people's lives with hasty words without having prepared the ground spiritually beforehand through prayer – often with tragic results.

Today's focus verse also reminds us of how Christians should use the tongue (now surrendered *to* and 'tamed' *by* God) to speak up on behalf of those in society who, for various reasons, have no voice of their own (Prov. 31:8–9).

For prayer and reflection

How can we love not just 'with words or tongue' but also 'with actions and in truth' (1 John 3:17–18)?

Words of **witness**

We saw, yesterday, how Christians can use the tongue to speak *to* God (and to the right people in society) *on behalf of* others. Now we begin looking at how we can use the tongue positively and fruitfully to speak to *others* on behalf of *God*, by offering words of comfort and compassion, blessing and peace etc. Today we see how important it is to speak words of personal testimony and witness.

On the breakfast news one morning I heard about the miraculous escape of a woman who was trapped overnight in her flood-swamped car. She shared quite openly with the radio interviewer how, for 12 hours, she had sung hymns and choruses (in her own words, 'songs that mean so much to me') to keep her spirits up. She went on to say, 'God was there with me, giving me His peace and keeping me calm. I prayed that He would rescue me and He did! He sent someone to find me – someone who never usually travels that way to work. Praise God that today he did! The Lord certainly had a hand in rescuing me. I still don't know why He saved me – only that He must have work for me to do and He'll tell me what that is when it's time to begin.'

How remarkable that these positive words of personal testimony were broadcast so openly for non-Christians to hear! Even more remarkable were the closing words of the interviewer: 'Sarah's faith was strong before today but after this it's rock solid!'

Like the man in our reading, God did for Sarah what she was totally powerless to do for herself and she couldn't wait to tell the world! I'm glad she did because her positive words of witness certainly lifted my *own* spirit in God that day.

Mark 5:1–20

'Go … and tell … how much the Lord has done for you, and how he has had mercy on you.' (v.19)

For prayer and reflection

Is Jesus living and at work by His Spirit in your own heart and life? Then go and tell those around you your own story in God. How else will they hear?

Words of **comfort**

**2 Corinthians
1:2–11; 7:4–7**

'... the God of
all comfort ...
comforts us ...
so that we can
comfort those in ...
trouble ...' (1:3–4)

saiah foretells what Jesus' ministry would involve before His death: for example, comforting the broken-hearted and those struggling with grief (Isa. 61:1–3). In today's upwardly mobile society, however, compassion and comfort seem to be in short supply. The emphasis is on so-called 'positivism' and 'spin' – where you 'tell it how you would like it to be' and not 'how it really is'. Sadly, few people have time for those struggling with real and raw emotions like disappointment and hurt. Thinking them negative and weak, most would probably say, 'That's life! Get over it!'

Jesus came for *real* people with *real* emotions and needs. We Christians are called to continue His work – to be His listening ear as people share how their hearts came to be broken, His loving arms holding those enduring sickness and pain, and His gentle voice speaking tender words to those sunk deep in grief and gloom.

Yesterday was a significant day in the life of my family. Three years ago my dad, whom we adored, died suddenly, leaving us struggling with the awful gut-wrenching 'mixture' of almost unbearable emotions that we all have to experience at some time in life. I will always be grateful for the comfort I received directly from God's own heart and from those whom He called alongside to minister in His name. Within weeks, however, whilst still coming to terms with my own loss, our compassionate Lord was already sending *me* to others who were also mourning the sudden loss of a loved one. '... he brings us alongside someone else ... so that we can be there for that person just as God was there for us' (2 Cor. 1:4, *The Message*). I was able to comfort and pray for *them* from a heart that truly empathised.

**For prayer and
reflection**

**What an awesome
privilege it is to
be able to 'be
there' for others
just as You are
always there for
us. Help me be
what You need me
to be, Lord.**

Words of **blessing**

The traditional Jewish greeting is the Hebrew word *shalom*. In Scripture this is translated as 'Peace be with you!' (eg John 20:19). *Shalom*, however, expresses much more than just 'peace'. It literally means 'wholeness, complete wellbeing'.

Many of Paul's letters begin: 'Grace and peace to you ...' (eg Eph. 1:2) whilst Peter and Jude are more generous: 'Grace and peace [Mercy, peace and love] be yours *in abundance*' (1 Pet. 1:2 [Jude 2], my emphasis). These words were never meant only as polite platitudes, as our 'Best Wishes' can often seem on cards and letters.

Peter, Paul and Jude really did want grace, mercy, love and peace to be poured into the lives of those to whom they were writing. Their words were actual spiritual blessings that they fully expected, in faith, to be released from heavenly places in response.

Powerful and often prophetic words of blessing were also spoken out in the Old Testament (eg Gen. 49:1–28). God declares to Abraham, 'I will bless you ... and you will be a blessing ...' (Gen. 12:2). As God's spiritual children through faith in Jesus, we are inheritors of that same promise. We are called to be both 'blessed' by God and to be channels of His blessing to those around us. As members of His 'royal priesthood' (1 Pet. 2:9) we are also able to share in Jesus' name the same blessing that the Levite priests were called to speak over God's original 'chosen people', the Israelites (Num. 6:24–26).

Whenever we speak words of blessing to others (providing that our motives are godly and what we say is in line with God's Word, His will and His timeline for them) the Holy Spirit can take what we have faithfully declared and make it a reality in their lives.

Genesis 12:1–13; Numbers 6:22–27

'... I will bless you ... and you will be a blessing.' (Gen. 12:2)

For prayer and reflection

Whom does the Lord want to bless through you today?

Words of **encouragement**

Isaiah 35:1–10;
Acts 27:13–25

'… say to those with fearful hearts, "Be strong, do not fear; your God will come …"' (Isa. 35:4)

Medical evidence suggests that children who are starved of encouragement and hope early in life can go on to suffer severe problems in health and physical growth as adults. Many become highly-strung and emotionally disabled because no one saw the need to support and encourage them during their most formative years.

And the same can be true within God's family. Sadly, there are Christians who never hear encouragement from their brothers and sisters in Christ and, as a result, struggle to mature spiritually. Many have little confidence in who they are in Jesus because no one has ever taken the time to accept and affirm them in the Lord.

We must never fail to keep in mind the fact that God's amazing love (that sent His Son to die for us) never looks solely for the negative in people. It never focuses on their faults and weaknesses. God's love looks only for the good in our lives, and if the Lord can look at us and always see something positive then surely we, too, should be looking for what is good and positive in the lives of others.

We can also use the tongue to encourage those who are in trouble and struggling with fear (Acts 27:22–25). Ted told me this story from his childhood: during the war his mother had to bring up several children on very few rations. One day she was so troubled that she was heard to cry, 'Lord, please strengthen my weary soul in You today.'

Later she was met by a complete stranger who smiled at her and said, 'Sister, our loving Father says to tell you: "… Christ in *you*, the hope of glory"' (Col. 1:27, my emphasis). He then walked away and she never saw him again. Ted said, 'You'd think he'd given my mum a million pounds that day. She was so blessed in Jesus!'

For prayer and reflection

Why not give a very special gift? Encourage someone in Christ today.

WEEKEND

Too old to make a difference?

For reflection: Luke 2:21–40

How do you think Mary and Joseph might be feeling here? Overawed by the vastness of the Temple? Embarrassed that they could afford only the poorest sacrifice (v.24; Lev. 12:6–8)? Overwhelmed by the 'craziness' of their relationship so far (Matt. 1:18–25)? Wearied by all their travelling in recent weeks (Luke 2:1–40)? Out of their depth as first-time parents? Confused yet excited by the strange things that have been happening (Matt. 1:18–2:23; Luke 1:26–2:20)? Wanting to do right by God and their very special Son?

Onto the scene come two elderly but very wise and experienced people (vv.25–26,36–37). Simeon and Anna have been chosen by God to speak blessing and hope into their lives (vv.25–38). How do you think Mary and Joseph might now be feeling, having met them (see v.33)?

A 98-year-old lady tells me that she can't do much for Jesus now. Yet I know that she prays for me daily and that God enriches my life with His grace and favour in response! Think you are too old to make a difference in His kingdom? Think again!

Optional further reading

1 Thessalonians 5:1–28; James 5:7–20

Words **of invitation**

Luke 2:1–20

'Let's go … and see this thing that has happened, which the Lord has told us about.' (v.15)

The well-known story of the shepherds out in the fields, 'keeping watch over their flocks at night' (v.8), has thrilled me since I was a little child. I loved to imagine the angels popping down from heaven (vv.9–10) to give those unsuspecting humans the 'good news of great joy' (as well as probably the fright of their lives!). In describing how the whole sky was instantly saturated with light, Luke writes simply, '… and the glory of the Lord shone around them …' What an amazing sight it must have been: as if the powerful floodlights of every sports ground and stadium in the whole world had suddenly been switched on at precisely the same time!

In sharing the good news, the angel told the shepherds exactly who Jesus was and where to find Him. They, in turn, encouraged each other to go and see if what they had been hearing was really true, 'Let's go to Bethlehem and see this thing that has happened …' (v.15). They 'hurried off' (v.16), found everything to be 'just as they had been told' and 'returned, glorifying and praising God' (v.20).

Thirty years later, a Samaritan woman had a personal encounter with Jesus (see John 4:1–42). This had such a profound effect on her that she invited everyone in her town to come and meet Him. Many did and ended up believing in Him because of what she had said (vv.28–30,39).

Can you testify to how someone's words of invitation helped to change the whole of your life? You were invited to repent and follow Jesus and you responded by putting your faith and trust in Him for salvation. As a result, you became a member of God's kingdom and your life was changed forever!

For prayer and reflection

Help me, Lord, to say: 'Come, see …' (John 4:29) to those who have never met You personally.

Words of **forgiveness**

The word 'compensation' meaning 'payment due for injury inflicted' is very popular today. Owed where physical, mental, emotional or spiritual injury is inflicted on an innocent party, payment can be made in ways other than simply handing over money.

Many of us may have paid compensation (or 'made amends') at some time in our lives. Or perhaps you were the innocent party and payment was owed to you for some offence or hurt inflicted by others? Had you been asked to give up your right to compensation, what would have happened? Giving up our rights to what we are genuinely entitled does not come easily, does it?

Yet God is willing to give up His right to compensation for hurt inflicted on *Him* every time He is sinned against – such a vast amount of injury caused and recompense owed that we could never ever pay it on our own. However, instead of demanding compensation (ie that we be punished for our sins), God willingly waives this for those who put their personal faith and trust in Jesus for salvation. In other words (see 1 John 1:5–10), *GOD FORGIVES*!

In His earthly ministry, Jesus *proclaimed* and *practised* forgiveness (Luke 7:48; 23:34) and He expects His children to do the same: 'Keep us forgiven with you and forgiving others' (Matt. 6:12, *The Message*). Whenever we allow Him, the Holy Spirit can and will empower us to offer our own sincere words of forgiveness to those who have hurt us (Matt. 6:14–15). Sometimes this may be a lengthy and painful process, beginning merely with a willingness to *want* to forgive – but the Holy Spirit will help us, as we are willing.

What an absolutely wonderful message to be taking out into the world every day!

**John 8:1–11;
Matthew 6:9–15**

"'… neither do I condemn you," Jesus declared. "Go now and leave your life of sin.'"
(John 8:11)

For prayer and reflection

Thank You, Father, for forgiving me in Jesus. Help me, please, to keep loving and forgiving others (and myself!) in His all-powerful name.

Words of **advice and warning**

'… if someone is caught in a sin, you who are spiritual should restore him gently.' (Gal. 6:1)

Are you someone who has always acted righteously, never chosen wrongly, never yielded to temptation and rigidly followed God's perfect plan for your life – wherever it has taken you? Then read no further.

Still reading? Then you must be the kind of person who greatly values the advice (and sometimes admonition?) of wiser, more experienced Christians. And how do they get the wisdom and experience to pass on to you in the first place? By hearing *and* heeding the wise and experienced words of others whom God has sent alongside them as mentors.

And who might be the best person for God to send alongside someone else with words of advice and warning in the future? You, of course! Why? Well, you already know the best way to handle this. You realise that to rush up, finger wagging, tongue tutting, to simply preach or quote pious scriptures at someone would be pointless. Your words would almost certainly fall on closed ears – and do no good at all.

If your approach is prayerful, gentle and humble, however, bearing in mind the awesome effect of God's love, mercy and grace in your own life, then your words, I'm sure, will not only be heard, but almost certainly be heeded – and a personal tragedy averted as a result.

Whenever the Holy Spirit gives us specific words of counsel or caution for another, we should never be afraid to share them as long as our motives and attitude mirror those of Jesus: for example, when He met the man in today's story (John 5:14) and the woman caught in adultery (John 8:11). And may we always remember to deal with the '*plank*' in our own eye *before* seeking to remove the '*speck*' in a brother's or sister's eye (see Matt. 7:1–5).

For prayer and reflection

Lord, thank You for entrusting me with vital words for others. May I keep in mind how much I need Your love, mercy and grace in my own life as I share them.

Words of **faith and victory**

Jesus spoke these words to His bemused disciples: 'In this world you will have trouble ...' (here He describes what will become stark reality for them – and us!) 'But take heart! I have overcome the world.' (He states here our amazing potential in Christ.) There will always be those in our worldwide Church family who are struggling with 'trouble' (v.33) at some time or other. It's inevitable!

How hard it is to be brimming with faith when you are battling with 'troubled' reality and its raw emotions. It's even harder to focus on 'potential in Christ' when you are right in the thick of difficult circumstances.

This, however, is when those of us who are spiritually stronger and *un*troubled at the time can help. Instead of condemning those who are struggling, we should get alongside and be God's heart, hands, listening ear and smile ministering to them at their point of need.

And we shouldn't stop there! We should then go on to speak Scripture-based words of faith and victory on their behalf into their troubled situation, eg 'This *is* possible in Jesus! Don't give up!' (see Mark 9:23); or 'God is right here with you, so trust Him' (see Isa. 41:10; 43:2). When *they* are struggling to do this, we should do it for them until they can manage on their own. Then when they are strong again and *we* find ourselves in trouble, they can speak overcoming words into *our* situation in return.

By doing this, we are helping to 'steer' each other's focus away from our problems and back onto 'potential in Christ' again. We are also asking God to release into our lives whatever we need to actually become the 'more than conquerors' that He promises in His Word (Rom. 8:35–39).

....

John 16:17–33

....

'... take heart,
I've conquered
the world!'
(v.33, *The Message*)

....

**For prayer and
reflection**

....

**Lord, please use
me to encourage
others to 'keep
keeping on' in
You today –
for Your glory.**

The choice **is yours!**

Psalm 139:1–18,
23–24

'Before a word is
on my tongue you
know it completely,
O LORD.' (v.4)

So how did you do in your 'spiritual health check'? Has an examination of your tongue shown that your heart is healthy in the spiritual sense or has the Holy Spirit been exposing areas that need attention? Are the words you speak usually godly and gracious because they flow from a heart that is spiritually contented and secure in His presence and love? If the answer is 'Yes!' then may the Spirit use them to direct others towards Jesus and His kingdom and may there be a rich, spiritual harvest as a result.

Or are your comments mostly negative, callous, critical or cross, causing needless embarrassment and hurt? It could be that these flow from a heart that is itself unhappy and in pain because *you* have suffered verbal cruelty in the past and have yet to have its effects fully dealt with in God. If so, why not offer your damaged soul to Him in faith-filled trust and begin to receive His comfort and healing in return?

Or perhaps your tongue produces spiritually unfruitful comments because you voice them carelessly without ever considering their effect on others? What would happen, I wonder, if you were to pay as much attention to the words you dispense from your mouth every day as the money you distribute from your purse?

For prayer and reflection

Whatever 'heart' problems we might have, the Creator who knows us as intimately as the psalmist describes is able to reveal not only their *source* and *symptoms* but also His own powerful *solutions* or *healing* to make them right again — when we allow Him. Are you willing to trust God to cleanse, heal and anoint your 'untamed' heart and tongue, and then to set them to work powerfully and fruitfully for Him? Seek Him now; He's waiting …

May my words and actions from now on convey only messages of love, grace, peace and hope, for Your glory.